Library
Knowledge Spa
Royal Cornwall Hospital
Truro
TR1 3HD

01872 256444

This item is to be returned on or before the last date
stamped below. To renew items please contact the library
Or renew online with your library card number at
www.swims.nhs.uk

21 DAY LOAN

)7.doc   v:18052005   geggro

D1346057

Also by Dan Goodley

SELF-ADVOCACY IN THE LIVES OF PEOPLE WITH LEARNING DIFFICULTIES: The Politics of Resilience

RESEARCHING LIFE STORIES: Method, Theory and Analyses in a Biographical Age (*with R. Lawthom, P. Clough and M. Moore*)

ARTS AGAINST DISABILITY: The Performing Arts of People with Learning Difficulties (*with M. Moore*)

DISABILITY AND PSYCHOLOGY: Critical Introductions and Reflections (*co-editor with R. Lawthom*)

ANOTHER DISABILITY STUDIES READER: Including People with Learning Difficulties (*co-editor with G. Van Hove*)

Also by Janice McLaughlin

FEMINIST SOCIAL AND POLITICAL THEORY: Contemporary Debates and Dialogues

VALUING TECHNOLOGY: Organisations, Culture and Change (*with P. Rosen, D. Skinner, A.Webster*)

INTERSECTIONS IN FEMINIST AND QUEER THEORY (*co-editor with D. Richardson and M. E. Casey*)

Families Raising Disabled Children

Enabling Care and Social Justice

Janice McLaughlin
Newcastle University

Dan Goodley
Manchester Metropolitan University

Emma Clavering
Newcastle University

Pamela Fisher
University of Huddersfield

First published 2008 by
PALGRAVE MACMILLAN

Palgrave Macmillan in the UK is an imprint of Macmillan Publishers Limited, registered in England, company number 785998, of Houndmills, Basingstoke, Hampshire RG21 6XS.

Palgrave Macmillan in the US is a division of St Martin's Press LLC, 175 Fifth Avenue, New York, NY 10010.

Palgrave Macmillan is the global academic imprint of the above companies and has companies and representatives throughout the world.

Palgrave® and Macmillan® are registered trademarks in the United States, the United Kingdom, Europe and other countries.

ISBN-13: 978-0-230-55145-9   hardback
ISBN-10: 0-230-55145-9   hardback

This book is printed on paper suitable for recycling and made from fully managed and sustained forest sources. Logging, pulping and manufacturing processes are expected to conform to the environmental regulations of the country of origin.

A catalogue record for this book is available from the British Library.

A catalog record for this book is available from the Library of Congress.

10 9 8 7 6 5 4 3 2 1
17 16 15 14 13 12 11 10 09 08

Printed and bound in Great Britain by
CPI Antony Rowe, Chippenham and Eastbourne

Contents

Tables

Preface

Aims of the book

This book explores the lived realities of parents of disabled children. The book emerges from an Economic and Social Research Council (ESRC) funded project *'Parents, Professionals and Babies with Special Care Needs: Identifying Enabling Care'* (RES-000–23–0129). This project had three key objectives:

1. To identify enabling principles of post-natal and subsequent care primarily from the perspectives of parents of disabled babies alongside a consideration of professional perspectives;
2. To critically examine interactions between parents and professionals in terms of the ways in which parents are empowered to take an active and enabling role in the care of their children;
3. To investigate how meanings of 'impairment' and 'dis/ability' are negotiated/constructed and consider how these meanings impact upon the provision of care, perceptions of the disabled baby and the resultant understandings of 'good' parenting and professional practice.

These objectives were tackled through the following aims of our empirical work:

- To engage with the retrospective narrative accounts of parents of young disabled children about their experiences of services, professionals and the related interventions during post- (and ante-) natal care;
- To investigate health professionals' views of the key strategies necessary for different services to provide enabling care and support as the baby develops into infancy and early childhood;
- To trace the experiences of care received and provided by parents of disabled babies over a period of 18 months through the use of narrative interviews;
- To explore the interactions between parents and a variety of professionals in negotiating the care of the disabled baby and notions of impairment and disability;
- To examine the wider support networks inhabited by parents of disabled babies.

Researching social lives alongside policy

Our research placed particular emphasis on the expectations, roles and rules governing the lifeworlds of families and professionals. The research project took place between 2003 and 2007 in two sites in England. This was a particularly turbulent time for parents, children and practitioners as a raft of new policies and legislation impinged upon health and social care services (e.g. Special Educational Needs Code of Practice, 2001; Every Child Matters, 2003; 'Together from the Start'–Practical Guidance for Professionals working with Disabled Children (Birth to Third Birthday) and their Families, 2003; The Children Act 2004; The National Service Framework for Children, Young People and Maternity Services, 2004). The National Service Framework, for example, states a clear conviction: 'At its heart is a fundamental change in thinking about health and social care services. It is intended to lead to a cultural shift, resulting in services being designed and delivered around the needs of children and families' (DOH 2004: p. 8). It outlines the national standards for children's health and social care across the National Health Service (NHS), identifying 'best practice' from across England and Wales; with the aim of generating high-quality services regardless of location (Mallett, 2006).

The standards target promoting social inclusion, healthy child development, supporting parents, strengthening families, improving participation in community life and increasing parental voices in service planning and provision. The National Service Framework is situated within Every Child Matters (ECM) (Department for Education and Skills, 2003, 2004a, b). ECM advocates mainstream and coordinated service delivery for children's services and early intervention. A core development within this is the creation of Children's Trusts, which will 'have a key role to play in co-ordinating and integrating the planning, commissioning and delivery of social, health, social care and education services' (DOH 2004: p. 10). Children's Trusts, backed up by the Children Act (2004), the Health and Social Care Act (2001) and the Health Act (1999), provide a framework for professionals across health and social care to work together via processes that allow for both multiagency and multi-disciplinary partnerships. It also allows for joint commissioning and planning of services across health and social care, including the creation of joint budgets. The Acts make it a statutory requirement for local authorities to create joint mechanisms for working and managing the needs of children.

Our work with parents and professionals has not been geared towards evaluating the progress and success of the government initiatives laid out above (see Mallett, 2006, for a detailed overview). Indeed, our research was taking place just as new initiatives such as Children's Trusts were being set up. Our concern, then, was not with an appraisal of policy. Other work is doing this and has raised concerns about the direction of cultural change (Williams, 2004); limits to financial resources from central government (Audit Commission, 2002; Education and Skills Select Committee, 2005); the level of training provided for professionals working with disabled children and their families (Parliamentary Hearings on Services for Disabled Children, 2006); and the lack of participation from parents and children in their development (Every Disabled Child Matters (EDCM), 2006; Parliamentary Hearings on Services for Disabled Children, 2006). Our research, instead, aimed to work closely alongside parents, their perspectives and their dealings with professionals, institutions and communities. This book acknowledges the importance of policy, guidance and legislation to families but moves beyond this to explore actualities and intersections.

Researching social lives alongside parents

In this book we have been drawn to theoretical ideas that neither portray parents as cultural dopes nor overemphasise their choices as agents unconstrained by social pressures. We recognise that parents are active in the creation of their identities and roles associated with the care of their disabled children. Parents are also very much aware of expectations and regulations placed upon them. We know that parenting a disabled child can be a very positive experience (Beresford, 1994). However, any analysis of parental identities should, by necessity, be considered in relation to wider social, cultural, political and historical factors. Sometimes our discussion will refer to mothers rather than parents. While fathers do, undoubtedly, contribute to care enacted in the home (Carpenter, 2002), mothers of disabled children are often the key players (Willoughby and Glidden, 1995). Hence, while the politics of disability are illuminated by any discussion of care and the social world, so too are feminist sensibilities of the relationship between mothers and caring practices. We do not use parents and mothers interchangeably. We do consider how mothers are positioned as key players in care. When we refer to mothers we aim to shine some light on the complex social and political systems that underpin the intersections of patriarchy, the welfare state, disablement and institutional constructions of family. Russell (2003) argues that it is important to access parents' expectations rather than simply their needs. Consequently, the arguments developed in this book consider the ambitions as well as the experiences of parents.

Structure and authorship

This book draws upon the empirical and ethnographic work of the project's researchers Emma Clavering and Pamela Fisher. In some places we also make mention of empirical work provided by Claire Tregaskis, who was involved with the first year of the project. Chapters 2 and 3 bring together insights from all members of the research team in order to explore the dynamics of method/ology and analysis. The remaining chapters of the book are written by Dan Goodley and Janice McLaughlin, who offer their overview of the literature, theoretical resources and analyses of the data collected.

Chapter 1 outlines the theoretical, orientational and disciplinary approaches adopted by McLaughlin and Goodley in the book. Chapter 2 describes the approach to research undertaken by the research team with a particular focus on the approaches of ethnography and narrative inquiry. Chapter 3 reflexively accounts for some of the relational aspects of the fieldwork. It draws together some of the field notes and research stories from Clavering, Fisher and Tregaskis to expose some of the tensions, dilemmas and impacts of working alongside parents, children and professionals. Chapter 4 begins the analysis of the material collected in the study and asks some challenging questions about the ways in which disabled children's identities are made and unmade through a host of relational, material and discursive dynamics of family and institutional life. Chapter 5 continues this focus on identity and personhood through exploring the many alliances adopted by parents with other parents, disabled people and their own children. This chapter indicates the richness of the encounters of parents as they shape and extend their parenting in ways that are responsive to their disabled children. It also recognises conflict. Chapter 6 examines some of the details of the cultures, communities and groups inhabited by parents. It considers the ways in which dominant, everyday community practices impact upon disabled families. In addition, through reference to parents' own accounts, the chapter also illuminates new, emerging communities and forms of participation constructed and developed by parents and their children. The tension between the diverse and the normative is analysed through notions of governance. Chapter 7 focuses in detail on the challenges facing professionals who care for disabled children and their families. It takes up (and takes on) the phenomenon of New Public Management in order to expose some of the processes, ethics, structures, practices and expectations imposed upon, and worked through, by professionals. It considers what kind of ethical practice parents should reasonably expect from professionals if they are to become partners in developing enabling care and social justice. Chapter 8 continues this engagement with professionals and professions and, with a specific eye on gender dynamics, articulates emerging visions of care that may be viewed as transformative but always shaped by the constitution of boundaries. The final chapter revisits the analyses of the book and evaluates the values that can and do underpin enabling and socially just forms of care. It also celebrates the richness of the journeys undertaken by parents, their disabled children and professionals as they seek forms of responsive care.

Acknowledgements

We are indebted to all the families for sharing so much of their lives with us. All parents showed a commitment to this project and clearly wanted their stories to help other families. We hope this book contributes in some small way to eradicating the disabling barriers faced by disabled children and their families. We would also like to thank the many professionals who acted as gatekeepers, participants and critical friends.

Hats off to Claire Tregaskis for her contribution to the project in its early days. Nicola Salkeld and Lisa Pass offered expert administrative and secretarial support to the project. Their contribution was very important. Nicola, in particular, contributed much to the support of the research. We would like to thank colleagues from our respective departments in Newcastle, Sheffield and Manchester Metropolitan University for their support, including Ann Marie Bathmaker, Tom Billington, Peter Banister, Tsitsi Chataika, Andy Gillespie, Erica Haimes, Peter Hannon, David Hyatt, Rebecca Lawthom, Michele Moore, John Nixon, Cathy Nutbrown, Peter Phillimore, Diane Richardson, Jon Scaife, Tom Shakespeare, Tracey Warren and Simon Woods. Thanks to Rebecca Mallett for her literature review of policy and legislation; Katherine Runswick Cole for proof reading of various project reports; and Gordon Grant and Paul Ramcharan for their encouragement and support of the project, particularly at the proposal stage. Thanks to colleagues in our institutions: The Research Institute for Health and Social Change (http://www.rihsc.mmu.ac.uk/) and The Policy, Ethics and Life Sciences (PEALS) Research Centre (http://www.ncl.ac.uk/peals/).

Finally, we would also like to express our gratitude to ESRC for not only funding the project on which this book is based but also for providing consistent constructive assistance throughout the duration of the project, including their agreement to extend its duration. They gave us wonderful support structures and our case officers were only too happy to help. Thank you.

Dan and Janice send love and thanks to Rebecca Lawthom, Katie Ash, Ruby Haf Lawthom Goodley and Rosa Cariad Lawthom Goodley for their unwavering support and patience.

1
Theorising Parents, Professionals and Disabled Babies

Dan Goodley and Janice McLaughlin

Introduction: Orientations

This chapter identifies a number of theoretical orientations and emphases that shape the arguments of this book. The orientations include critical disability studies, feminisms and critical community psychology. The emphases illuminate a number of key relational, social, identity and cultural nodes of analysis. We develop these interconnections throughout the book – methodologically and analytically – but at this stage outline some key starting points for our conceptualisation of parents, their disabled children and their relationships with institutions, communities and professionals.

Critical disability studies

Disability has emerged as a socio-political category through the agitations of the International Disabled People's Movement (see http://www.dpi.org/, Campbell & Oliver, 1996). While genetics continues to increase possibilities for preselecting embryos or identifying congenital conditions during pregnancy, in order to avoid giving birth to disabled children, the movement troubles the values society attaches to the lives of disabled babies (Shakespeare, 2000, 2006). Consequently, questions are raised about the ways in which professionals and parents contribute to the 'quality of life' of disabled children. The actions of organisations of disabled people and associated scholars and researchers have clearly influenced the development of recent policy and legislation aimed at children, families and disabled people (Brazier et al., 2006). Crucially, the British Disabled People's Movement distinguishes between impairment and disability. 'Impairment' refers to lacking some part of or all of a limb, or having a defective limb organism or mechanism of the body (including 'learning disabilities') whereas 'disability' refers to societal exclusion of individuals with impairments (UPIAS, 1976). Health and social care professionals, service interventions, care packages and parents' own care all contribute to meanings associated with 'impairment' and 'disability'. Recently, Thomas (2006) has suggested that the term 'disablism' – rather than 'disability' – more clearly captures the social, political and cultural nature of the exclusions faced by people with impairments and their families. The work of families and professionals, then, is often exercised in reaction to disablement. In Britain, the development of the social model of disability helped to form an intellectual, epistemological and practical foundation for the organisation of disability theory, politics, culture and discourse (Barnes, 1990; Barnes & Mercer, 1996, 1997, 2003; Barnes et al., 2002; Barton, 2001; Morris, 1996; Oliver, 1990, 1996; Oliver & Barnes, 1998; Shakespeare, 1998, 2000; Swain et al., 2003a, 2004; Thomas, 1999a). The social model was the disabled people's movement's 'big idea' (Hasler, 1993). This encouraged policy, politics, research, arts, care, attitudes and legislation to move away from a focus on the disabled body and mind (the traditional individual model often found in medical contexts) and instead turn to understanding and challenging disablism (located in the social world). The social model provided the platform for theoretical work on disabling society and was eagerly taken up by theorists from diverse foundational positions including materialism, structuralism, social constructionism and interpretivism (Shakespeare, 1998; Skrtic, 1995).

This book is written at a crucial time in British disability studies. The late 1990s and noughties saw disability studies come of age as an intellectual paradigm. Contributors from diverse academic disciplines, activist contexts and professional places have debated a number of key issues. A number of these debates are of relevance to the arguments of this book. The first debate concerns the future of the social model. The relative strength or immanent death of the social model of disability continues to fire argument (e.g. Barnes, 1990; Barnes & Mercer, 1996; Barnes. et al., 2002; Oliver, 1996; Shakespeare, 2006; Shakespeare & Watson, 2001; Watson, 2002). For some, the social model obstructs thinking, through its rigid adherence to the material bases of disablement, and fails to acknowledge diverse experiences of disabled people which are not best explained in terms of social oppression. For others, the social model's potency resides in its attention to the material conditions of marginalisation. Attempts to dismiss it are tantamount to rejecting disability as a political category. The second debate is about the increasingly questionable relationship between disability studies and disability politics

(Traustadóttir, 2006a). While many proponents would assert that the social model's strength grew as a consequence of the close relationship of activism and the academy, anxieties about the future of disability politics complicate this relationship and, hence, the social model. When the Greater Manchester Coalition of Disabled People asked, 'Where have all the activists gone?', one wondered if the social model of disability had become more the possession of the academy (Cunningham, 2000; Oliver & Barnes, 2006). Moreover, the growth of organisations of parents of disabled children raises some interesting questions about how disability theory feeds into, reflects and is energised by the activism of parents. The third debate is about the place of 'impairment' and 'embodiment' in discussions of 'disablement' (Abberley, 1987; Barnes & Mercer, 1996; Brett, 2002; Crow, 1996; Hughes & Paterson, 1997; Marks, 1999). Many debates have emerged in relation to the primacy the social model gives to the disabling world at the expense of the effects of an impaired body or the experiences of embodiment. For some professionals, parents and researchers, the social model is in danger of jettisoning any discussion related to illness or impairment. It ignores discussions of impairment effects (Thomas, 1999b) and does not allow disabled people to speak openly about their bodies. Others suggest that the social model should promote a discussion of bodies and impairment but in ways that do not slide back into biological determinism, medicalisation and tragedy discourses. Hence, a number of writers have promoted theories which recognise the complicated nature of impairment through bringing together psycho-social, emotional and relational understandings of impairment and disability.

The fourth current debate in disability studies centres on the inclusive nature of the social model. A number of commentators have attacked the apparent exclusion of some disabled people from dominant theories of disability, including people with learning difficulties (Chappell, 1998; Goodley, 2001), survivors of mental health systems (Wilson & Beresford, 2002) and black disabled people (Stuart, 1992). While some have defended the social model against those attacks – suggesting that if we look carefully enough then we will find an inclusive epistemology – critics have called for the development of theories and modes of research production which are open to diverse experiences across the spectrum of the disabled population. The fifth debate is about interdisciplinarity. Much of the writing associated with the social model emerged in sociology and social policy. More recently disciplines such as anthropology (Landsman, 2003), cultural studies (Skrtic, 1995; Tremain, 2002), philosophy (Silvers & Francis, 2005; Silvers et al., 1998) and others have begun to have a presence within disability studies. Perhaps more contentiously, ideas from within practitioner frameworks, which have historically pathologised disabled people, including psychology (Goodley & Lawthom, 2005a, b), social work (Oliver & Sapey, 2006; Sapey & Pearson, 2005), physiotherapy (Swain et al., 2004; Swain & French, 1999) and psychotherapy (Swain et al., 2004, 2003b) are being brought into disability studies. Those critical of such interdisciplinary fusions suggest that disability studies might lose its politicised nature if it allows itself to be colonised by these omnipotent disciplines. Those of a more eclectic mindset suggest that drawing on such approaches can aid working with professionals to educate them to work more receptively and respectfully with disabled people. The sixth debate worth mentioning is the global place of the social model. The last few years have seen the social model experience a growing migration of ideas from other models of disability, including the cultural and relational models of North American (Albrecht et al., 2001; Linton, 1998; Longman & Umansky, 2001) and Nordic countries (Scandinavian Journal of Disability Research, 2004; Traustadóttir, 2004a, 2006a). Such ideas bring with them not only new conceptual challenges but also different models of professional practice, service provision and welfare in the lives of disabled people and their families.

This brief synopsis of disability studies in Britain should, we hope, give a flavour of some of the key challenges and controversies we face in researching the lives of disabled babies, their families and associated professionals. We embrace these debates. Clearly, understandings of disability and impairment that we develop in our work should be mindful of the responsibilities we have towards disabled people who have fought long and hard for disability to be taken seriously as an issue of marginalisation, oppression, exclusion and discrimination. Our analyses should also be attentive to the challenges and needs of families of disabled people. But, at the very same time, disability studies must connect more overtly with other minority writings and perspectives, including postcolonialism (Chataika, 2007; Sherry, 2004b), queer theory (Guter & Killarky, 2004; McRuer, 2002; Overboe, 2007; Sherry, 2004a; Whitney, 2006), critical race theory (Lynn, 2006) and feminism (Garland-Thomson, 2005). This may well shift thinking towards a *critical* disability studies perspective which maintains an emphasis on the social, cultural and political foundations of disablism but unites this with the nuanced analyses of other transformative approaches (for a detailed argument of critical disability studies, see Goodley, forthcoming). We now turn to one such approach, which we broadly define as feminisms.

Feminist critique

Our adoption of a critical disability studies perspective is broadened and reviewed through our acknowledgement of the importance of feminist analyses of caring practices. Clearly any engagement with disabled families demands us to think critically about the association between gender and care (McLaughlin, 2006; Traustadóttir, 1991, 1995, 1999). In particular, there are three areas of work which influence the discussions in the book. The first is work that began in the 1970s and 1980s arguing that care, and women's role in the provision of it, was a major factor in gender inequality (Finch & Groves, 1983; Land, 1978; Ungerson, 1987, 1990). Stories of women's 'caring nature' and 'selfless love' were replaced with detailed accounts of the 'material practices' and 'labour' of caring (Graham, 1983). The second is work from the late 1980s and 1990s which focuses on the intricate processes at play within family life (Finch, 1989). Finch and Mason (1993) argue that the processes through which women become the predominant carers involve 'negotiations' within families, negotiations which often leave women with the least socially acceptable excuses to leave care to others outside or inside the family (Baldwin & Twin, 1991). For many women, the role of carer gives them value and appreciation, providing them with a socially acceptable identity which is not available elsewhere:

> People's identities are being constructed, confirmed and reconstructed – identities as a reliable son, a generous mother, a caring sister or whatever it might be ... If the image of a 'caring sister' is valued as part of someone's identity then it eventually becomes too expensive to withdraw from those commitments through which that identity is expressed and confirmed.
>
> (Finch and Mason, 1993: p. 170)

Skeggs (1997) also explores the gendered subjectivity of the carer and the social conditions that support and legitimate particular identities. Being a carer becomes something that is not just incorporated into things women do. It is also translated into aspects of the self, providing respectability and recognition. In contrast, Campbell and Carroll (2007) argue that practices associated with hegemonic masculinity (Connell, 1987) make it difficult for men to incorporate care as a legitimate aspect of their identity, even if they are involved in significant caring activities.

The third area of feminist work, the ethics of care debates (Gilligan, 1987, 1993; Larrabee, 1993; Noddings, 1984), has developed a productive understanding of women's role in caring. In contrast to seeing care as a barrier to women's personhood and identity, writers such as Gilligan have proposed that caring practices can be the basis to both a positive sense of self and also the emergence of moral frameworks that challenge the instrumentality and individuality of the public sphere. Others have taken this work forward to use it to call for different understandings of citizenship, justice and social responsibility (Lister, 1999; Sevenhuijsen, 1998; Tronto, 1993).

However, feminist accounts of the significance of care have been heavily criticised by disability writers. It is worth acknowledging that Black feminists (Carby, 1997; Glenn, 1992) also felt marginalised by discussions of family dynamics of care which had little to do with non-white patterns of family relationship and care. The work on the gendered division of labour and caring subjectivities has been criticised by disability writers because of its sole interest on the 'burdens' placed on the carer (Morris, 1996; Sheldon, 1999). Skeggs proposes that the 'caring self is a dialogic production: a caring self cannot be produced without caring for others' (1997: p. 56), but within the text she does little to explore the identity of the (disabled) 'others' she speaks of. These criticisms led Graham (1993) to acknowledge the limitations identified by disability writers in her and other feminists' work.

The ethics of care arguments are criticised for falling into similar ways of thinking about care and the superior morality of the carer as found in charitable care discourses. Charitable care is deeply problematic for the disability movement because it presents care as involving the noble carer, pity and optionality. Care is a benevolent gift the receiver should be grateful for and accept without question (Hughes, 1999). As Lindemann argues, charitable care is 'something of an "extra" action; something not quite required' (2003: p. 507). Charitable caring for Hughes 'mobilised the emotions invested in the tragic and the pitiful' (2002: p. 577) while Kittay suggests that care is not a right but instead is provided 'out of a gratuitous kindness, a kindness they have no right to demand' (2002: p. 271). This disconnection between feminisms and disability studies might explain the reticence within the latter orientation to use care as a concept to explore the lives and identities of those who support disabled people. Instead, the talk is often of assistance (Watson et al., 2004).

This unwillingness to debate the significance of care has created a lack of engagement with, and even hostility towards, parents of disabled children. At times, in the disability studies literature, non-disabled parents of disabled children have been presented as part of the problem, anxious to talk of their own burden and side with professionals against the needs and interests of their children. This is not a useful situation and does little to help understand the significance of parental experiences of caring roles to the social position of disabled children. It is based on an assumption that there exists a binary opposition between all aspects of disabled and non-disabled people's experiences, ignoring the reality of the stigma, social deprivation and exclusion that non-disabled family members may face alongside their disabled relatives (Beresford et al., 1996; Brett, 2002; Dobson et al., 2001; Murray & Penman, 2000). While feminist literatures may well have failed to engage with the demands of disabled activists and researchers, there are still many important lessons to be drawn from them. Shakespeare (2000) makes a convincing case for fusing the agendas of disability studies and feminist ethics of care. Similarly, Reindal (1999) attempts to combine both in order to conceptualise notions of interdependence. We would argue for a careful bringing together of feminisms and critical disability studies (and have developed this in detail elsewhere, McLaughlin, 2006). We are mindful that mothers remain the primary care givers for many of the families described in this book. Caring remains a gendered activity and enacting care is a common part of doing gender (West & Zimmermain, 1987). This amalgamation is strengthened through an engagement with other feminist analyses, such as the social construction of motherhood (Phoenix, 1991; Phoenix et al., 1991).

Critical and community psychologies

A further orientation of this book is critical community psychology. This is an arena for theory and practice that can be usefully colonised by critical disability studies. Recent work has aimed to articulate forms of psychology that understand and theorise disabled people in terms of their cultural and political context (Goodley & Lawthom, 2005a, 2005b, 2008; Lawthom & Goodley, 2005). Goodley and Lawthom (2005a), for example, describe community psychology as a revolutionary paradigm of psychology; a counter-hegemony to mainstream psychology's individualism; and an interdisciplinary context that brings together politics, sociology, social policy, health and social welfare (Duffy & Wong, 1997; Heller et al., 1984; Kagan, 2002; Levine & Perkins, 1997; Orford, 1992; Prilleltensky & Nelson, 2002; Rappaport, 1977). Crucial to most conceptions of community psychology is the idea of working alongside the primary source of knowing and instrument of research: 'the self-directing person within a community of inquiry' (Reason & Heron, 1995: p. 123). Community psychology researchers align themselves with members of excluded communities to understand and challenge oppression and marginalisation. The view of psychology promoted here is inherently political. It considers psychology as a liberatory space (Kagan, 2002; Martin-Baró et al., 1994), in which researchers, who are armed with theoretical and practical knowledge of the social and interpersonal world, aim to work alongside communities towards positive social change. Psychology is up for grabs, particularly by those communities whose psychologies have been pathologised and alienated by labour markets, poor housing, welfare dependency and material poverty.

For this book, community psychological perspectives provide a deep engagement with the meanings of inclusive and exclusionary contexts for parents and their disabled children. The related agendas associated with critical psychology further enhance an analysis of the exclusion of disabled children and their families. In Goodley and Lawthom (2008), for example, it is suggested that critical psychology provides a number of necessary theoretical resources for understanding the construction of the (disabled) human subject. The first, *social constructionist psychology*, has challenged the concept of the self as an embodied and unitary human subject and opened it up as a distributed self, dependent on different contexts and the meanings in those contexts at given times (e.g. Burr, 2003; Nightingale & Cromby, 1999). The self, identity and psychology are understood as constructed phenomena through meaning-making, language and human practice. The very concept of personality, for example, is therefore ripped out of its usual embodied site and recast as a socio-cultural formation. Personalities are increasingly consumable entities of a society obsessed with identity. In contrast, the supposed undesirability of a disabled identity raises questions about what identities are deemed socially valuable. The second, *discursive psychology*, furthers an engagement with constructions by positing that there can be no truth without language and the ideologies and institutions implicated in the production of language. The various forms of discursive psychology are beyond the remit of this chapter (see Nikander, 1995, for a useful overview). Parker's (2002) approach to discourse analysis, for example, is concerned with providing a social account of subjectivity. In an associated text, Parker et al. (1995) unpick the ways in which psychopathological conditions are the product of normalising institutions and professional practice. Mental illness is not a condition that exists prior to the psychologist intervening – mental illness is a social creation of institutions within society that psychology has helped to construct. The task for critical psychologists is to confront the practices of psychology – and other associated professions – that sustain oppression through the naming of disability and deficit. Instead, we are encouraged to promote a politicised and aware psychology, work alongside users and survivors of psychology and link into wider social justice agendas as ethically responsible psychologists.

Combining disability studies, feminist ideas and critical psychology perspectives encourages us to view the lives of parents and disabled children in a number of ways. It encourages us to

- Attend to the kinds of subject positions that parents are pushed into and/or create;
- Deconstruct objects such as 'parent', 'impairment', 'disability', 'professional' and 'institution';
- Be mindful of the ways in which phenomena such as 'care' are imbued with material and discursive meanings and practices;
- Be sceptical of 'truth claims' associated with such phenomena as diagnosis and prognosis;
- Explore the ways in which parents' and professionals' knowledge of and life with disabled children link into the creation of different elements of subjectivity, personhood and identity;
- Treat new forms of knowledge production, including those associated with the Internet and the network society, with the necessary criticality.

Emphases

From these orientations and through our in-depth work with parents, professionals and disabled babies (which we introduce in the next two chapters), this book engages with a number of analytical and theoretical considerations. We now introduce some of these emphases.

Disabled families, contextualised parents

Parenting takes place in and through complex relationships. For example, Kittay (1999b: p. 205) views parents, especially mothers, as being nested in sets of reciprocal relations and obligations. Parenting disabled children troubles orthodox notions of autonomy and ability and, consequently, for Gottlieb (2002) contests the normative rational subject of Western philosophy. Shildrick (1997) calls for an understanding of human subjectivity that embraces rather than rejects vulnerability. Vulnerability is not something that should be done away with – as the abject other of the modern sovereign self – but embraced because, as Shildrick observes quoting Nussbaum (1986: p. 86), 'the peculiar beauty of human excellence...is its vulnerability'. Hence, while parents undergo many difficulties and struggles, we should not dismiss the ways in which this makes them vulnerable or at risk. Instead, we should consider the ways in which their vulnerability is an essential part of the interconnectedness of life. If parenting is situated, vulnerable and interconnected, then this raises questions about marginalisation and social justice. Existing social hierarchies, such as those located in terms of class or capital (Gillies, 2005; Sharma, 2002) and ethnicity (Chamba et al., 1999; Shah, 1995), have inevitable consequences for access to resources and support for the family. The increased risk of poverty has been well documented in other studies (Beresford, 1994; and Preston, 2006). It is therefore essential to remain aware of material, cultural and discursive factors which will become wrapped up in the act of parenting. McKeever and Miller's (2004) Bourdieusian analysis highlights the varying qualities of community engagement experienced by parents of disabled children. They analyse the worlds of parents through the use of concepts including habitus (subjective dispositions or background understandings that are in some way informed by social structures), fields (everyday contexts and institutions politicised and contested, e.g. the family, law, medicine) and forms of capital including, economic (e.g. wealth), cultural (e.g. education, bodily norms, bodily comportment), social (e.g. networks and the extended family) and symbolic (e.g. authority, prestige and legitimacy). They found that parents' – and in particular mothers' – agitation for resources on behalf of their children occurred in the fields of health, education and local neighbourhoods, appropriating forms of capital and occupying often newly found and, at times, contradictory habitus. Parenting a disabled child may well move the focus away from romantic notions to more broad politicised understandings of parenting. In this sense, then, parents may be viewed as occupying a minority group status (Partington, 2002).

At the same time, Read (2000) and Runswick Cole (2007) draw our attention to the ways in which a disabled family is so often considered, by definition, as a dysfunctional family. Such pathological views fail to attend to the subtle pressures of disablement and their wide-reaching influences on the relationships within families. Traustadóttir (2006b) argues that historically much social scientific and healthcare research on disabled babies has focused on the perspectives of parents, professionals and other adults rather than children. This has had the effect of viewing disabled children through the eyes of adults and ensured that the voices and experiences of disabled children and youth remain ignored. In addition, studies of disabled children have tended to be preoccupied with impairment, vulnerability and dependency and have thus constructed them as a 'burden' to the family and community at large. This reliance upon an individual model perspective of disability perhaps explains an over-interest with health, social, welfare and educational services (rather than wider community and societal responses) and a tendency to view disabled children as a homogeneous group, denying their sophisticated identities and ignoring the complexities of their families. Parents have also suffered at the hands of research that medicalises and individualises their disabled kids. Fortunately, a growing body of literature has developed, particularly across the minority world, in which the experiences of disabled children and their families are not only taken seriously but are understood in terms of their location in a disabling world. In the US, the Syracuse Center on Human Policy has a long history of researching disability from cradle to grave (Bogdan & Taylor, 1976, 1982; Ferguson et al., 1992; O'Connor, 1995a, b; Taylor & Bogdan, 1984; Taylor, et al., 1995). Their work with families has been particularly powerful in taking seriously the stories and qualitative accounts of disabled children and unearthing the details and complexities of services and family life through the long-term involvement of researchers. From this work has emerged the notion of the 'disabled family' which conceives of the family unit as a whole and takes this as the starting point for analysing the material, cultural and personal challenges faced by disabled children and their families. In the Nordic countries, Traustadóttir and others have combined interests in interpretivism, feminism and disability studies in order to promote receptive forms of professional practice and enabling theories in the Icelandic context and beyond (Kristiansen & Traustadóttir, 2004; Traustadóttir, 1991, 1995, 1999, 2004b, 2006b). In Australia, The Family Support and Services Project at the University of Sydney, brings together professionals from occupational therapy, psychology and social work committed to identifying, promoting and addressing the issues faced by families where a parent or a child has a disability (Llewellyn, 1997; McConnell & Llewellyn, 1998; Strike & McConnell, 2002). Meanwhile, in Britain, a plethora of work has emerged over the last ten years which has taken seriously the lives of disabled children and their families (Beresford, 1994, 1997; Beresford et al., 1996, 2005; Brett, 2002; Dale, 1996; Davies & Hall, 2005; McConachie, 1999; Middleton, 1992, 1998, 1999a, 1999b; Read, 1991, 2000, 2002; Read & Clements, 2004a, 2004b; Sloper, 1999, 2004; Sloper et al., 2006; Sloper & Lightfoot, 2003; Sloper & Turner, 1992; Speedwell et al., 2003). Clearly, each of these examples from the literature brings with it a specific and unique analysis

of disabled families. We shall return to some of their details throughout this text. For now, it is possible to identify a number of recurring
findings:

- Families are often reliant on state benefits, which can be complex to
  claim;
- State benefits that families do receive often do not meet the addi-
  tional outgoings associated with having a disabled child;
- Families of disabled children often live in poverty;
- Parents' lives and the children's education are disrupted by recurring
  appointments and professional treatment;
- Families report widespread parental stress, lack of sleep, lack of respite
  care and reliance upon extended family (if they are present);
- Families often lack access to accessible leisure pursuits and housing
  and responsive respite care;
- Children are excluded from friendship groups and parents may be
  marginalized by other parents.

In light of such findings many researchers reposition the perspectives
of parents at the fore of consideration (e.g. Avery, 1999; Case, 2000).
This call has been taken up, in a dramatic fashion, through the writings
of parent-researchers and parents' representative organisations (e.g.
Murray & Penman, 1996; Murray & Penman, 2000; Runswick Cole,
2007; Ryan & Runswick Cole, 2008; Ryan, 2005b). These analyses have
further politicised research on disabled children and their families,
demonstrating that issues of inclusion and disability politics are as
much a part of private family affairs as they are the public educational
worlds.

The social construction of (disabled) childhoods

The sociology of childhood and critical psychologies of child development have excavated the social construction of childhood. This has
led to examinations of the changing boundaries made and drawn
between childhood and adulthood (Heywood, 2001; James, 1993;
Wyness, 2006). Childhood is constructed within a range of spaces and
practices, from clothing and toys, through to educational rhetoric and
cultural representations of the asexual and innocent child (James,
et al., 1998; Jenks, 1996). The construction of the child within the
family is always in a context of broader societal and state versions and
valorisation of what the good child and family embraces and evokes.
Such constructions are predicated on the equally demonised versions

of the bad child and family (McCarthy et al., 2000). At the heart of the social construction of childhood are questions about what kinds of children are valued by particular societies, at given times. Gottlieb (2002) asks, 'What is the typical moral subject?'. In terms of Western philosophy he briefly defines five positions: the Greek tradition which emphasises an individual's natural development and fulfilment; the Rights discourse which celebrates the rational autonomy of the citizen; Marxism with its commitment to collective liberation and fulfilment of the working class; feminist associations with mutuality and empathic connection; and the Judeo-Christian tradition which commits a person's humanity to freely submitting to God. Gottlieb argues that disabled children do not fit well with the developing, rational and autonomous subject position so highly valued by some of these discourses which underpin contemporary attitudes. The implication is that their prognosis for moral development remains poor. Disabled children are frequently understood as asocial, unable and lacking, and research in this area reflects these pernicious assumptions. Indeed, in New York State and many others in the US, parents of newborn babies with Down's syndrome are routinely offered fosterage or adoption placements (Rapp & Ginsburg, 2001).

However, in studies exploring the lives of disabled children, there is growing appreciation of their scope to define and articulate who they presently may be, what they value and who they currently wish to become (Landsdown, 2001). It is important, as Kelly argues drawing upon Merleau-Ponty (1962), to think of the disabled child as an 'experiencing agent – a site of meaning and knowledge of the world' (2005: p. 182). One example of this is the work of Colver and his research team exploring how children with cerebral palsy define and understand their quality of life. Existing medical models of what constitutes quality of life use criteria that emphasise the deficit model of disability, judged against a 'normal life' (McConachie et al., 2006; Moons et al., 2006). An inability to reach particular markers of development becomes a proxy for poor quality of life (Koch, 2000). The achievement of goals, made against markers of medically and psychologically defined physical and mental development, is privileged over broader criteria of what makes for a reasonable quality of life. If we begin with the children's point of view, their version can be differently imagined (Eiser et al., 2000). In Colver's work (Dickinson et al., 2007), involving both qualitative and quantitative analysis of the perspectives of children and their parents across Europe, children consistently defined their quality of life as higher than that assumed by their parents and by professionals in other studies. The children were neither in denial nor living in a condition where they did not know better. Instead, active in finding a life meaningful to themselves, they had developed a positive sense of self, which others who did not live with a disability could not imagine possible. This positive narrative of living with disability can spread from the child out, via the life they lead and values they articulate. At various points this was seen within the families we worked with and was particularly noticeable with non-disabled siblings. Much of the literature on the siblings of disabled children concentrates on problems such as the sibling forced to be a carer for the child and given relatively little attention in comparison. While we would not want to argue such problems do not exist, it is important to also stress the positive difference the disabled child can make to the lives of other siblings; in particular, in providing ways of thinking of disability in non-tragic or non-pathological kinds of ways.

Beyond coping and stress: Negotiation, productive parenting and community practice

This book moves away from a simplistic and static conception of the tragic parent of a disabled child. Brinchmann (1999) typifies a body of work that characterises parents as 'suffering' through life with their disabled children. Parents are understood to enter a life trajectory across which they are obliged to grapple with forms of mastery and adaptive behaviours to counter commonly held feelings of parental guilt, shame and hostility (Canam, 1993; Dyer, 1996; Hannam, 1988; Partington, 2002; Snell & Rosen, 1997). Delving deeper we find complexity in this presumed helplessness. Elllis and Hirsch (2000) found, in seeking to examine the relationship between having a disabled child, psychological trauma and suicidal thoughts (note the assumption, here, that they are inevitably related factors), that no actual difference existed between parents of disabled and non-disabled children. They conclude that having a disabled child might actually promote adaptive characteristics. Similarly, as Murray (2000) observes, it is increasingly possible to find accounts in the literature of parents' experiencing their children in more positive ways (see also Murray, 2003). Parenting a disabled child may not be the moral problem promulgated by popular philosophical, professional or lay truths. Notwithstanding this observation, parents do seem to occupy a 'no-win situation'. They are characterised as either unable to cope or, for those who appear to be coping well, as deluding themselves about the extent of their child's difficulties, sometimes disguising their rejection (Runswick Cole, 2007: p. 317). Larson (1998: p. 865) reflects on this situation and suggests that parents may well find themselves embracing a paradox:

> The management of the internal tension of opposing forces between loving the child as he or she is and wanting to erase the disability, between dealing with the incurability while pursuing solutions and between maintaining hopefulness for the child's future while being given negative information and battling their own fears.

This book aims to understand how parents work through, and beyond, this paradox as they define their lives and their children. McKeever and Miller (2004) have argued that hitherto much research has ignored the socio-political context of disability and has, as a result, interpreted parental feelings and behaviour in pathological ways. Having disabled babies is commonly associated with painful processes of acceptance, denial or rejection. Yet, such simplistic views ignore the very complex ways in which parents negotiate, work through and understand their children (Case, 2000; Read, 1991, 2000; Traustadóttir, 1991). Families are not simply microcosms of society or community: they exist potentially as spaces through which dominant ideas associated with autonomy, choice, individuality and freedom are understood and contested. The family allows a place to work out ways of living, drawing on and challenging ideas about childhood, disability and parenting that exist in the public domain. For Vanobbergen et al. (2006: p. 425), a key emerging practice associated with the contemporary family is the growing adoption of the negotiation model:

> Parents represent a generation of 'negotiators' with their children. This means, on the whole, more communication between parents and children and also more reflection by parents on their educational aims and strategies.

The family household, then, becomes a place in which meanings of parenting, constructions of disability and expectations of support are negotiated. Relationships include not only parents and their children but also those across and between generations of family and friends. Such a model of negotiation encourages debate and discord about the practice of parenting. And, as we shall see later, this also extends parenting relationships outside of the household to connect with parent groups, and online and self-help communities. In so doing, and following Yuval-Davis (2006), we are able to pick up nuances of community belonging including location, identification and shared values. Parenting involves far more than developing coping strategies. It draws parents into different community spaces. Some are more accepting than others. Parents therefore have to take some decisions about how they participate, fit, accommodate or change these community contexts.

Governance and regulation

Where there is agency there is always governance. According to Ruddick (1984) cited in Lauritzen (1989), parenting, particularly mothering, should be understood as a social practice precisely because it is a human activity governed by certain interests and defined by certain ends. A social practice engenders particular ways of being and acting. This relates directly to the notion of governance, a concept closely linked to the work of Foucault (1982, 1991). While a fuller explanation of Foucault's work and its application in the area of critical disability studies is not possible here (see instead Tremain, 2001, 2002, 2005), governance is a useful concept because it fits with some of the accounts of identity work on the part of parents that we collected in our research. In short, while parents can and do occupy particular subject positions, they simultaneously face a variety of disciplinary practices associated with 'parenting' the 'disabled child'. The scare quotes recognise the socially constructed nature of practices, subjects, objects and their consequences, understood in relation to the processes of governance. The notion of governance relates directly to the rise of assessment, professional power, surveillance, standards and norms promoted through the ideology of liberalism and the marketised practices of capitalism, where particular kinds of subjectivities are valued, expected and anticipated. A key feature of contemporary society is the progressive extension of ways of understanding ourselves. While this is often seen as a positive feature of the civilising tendencies of modernity – we have more and more ways of understanding how we should live our lives – Foucault's work intervenes to highlight the oppressive and containing nature of this apparent psychological enlightenment. Tremain (2006: p. 50) captures this well by arguing that these ways of understanding constitute human subjects whose actions are governed through the exercise of their own capacity to choose in accordance with the norm(al). So, while we are free, we are free only to govern ourselves. At the intersection of parenting and disability, professional intervention and policy guidance, associated discourses introduce concepts, vocabularies and practices for self-management:

> The discourse that is generated frequently appeals to certain conceptions of responsibility, self-control, self-interest, and self-determination; moreover, many people who become ensconced in this self-management characterize the lived reality that they experience in terms of a genuine increase in their personal power and decision making.
>
> (Tremain, 2006: p. 45)

Behind self-management are the practices of bio-power. Armstrong (2002: p. 444–5) argues that Foucault's notion of bio-power is useful in describing the 'shift in the nature of power' in which 'the pastoral' becomes merged with 'the disciplinary' as part of 'a technology of care and control'. She quotes Peim's summary:

> The point of bio-power is that it represents a shift in the very nature of government and in the very nature of power. Bio-power works through the dual, but necessarily combined, forces of pastoral discipline and its end point is the production of *self-disciplinary, self-regulatory citizenry overlaid with an array of attributes*.
>
> (Peim, 2001: p. 183, our emphasis)

An example, for Armstrong, of 'bio-power' is the role of labelling in the creation of deviant and marginalised identities as a mechanism for the management (i.e. education, care and treatment) of disturbing others. Key examples for Tremain (2006) are those disciplinary powers of discourses associated with disability and parenting that lead to forms of parenting governance or governed parenting. The arguments developed in this book are therefore mindful of the pressures and resistant potentialities of governance on disabled families and professionals. This in particular is the case in the un/making of children's identities, the shaping of productive parental alliances and the making of professional ethics.

The psycho-emotional register

Parenting is as much an emotional form of labour as it is material, cultural and political. From a critical disability studies perspective, research and practice must take seriously the complex psychological impacts of living with an impaired child in a disabling and exclusionary world. One way of engaging with this complexity is to turn to what has been termed the psycho-emotional dimensions of disablism (Goodley & Roets, 2008; Thomas, 1999a, b, 2007). This refers to those psychological and affective realities that undermine the emotional well-being of disabled people which can be just as disabling as structural barriers. Emotional disablism might be expressed through internalised oppression, anger, uncertainty, fear or shame. It can impact upon self-esteem, personal confidence and ontological security (Thomas, 2007: p. 72) and in some ways makes for difficult and potentially spoilt identities (Reeve, 2002, 2005). Thomas (2001: p. 55) argues that a preoccupation with the public and the material in a lot of British disability studies literature has ignored whole areas of disability experience, and thus of disablism, because they are located in the private domain of life. Tregaskis (2004b) notes that many disabled children differ from children of other minority groups (except, probably, many gay and lesbian children) in being the only family member who belongs to that minority:

> Even for well-loved disabled children, there might be nobody at home with whom to 'compare notes' on how to deal with oppressive practice within wider society, thus rendering the person with impairment even more isolated. In such a situation it is unsurprising that many disabled people with no positive role models have experienced internalised oppression … turning feelings of guilt at having been born at all and changing their family's life for ever onto themselves in damaging ways.
>
> (p. 3)

Any analysis of the psycho-emotional must resist psychologising and individualising parents' accounts. Critical community psychological ideas are useful here, not least, in shaping the kinds of understandings we develop around notions of distress, burden and anxiety, as well as alliance, support and empathy. Instead of understanding parental distress, for example, as an inevitable psychological reaction to a diagnosis of their child's impairment, we want to ask questions about the relational, cultural and institutional discourses and practices that influence how parents feel about their children (see Orford, 1992; Kagan, 2002). Furthermore, we would want to acknowledge that affect is constantly shifting, always moveable and social in character (Burr, 2003). How parents feel about their disabled children – and how disabled children feel about themselves – will say much about how their emotional worlds respond to, and are structured by, disabled discourses of quality of life, community belonging, familial responses and institutional location.

Burman (2008) conceives the child as the subject of a whole host of explanatory ideas associated with development, achievement and progress. Parents will internalise these ideas in their emotional lives with children. This may influence how they feel about their child's diagnosis; their family's response to the diagnosis; the norms surrounding behaviour and bodily comportment in public spaces; expectations about schooling and the meaning of education; and ideas and plans for the future. We emphasise the psycho-emotional in this text to acknowledge the socially constructed nature of emotional life in ways that will also sensitise us to the ways in which parents resist normative modes of feeling about their disabled children, as they seek out productive alternatives.

Critical professionals and professions

Professionals play a huge role in the lives of disabled families. How, why and what they do require sustained analysis. The study of professionals has a long history within sociology (MacDonald & Ritzer, 1988), while the disability movements have had their own critique of professional practice and the role of institutions in the maltreatment of disabled people in both community and residential settings (Illich, 1977; Morris, 1993b). Marxist sociology identified professionals as key actors within institutions that solidified power inequalities and acted in the self-interest of capitalist powers (MacDonald, 1995; Perkins, 1989). Disability studies adapted this critique to argue that the institutional power of professionals was crucial to pathologising disability and the creation of dependency (Drewett, 1999). Within sociology the Marxist approach has been widely criticised for failing to recognise the practices of power and negotiations within institutions, which cannot be solely explained via a structuralist approach that privileges capitalist requirements (Savage et al., 1992; Witz, 1992). New ways of understanding how and in which ways professionals can be powerful, create professional boundaries, conceptualise their influence, and act as resistant actors have developed, some of which have found their way into disability studies (Deeley, 2002; Fournier, 2000). An important aspect of such work is to see professionals from a multidimensional perspective, which recognises them as socially embedded human actors, involved in making day-to-day complex ethical decisions, in conditions of uncertainty and as members of institutional contexts (Kalvemark et al., 2004; Pols, 2006). There is now greater recognition of the ways in which both individual professionals and professional organisations labour to construct areas of practice, knowledge and expertise as both theirs and useful (Reed, 1996). Research explores how professions shape the work they do, rather than how professions gain and lose importance because of the intrinsic value of their expertise (Artaraz, 2006; Freidson, 1994; Hanlon, 1998). Claims to particular sets of practice – for example, empathetic care for social workers and nurses, and clinical expertise for medical professionals – allow for the articulation of professional boundaries, which assert the importance of individuals and groups to the institutional fields within which they operate (McLaughlin & Webster, 1998). Later on in this book, we explore the reflexive processes undertaken by a host of practitioners when they are reflecting on their professional ethics. This highlights a host of issues associated with moral values and how these fit or jar with the realities of professional practice, policy governance and institutional expectations. Pols' (2006: p. 426) notion of 'contextual reflexivity' is useful here and allows a methodology for grappling with the practice of professional ethics.

Conclusions

This chapter has outlined some of the epistemologically, theoretical and analytical resources that underpin our analysis of parents, professionals and disabled babies. Crucially, this book also engages with the realities of caring for a disabled child through reference to in-depth qualitative work with families and professionals. The strong empirical focus of the book is explored further in chapters 2 and 3 as we introduce the methodological and relational details of our Economic and Social Research Council (ESRC) funded study.

2
Methodology

Dan Goodley, Janice McLaughlin, Emma Clavering and
Pamela Fisher

Introduction

In this chapter we will briefly provide an overview of the research project, upon which this book draws, in order to consider issues of theoretical background, ethics, methodology and analytical frameworks. In Chapter 3 we turn to some of the relational processes and stories of the research. The research team worked with families of disabled children and a number of associated professionals over a period of three-and–a-half years. The research was based in two English regions (the North East and the Midlands). Researchers responsible for the day-to-day fieldwork were Emma Clavering in the North East, who worked throughout the duration of the project, and Claire Tregaskis and Pamela Fisher who spent, respectively, a year and just less than two years on the project in the Midlands.

At the heart of the fieldwork were 39 families. The first group of 23, who had disabled children aged two or over, provided us with retrospective accounts of their experiences, including medical, social care and educational services, which had occurred since the birth of their children. The second group of 16 families, had children up to two-and-a-half years old at the start of the project, and they had a long-term involvement with our research. They provided a longitudinal perspective through participating in a number of interviews conducted over a period of two years. People's lives and experiences do not easily fit into research categories and protocols. The research team quickly recognised that families' lives were not static, nor were diagnoses or prognoses (whether medical, social or educational). From initial encounters with those families first intended to offer a retrospective view, looking back on their experiences over the past two years and beyond, we realised that a great deal was still in flux and unresolved for them. In recognition of the need to explore the fluid context in family worlds, it was decided to also follow up some parents in the 'retrospective' group over time.

The parents were recruited from a variety of sources, including support group and voluntary agency newsletters and contact via health and social care professionals and National Health Service (NHS) trusts, following ethics and governance approval. When recruiting the parents the deliberate step was taken not to recruit one form of childhood impairment or condition, as this fitted too rigidly with a medical model of impairment/disability. Instead the basis for a family's inclusion was that they defined their child as having specific care and support needs. A range of labels and impairments were represented, including the labels of autistic spectrum disorder, Down's syndrome, cerebral palsy, a host of different genetic conditions (not always definitively diagnosed during the period of the study), brain damage and a range of physical and learning impairments. Three families had more than one child who was disabled. The participating parents came from a range of different locations and backgrounds that did not sit easily with fixed social classifications. Most were co-habiting heterosexual couples; a few were single mothers, and one parent self-identified as a disabled person. There was a range of ethnicities within and between the different families. In three cases we worked with immigrants to the UK whose first language was not English; interpreters of the family's choosing were used for two families (in the other case the researcher spoke the family's first language) and translations of interview materials provided. The total amount of fieldwork is summarised below (see Table 2.1).

There was also a strong ethnographic component to the methodology, involving (1) the observation of parents, children and professionals in a variety of clinical, social service and home settings and (2)

Table 2.1   Fieldwork Summary

	No. of Families		Interviews		Observation		Professional
	Retro	**Long**	**Retro**	**Long**	**Retro**	**Long**	**Focus Group**
Newcastle	8	4	28	12	13	12	3
Sheffield	15	12	18	35	2	28	3
Total	23	16	45	46	15	40	6
Overall Total	39		931		55		6

Note: 'Retro' indicates retrospective parents and 'Long' refers to longitudinal parents.

immersion within the wider support networks of parents. In addition, six focus groups were conducted to include the perspectives of a range of medical and social care professionals working with the families. Below we discuss how the research was influenced by the theoretical and methodological priorities of an ethnographic approach.

Ethnography

Ethnography has a long history within disability studies and has been used to explore healthcare settings (Bartolo, 2002), inclusive education (Vlachou, 1997), special education (Duncan, 2003), segregated institutions (Edgerton, 1967, 1984), community settings (Angrosino, 1994; Tregaskis, 2004a), organisations of disabled people (Goodley, 2000; Priestley, 1999) and parent groups (Vincent, 2000). In other work, one of us has described ethnographic work as an epistemological journey (Goodley & Lawthom, 2005a), where different epistemological places are visited in order to address particular questions, interests and aims of the research at given times. Ethnographers are encouraged from the very outset of their research to tease out and illuminate their epistemological and theoretical agendas. For example Coffey (1999), Atkinson et al. (2001) and Evans (2002), acknowledge that ethnographers will inevitably combine 'observational notes' (the who, what, when, where and how of human activity) with 'theoretical notes' (interpretations, inferences, hypotheses and conjectures) and 'methodological notes' (the timing, sequencing, stationing, stage setting and manoeuvring of research).

In order to identify the theoretical underpinnings of ethnographic work, Gordon, et al. (2001) identify a number of epistemological persuasions, often overlapping, which direct researchers towards the analysis of particular facets of the social world. Because we had a number of researchers in the team (with their own theoretical predispositions and interests) and the research was longitudinal by design (so our participation shifted and changed, in and out of a host of individual, relational and institutional places), it is possible to account for our ethnographic work in relation to each of the persuasions identified by Gordon et al. (2001).

First, social interactionism encompasses a number of theoretical persuasions such as ethnomethodology, symbolic interactionism and phenomenology that prime the ethnographer to attend to the construction of meanings by social actors within particular contexts. Cultural and social dynamics are understood as processes of negotiation of the 'order that is to be': where individuals come to a common definition of the situation, draw on similar commonsense knowledge and make assessments of appropriate action. The aim is to elicit the constituent actions and dynamics that contribute to the making of culture. Hence, this approach is often termed 'constitutive ethnography'. In our research, we embraced some of the micro-cultural and phenomenological experiences of parents, children and professionals, which raised a number of questions including:

- How do parents and professionals negotiate forms of care?
- What do people do in healthcare settings and what do they do to each other?
- How are the phenomena of 'disability' and 'impairment' (re)produced in the interactions between professionals and parents?
- What roles and identities do professionals and parents occupy in trajectories and packages of care that contribute to outcomes of empowering/disabling visions of the life chances of impaired babies?
- What phenomenological accounts emerge of being a parent of a disabled child or a healthcare professional?
- How are comportment, diagnosis and prognosis of the disabled body accounted for?

Interactionist approaches have been criticised on the basis that they struggle to come up with theoretical and structural accounts of culture. This is addressed in what Gordon et al. identify as the second epistemological persuasion of ethnographic work: cultural studies and critical theory. For Gordon et al. cultural studies question the structural logic of the taken-for-granted view that cultures already exist and are functioning well. In Britain, the *Centre for Contemporary Cultural Studies* in Birmingham (from which the renowned work of Stuart Hall emerged) built a reputation for capturing this purported preoccupation with the 'bigger questions' of cultural formation. The aims here are to theorise social, economic and cultural constraints on human agency. Unlike the constitutive ethnographies of interactionists, critical ethnographers begin with the premise that human actors are essentially unfree and inhabit a world rife with contradictions and asymmetries of power and privilege. As well as theorising the inter-relationship between structure and agency, Marx's notion of praxis is drawn upon. Here the aim is not simply to understand the contradictions and oppressions within particular groupings but, as with action research, to promote empowerment. These theoretical resources appear to offer structural and transformative qualities for ethnographers. The priorities of critical theory do, at times, leave little space to acknowledge individual agency. In our ethnographic research we found spaces for working closely with parents to not only understand their experiences of disabling (or enabling) practice but also, at times, to explore possibilities for changing family lives for the better. We discuss some of these incidents in Chapter 3. For now, it is helpful to outline some of the ways in which our own ethnographic work engages with critical questions:

- In what ways does power circulate, reproduce but also provide opportunities for resistance in the lives of families?
- To what extent are professional hierarchies present but also challenged at the interface of parent-professional interactions?
- How do certain policy frameworks promote muted forms of care?
- Can parent groups provide alternative frameworks of meaning and valuing for parents of disabled children?

Gordon et al.'s (2001) third persuasion is associated with feminism, postmodernism and poststructuralism. Feminist theorists have developed a self-reflexive philosophy to research (Stanley & Wise, 1993). Ethnographers' claim that their presence in people's lives has the potential to support emancipation, has strong overlaps with feminist advocacy of research that has political possibilities (Haraway, 1991; Harding, 1991; Hartsock, 1998; Kenney, 1997; Mann, 2000). Feminists have opened up crucial debates about the relationships between researchers and participants (Alcoff & Potter, 1992). Ethnographers are challenged to work together with participants in order to develop shared subjective understandings of a given culture, breaking down power relationships between the researchers and the 'researched' and to work critically and closely with subjectivity as a resource of the ethnographic project. Feminisms recognise a whole host of structural and agency concerns within the doing of research and call for researchers to open up their own agendas for public viewing (Smith, 1987). Alongside these encounters has been an accompanying and not altogether comfortable relationship with the rise of postmodern and poststructuralist accounts. A 'turn to the textual' has problematised the interactionist vision of the ideal 'objective' ethnographic account (Barrett, 1992). Malinowski's vision of capturing the 'native's vision of their world' is directly contravened by postmodern and feminist demands for researchers to openly and critically write themselves into their ethnographic accounts. If we accept the presumption that life is a collection of narratives then researchers need to own their narratives of a given part of the social world. The questions these approaches provide for our research are:

- How do families negotiate roles and rules?
- To what extent do the roles and identities of parents – especially mothers – reproduce dominant patriarchal forms of gendered care?
- Are parents increasingly able to access multiple identities and subject positions in the care of their children?
- What are the costs and benefits of adopting the role of an extended caregiver for parents of disabled children?
- To what extent are parents and professionals governed by normative discourses of parenting and professionalism?

The priorities of postmodern considerations are not without tensions. Prominent feminist critics are unhappy with a turn to the text that has led to the death of the subject (Chancer, 1998; Riley, 1988; Stanley, 1990). The reflexive, embodied, human agent is replaced by an attention to the ways in which (human) subjects and (social, cultural) objects are constructed through a variety of inter-relating stories and practices: or discourses (Jackson, 1999; Wilson, 1993). Recently, in response to the relativist claims, there has been a revival in the contribution of materialist analyses to these textual ethnographies (Bannerji, 1995; Hennessy, 2006; Jackson, 2001). In this work we are encouraged to consider the underlying structures, material conditions and conflicting historically specific power relations and inequalities that give rise to certain forms of socio-cultural inclusion and exclusion. We have taken up this issue in relation to disabled babies and parents in a recent piece (McLaughlin & Goodley, 2008). In short, while we are interested in the social and institutional constructions of phenomena of impairment, diagnoses, disability, care, professional practice, policy, parenting, identity and community, we also are mindful of the very real material realities that underpin these constructions.

Having provided an overview of the theoretical background to the design of the project, we can now move on to discuss some of the practical processes and approaches involved in developing the fieldwork.

Methodological approaches

The empirical work raised a number of interesting methodological considerations, some of which we tackled in articles published during the lifetime of the project, including the relationship between on-disabled/ disabled researchers (Tregaskis & Goodley, 2006); the interconnections of a researcher's biography as a disabled child and emergent accounts in the interviews (Tregaskis, 2005) and working with the heterogeneity of focus group membership (Clavering & McLaughlin, 2007b). In this section we consider more broadly the methodology of the study.

Ethics and access: formal procedures

Ethical approval from NHS' Local Research Ethics Committees (LRECs) was required. In all, due to multiple sites of access, three LRECs considered and approved the project, involving substantial written applications and oral defence of the application at committee meetings. LREC approval also required registration of projects with NHS Trust Research and Development (R&D) offices. The project began as research governance of research projects in NHS contexts were increasing in significance following the scandals in Alder Hey and Bristol (where tissues and organs were taken from deceased children without parental consent). There was considerable variation in how Trusts were pursuing research governance and speed in putting new processes into play. The Midlands-based researchers encountered significant initial delays due to the requirements of their local R&D office. The R&D approval required Honorary NHS contracts for the researchers (as is now common practice). This meant, among other requirements, additional medical and Criminal Records Bureau checks. Working in the Midlands team around this time was Claire Tregaskis, who wrote in her fieldwork diary:

I really didn't see why we had to go through all this when we were both already members of University staff who had gone through medical vetting prior to appointment. It felt like the NHS trusted neither the University's procedures, nor our own individual integrity. Further, for me as a disabled person the prospect of yet more medical surveillance was terrifying, and my previous largely negative experiences with the medical profession made me suspect they would be looking for any reason they could that was connected to my impairment to deny me permission to do the research.

Until R&D approval was granted, six months into the project, the Midlands-based researchers were unable to access parents or professionals in the Trusts. A positive knock on effect of these drawn out ethical processes, was an increased engagement with parent organisations. They became our key gatekeepers in these early days and this allowed us to publicise the project, share our aims and ambitions with parents and work up clear ideas about the possible impacts of the research project.

All parents and professionals, across the two sites of the research, who were approached to participate in the study, were provided with participant information sheets, consent forms and an accessible introductory leaflet. The information sheet detailed the purpose of the study, why participants had been chosen, explained withdrawal, the impact of research and our plans to disseminate research findings in order to promote best practice for disabled children and their families. It also reassured parents that their involvement in the research would not impact negatively on their care or services they were accessing. Where time permitted, initial meetings were arranged by the researchers with parents who were considering taking part in the study. These meetings, with no tape recorder, were seen as opportunities in which the parent was able to freely voice any concerns and questions about the research before committing themselves. However, they also worked as a way of introducing both the researcher and the research approach to potential participants so, if the parent did decide to take part, one layer of rapport had already been established, which then helped develop further trust at the first interview. Parents were not considered part of the research until they had signed the consent form after this meeting had taken place. The consent form garnered individuals' initial agreement to participate, while a longer process of ongoing informed consent was adhered to (see Nelson & Prilleltensky, 2004). We return in Chapter 3 to the more relational aspects of building ethical relationships with parents and their children.

Interviewing

In-depth narrative interviewing was a major methodological resource in this study. Retrospective parents were interviewed up to four times in order to allow them time to reflect back on their experiences from the birth of their child. Longitudinal parents were interviewed at least three times over an 18-month period (circumstances and continued participation permitting). In the book we identify which interview a quote is taken from by placing IV1, IV2 etc. following the quote. As a team we were inspired by a myriad of literature associated with in-depth interviewing, including oral historians (Parker, 1963, 1990; Parker, 1994; Thompson, 1988), biographical sociologists (Bertaux, 1981; Clandinin & Connelly, 1994; Plummer, 1983, 1995) and qualitative disability researchers (Bogdan & Taylor, 1976, 1982; Booth & Booth, 1994, 1998). We also drew upon our own experiences of using this methodology (e.g. Goodley, 1996, 2000; Goodley et al., 2004).

Different researchers approached the in-depth interviews in their own ways. Pamela explained her approach as applying techniques familiar to those working within the oral history tradition, while Emma drew from social anthropology techniques she had used in previous research with families. From the different backgrounds came a shared focus on providing the interviewees with freedom to talk about their lives, prioritising whatever issues or topics they held to be important. They were encouraged to go beyond a merely descriptive approach, and to place their own interpretation on events and situations. In this way the intention was to reveal experiences and perspectives which might have otherwise remained hidden. Very little can be known about the everyday routine existence and concerns of ordinary people without narrative evidence from oral testimonies. In this respect, interviews have provided an invaluable source for uncovering and exploring experiences which have been in Rowbotham's (1973) resonant phrase, '... hidden from history'. Narratives resulting from this type of approach to interviewing should therefore constitute a democratic epistemology which gives a voice to groups which more traditional methods have neglected. While this is worthwhile in itself, narratives of this kind offer another considerable advantage which should not be overlooked: oral testimonies make connections between separate spheres of life which collapse boundaries of private and public.

Observation

The study used the ethnographic tradition of observation in order to analyse the lifeworlds of parents of disabled children in a variety of community and institutional contexts. The research team carried out 55 days of ethnographic research with a host of events and activities, some of which are detailed below in Table 2.2.

In addition to these days we also carried out documentary analysis of national, regional and local policy documents; reviewed guidelines and good practice produced by statutory and voluntary organisations; assessed Internet sites produced by parents, professionals and disability people's organisations from a host of countries; consistently reviewed publications of government websites; and commissioned an analysis of policy and legislation by a disability studies researcher. Through combining analyses of the public/private and formal/informal we were able

Table 2.2 Summary of Observational Settings

Formal settings of health, social care and education	Informal settings of family, leisure and community
Observation of a specialist nursery at a Children's Centre	Visits to family homes for coffee
Attendance at a parenting class for parents of children with autism	Presence during home visits from health visitors, midwives, social workers, portage workers, physiotherapists, speech therapists, and pre-school Library service
Accompanying parents to medical appointments with GPs, Consultants, and specialist teams	Meeting with the family at the Mainstream community morning toddlers group
A visit to the citizen's advise bureau to find out about entitlement to Disability Living Allowance	Helping with the shopping in supermarkets and shops
Visits to observe neonatal intensive care units, including discussions with registrars and nursing staff	Lunch with the family in a local restaurant
Observation of a child's physiotherapy and speech therapy sessions at the hospital	Observation of a parent/carer forum
Meeting with a mother at the new Disability Information Service office to find out about accessible leisure facilities	Watching the kids during swimming lessons
	Observation of a parent- group meeting in the local community centre
Invitation to observe a staff meeting of Portage workers	Invited to attend a child's birthday party and meet the extended family and friends
A visit and look around the facilities of a respite care centre	Afternoon in the park with a family
A trip on a service minibus	Visiting a family to celebrate the birth of their new baby
A look around the Premature Babies Unit under the guidance of the consultant and three registrars	Invitation to see a family's new home
	On the school run with parents
Observation of staff meeting for Community Paediatric Nursing Team, followed up by several visits to give feedback to group about research	In the kitchen being taken through the form filling for an application for respite care

(Continued)

Table 2.2 (Continued)

Formal settings of health, social care and education	Informal settings of family, leisure and community
Interview with the Education Officer of an Early Years Special Education Needs (SEN) strategy	Meeting at the University to discuss the transcript from the last interview
Question and answer session with an early support team and Down Syndrome organisation	Two hours on-line with a mother as she fires off emails to members of her Parent group on-line community
Visit to see facilities offered by Special Educational Needs Teaching and Support Service (SENTASS)	An hour of MSN messaging with a parent
Observation during an assessment by the respiratory consultant	Attendance at an open forum of the Care Co-ordination Network
Observation of support group for parents and pre-school children run by the Toy Library	Evening out with several family groups for a trip to a local soft play venue – organised by one of the parents
Visit to social services Children with Disabilities Team (CWDT)	Numerous telephone conversations
Visits and observations at Sure Start projects	
A conversations with a group of parents at the child development centre	
A trip to hydrotherapy pool with a Mum and son	
Numerous telephone conversations	

to produce a qualitatively rich analyses of many aspects of living with a disabled child in the UK between 2003–07.

Focus groups

One use of focus groups is to provide a context within which the interaction between individuals generates data unavailable through one-to-one interviews (Kitzinger, 1994; Wilkinson, 1999). Focus groups have become popular within health research because they are time efficient and provide a useful vehicle for researchers to explore deeper aspects of health professionals' work and the cultural dynamics of healthcare settings. To capture professional perspectives on the family's lives we decided to use focus groups as a space within which professionals could discuss together their understandings and values. Some focus group researchers advocate homogenous membership (Carey, 1994), where participants share similar perspectives and beliefs and discussion is not inhibited by power hierarchies created by differences in professional or social status. While planning our focus groups, various researchers advised us to meet with consultants and nurses separately to avoid the nurses being silenced. However, as discussed in Clavering and McLaughlin (2007b) we rejected homogeneity and instead sought to include a range of professionals and practitioners from across health, social care, education and the voluntary sector in each focus group. This proved to be highly productive in identifying differences in professional perspectives and challenged assumptions made about the impact of differences in professional status; nurses were far from silent in the presence of consultants. In each location a focus group was formed, which met three times (in the text they are referred to as focus groups A and B, with a number to indicate which session the quote is taken from). The dominant tool was the use of composite narratives of stories drawn from the fieldwork (we discuss this further below under 'narrative inquiry') which were sent to participants prior to the focus group session and provided a challenging context to the discussions.

The focus groups had a series of unintended benefits. Recruiting participants involved a series of meetings with many different professionals and practitioners. These meetings became an opportunity to discuss the project and subsequently linked directly into policy dissemination of the project findings. This occurred through subsequent meetings, sharing of the project summary and attendance at a one-day workshop for professionals, practitioners and parents we held at the end of the project. In addition, when planning the focus groups, our main concern was how difficult it would be to get participants in the same room at the same time. To help entice people, sessions were always scheduled to end with lunch, however we assumed participants would probably dash away as soon as they could. Instead we found that the majority of the participants stayed for lunch. The focus groups turned out to be an opportunity for the participants to network. Finally, at the last focus group meeting in the North East the participants discussed the value they had drawn from the meetings and the wish to continue on, by taking what they had learnt in the discussions back into their workplace:

> The stories we have read ... they are hugely challenging, they have had an emotional impact on all of us, reading the stories of people and their lives as they see them, identifying other people that we work with within their stories. As grassroots workers we are challenged by that and I would like to see us having a role taking this agenda to another tier of management. So that they would have a greater understanding of the reality of the things they are actually doing.
>
> (Focus Group, 3B)

Narrative inquiry

Narrative inquiry pervaded all aspects of the research design. It can be argued that stories fundamentally capture the uncertain, diverse and changing nature of individual and social lives at the start of the twenty-first century (Bowker, 1993). Bruner (1986, 1990) argues that the telling of stories is the principal mode through which people make sense of their lives. Narrative inquiry deals with the collection, writing up, presentation and analysis of stories. It is both a methodological approach (it permits the storying of ethnographic observations and interview transcripts) and an analytical venture (it allows for the narrative construction of particular theoretical accounts). Drawing upon Goodley and Clough (2004) and Goodley et al. (2004) it is possible to speak of a number of narrative forms that provide insight into the problems being studied and reflexive analysis of the dynamics of research production; each of which have been used in this research and are represented in the analysis developed in chapters 4 through 8.

Autobiographies

Undoubtedly parents have numerous well-rehearsed stories. Many parents were very used to being asked about their experiences by professionals, family, friends and researchers. Stories of diagnosis, for example, were often well-worn accounts. Many parents turned up for the interview with ready-made autobiographical accounts. Sometimes these had already found their way onto public discourses of Internet communities and the oral histories of parent groups. An interesting aspect of the longitudinal nature of interviews allowed us the chance to see how these stories evolved.

Interview-based narratives

A number of narratives are brought together following transcription of audiotaped interviews. Professional transcribers are used to type up the interview material, the researcher constructs a story and the informant reviews the form. For an account of writing stories from interview to finished narrative see Goodley (2000).

Composite narratives

These stories bring together a variety of ethnographic material collected by the research team. They refer to real people, events and experiences that are then put together in a narrative of a pseudonym. This approach is captured well in Clough (2002). These narratives are particularly useful in capturing controversial and thought-provoking stories in ways that maintain the anonymity of the storytellers. Composites were used in most of the professional focus groups. Stories were sent to professionals prior to a focus group with the following covering note, 'We present this story not as a representative account of all parents' experiences with professionals but as an illustrative narrative'. When professionals felt that they 'knew who this story was about', we could appeal to fiction in order to maintain anonymity.

Ethnographic vignettes

Throughout the period of fieldwork, researchers kept diaries. Ethnography refers to a process of immersion within a culture, where the researcher attempts to capture the wordy nature of the meanings within that culture. Interactions, observations, conversations, documentary evidence are all brought together. Consequently, a number of ethnographic vignettes can be drafted. Ethnographic writing is considered in detail in Goodley (1999). Trawling through the raft of ethnographic data for the writing of this book has revealed big stories, recurring barriers experienced by a number of parents, methodological dilemmas, tentative theoretical accounts of the data and intimate accounts of family and professional life.

Conversational narratives

These stories bring together striking dialogue and discussion between our informants. This might include tensions and debate in the professional focus groups and parent interviews, or during observations of parents' social networks and dealings with professionals. How well one captures such conversations depends on the ability to script the encounters, and much can be gained here from dipping into research accounts of and by the arts (see for example Banks & Banks, 1998; Matarasso, 1977; Schutzman & Cohen-Cruz, 1997).

Themed narratives

The material we collect may allow us to provide themed stories, which pick up explicitly on analytical themes we are developing and capture some of the different engagements of parents. Examples that emerged in the process included 'the medicalised parent', 'the heroic struggler', the 'flexible activist', the 'professional mother' and the 'enabling professional'. These were held as tentative and transitional themes rather than as fixed and permanent analytical categories.

Approaching analysis

We have already seen that analysis starts right at the beginnings of research. There was also a distinct phase of analysis on the part of the research team which permitted opportunities for reading the emerging data in order to answer the research questions and identify further questions emerging from the data itself. Interview and focus group transcripts and observation notes were entered into Nvivo, alongside team discussion of fieldwork material and conceptual ideas developing from them. Observational notes were examined alongside interviews to explore lived experiences that exemplified the dynamics parents discussed in interviews. At times this approach to analysis was formalised through the workings of 'node meetings'. This involved subjecting narratives and ethnographic data to points of analysis or themes that were drawn together by the research team as the data were collected (Snow et al., 2003). The range of analysis and discussion allowed ongoing consideration of whether we were developing the most appropriate forms of interview; it allowed us to capture the complexity of the cultures we were investigating; it highlighted new ethnographic spaces to explore; it aided making the data collectively meaningful to us; and it enabled us to reflect on our research questions and through it we began to make the connections between what we were finding and the broader theoretical and policy literature.

Conclusions

In this chapter we have considered some of the methodological underpinnings of our research project. In Chapter 3 we consider some of its relationships.

3
Research Encounters

Dan Goodley, Janice McLaughlin, Emma Clavering and Pamela Fisher

Introduction

We were conscious from the outset that parents of disabled children, especially very young or poorly children, demand forms of respect that go way beyond the normative ethical criteria of consent, withdrawal and anonymity. Research design required reciprocity, mutuality and the development of practices which sought to place decision making about participation in the hands of parents. Early encounters with parents demonstrated the active impact that they would have, not only on the findings, but also on the relationships that would develop. For example, in the first few weeks of the study, a sizeable number of newly recruited parents raised issues about the terminology we were using in our project. They were unhappy with the use of the words 'disabled babies'. While other parents were happy with the term when we explained its origins in the critical disability studies literature, we decided it was important to respond to those parents uncomfortable with it by ensuring that project related documentation would refer to 'babies with specialist healthcare needs'.

The qualitative and ethnographic nature of the research meant that we spent a lot of time checking with one another about the types of relationships that were being formed and the extent to which we were (not) encroaching on the privacy of families. Furthermore, as our analyses became more developed, our team discussions would question the ways in which we were conceptualising families in enabling or disabling ways. We asked similar questions about our work with professionals. We did not want to work in ways that meant we ignored their good practices with parents of disabled children. Yet, our most developed, long-term commitments and relationships were with families. This chapter outlines how we worked with the families, what we learnt from them and what challenges emerged during the fieldwork.

Relational ethics

From the beginning we knew our fieldwork would have to be adaptable to the complex lives of the families. Researching children – and specifically disabled children – meant that research involvement had to be moulded around them and their families' needs. This pattern of adaptation was an important aspect of seeking to build a form of relational ethics with the families, which moved on from the formal ethics and governance procedures discussed in Chapter 2. In describing this approach, we do not want to suggest we always achieved this, or that we were ethically perfect; instead this was what we sought to achieve. In practice, it influenced our choice of open-ended interviews, which sought to situate power in the hands of participants, especially with regards to timing, and to the range and depth of issues discussed. The fieldwork approach of interviewing people over time and carrying out observations with some, provided a space within which there was scope to build a relationship with the families. Such relationships were not without tensions or boundaries, as is discussed later in the chapter. Nevertheless, the time spent with parents meant that connections could be made, similar experiences shared and, at times, resources provided. From when we first met with parents, there was a need to find ways to build a relationship, aided by the practice of meeting parents before their participation in the research began. While we never sought to refute the role we played as researchers, we also did not refute other aspects of who we are as individuals. In doing so, as within feminist and critical disability studies approaches, the aim was to be open to parents in the way they were open to us. There was a rawness, depth and honesty to what parents told us, which required a response from us and which acknowledged their lives and their children's lives as valuable.

Eva lives on a council estate that many in the city refer to as the rough side of town. I arrived at her house at about 11 am and parked my car on the curb outside her front door. When I knocked on the door (no bell), there was no reply and was I was fairly sure that the house was empty. More or less resigned to this being a 'wasted' visit, I nevertheless phoned Eva's home number on my mobile. She answered the phone fairly quickly – she was at home and was ready to be interviewed but after a broken night with her baby daughter, who sleeps only restlessly, Eva had dropped off in a chair … Eva told me that shortly after Cindy's birth, the doctor had bluntly stated, 'She'll never open her eyes, she'll never cry, she'll never sit up, she'll never walk.' Eva had been devastated. As she told me this, she broke down in tears. The doctor had, however, been wrong. Cindy, although unable to move with much ease, observes the world through her beautiful blue eyes.

(Pamela's fieldwork notes)

Building ethnographic relationships can flounder or prosper on perceptions of commonality. All the members of the research team were female bar one. All of the fieldworkers involved in the day-to-day fieldwork were women. Many of the participants were women. There were clearly times when mothers seemed to open up to female researchers because of assumed common identities associated with gender. One of the field-workers, Emma, is a mother of a young non-disabled boy, similar in age to many of the children. The commonality and difference this created became a significant aspect of the relationships she developed in the study, as Alec (Emma's son) became part of many interview discussions and ongoing conversations with the parents. It also became a resource in Emma's developing analysis:

I found myself comparing my child's rate of development and personality traits to his contemporaries in the study. What struck me more than anything was the diversity, and the way labels might be hung on a child, any child when minor queries become recognised as major issues. One example of this was when I was talking to Maria about Luke's progress. She had just been told what Luke could not do, and this included using cutlery and keeping his attention on one thing for a given length of time. I could not help but think about Alec, who was the same age as Luke and was ready to go to school, no questions asked, no statementing forms, no special measures. But he was not holding his knife and fork properly. Yet no professional had ever come into my home and measured his ability to do this. So, Alec is just Alec – no label, no diagnosis and we continue our lives relatively unmonitored.

(Emma's fieldwork notes)

Claire Tregaskis, who was involved in the research during the first year of the study, identifies herself as a disabled researcher. As has been discussed elsewhere (Goodley & Tregaskis, 2006a), this created, at times, opportunities to share a mutuality of experience, indicated here in this excerpt from an interview with a mother called Mags:

> Claire: I can't believe how fast he is on the floor, he's like a little motor, isn't he?
> Mags: He has to be, he can't stand up so ...
> Claire: Well, apparently I did that until I was about 4, I was always going round on my bum.
> Mags: Yes.
> Claire: I think mum was just quite laid back and thought, well, she'll do it when she is ready, and of course I did.
> Mags: You can't push if they aren't ready. I have found that, you will sort of try some things with him and he will just blank and is not interested in doing it and then you will forget about it and you will leave it and he will do it and you will think ... he has done it. They do things when they are ready.
>
> (Mags, IV2)

Claire was able, like Emma, to draw on her own experiences to analyse the experiences of families. For example, Claire quickly identified the presence of the persistent professional panopticon (Foucault, 1991) when she travelled into the professionalised spaces that the families inhabited:

> *When we arrived at the children's centre and were shown into the 'Parents' Room', I noticed immediately that there were one-way observation windows along one wall. From previous professional experience I knew this meant there was the possibility that people (e.g. behavioural psychologists) could be sitting in that room and observing the interview. As a result, we closed the blind over one of these two windows, and at the other (where the blind was missing) Rosemary [Claire's support worker] hung her coat to minimise what could be seen. She also checked the room next door, which was marked on the door as being unoccupied. Only after we were sure there was nobody there did we invite the parent into the interview room.*
>
> (Claire's research diary)

These elements of commonality – gender, parenthood and disability – were complicated by matters of difference associated with class, ethnicity, age, regional belonging and our status as academic researchers. We approached some parents who refused to be involved. One explanation may be that they were 'talked out' due to having so many interactions with professionals. On a few occasions parents remained fairly distant, perhaps associating us with the myriad professionals who constantly invaded their private lives. Friendships and acquaintances were quickly made with other parents. The depth of relationship and the scope of shared experiences were led by parents. We sought neither to obtain more than they were comfortable discussing, nor impose any more from our lives than they wished to hear.

This relational approach achieved a depth of material and insight in the families' lives. What happened during the first interview with Sarah and Nick indicates the kind of depth the relational approach made possible. The interview was four hours long, but was spread throughout a day Emma spent with them. The interview stopped and started to make way for children to be taken and picked up from school, lunch to be made and phone calls to be answered. At the beginning, Sarah and Nick told a relatively standard story of day-to-day challenges and coping. However, after two hours with them, a more complex picture began to appear. While Sarah was out of the room, Nick started talking about the way one particular professional had behaved. This behaviour had been extremely judgmental and negative. When Sarah came back the interview went back to where Sarah had left off. As the interview continued, Nick dropped into the conversation a comment that told Sarah he had let Emma know what had happened with this professional.

The composure of Sarah and of Nick was all of a sudden lifted, and they spoke about a single moment of crisis that they had never spoken about in such detail to anyone before. The emotions were raw. They both knew they were taking a great risk telling this comparative stranger about a time when tragedy nearly overwhelmed them. But I was not a professional who could use such a story to take their children away (the crisis had been dealt with by formal services and Sarah and Nick said nothing that indicated a current risk to their children, which would have required me to act by informing services). I was simply a person they knew would listen, and who they felt they could trust to not be judgmental.

(Emma's fieldwork notes)

This was a difficult story for the researcher to hear:

Not for the first or last time I questioned my role as researcher – being entrusted with such detailed and personal stories.

(Emma's fieldwork notes)

The interview brought to the fore how much stress and pressure can fall onto the shoulders of individuals when they are failed by services and service representatives. Sarah and Nick's involvement in the research, and the trust they placed in the in-depth approach taken, helped shape and develop the research and the research team's understandings of the complexities experienced by families.

Longitudinal lives and methodological matters

A clear benefit of ethnographic and longitudinal research is the insight it provides into the complexity, conditions and meanings of people's lives. At times, the methodological experiences are indicative of the very challenges faced by families on a day-to-day basis. We shared with parents their social reality of spending much of their time waiting around for others to be available. This ranged from consistently late appointments on the part of professionals, to the delay in turning practical decisions into actions. We also witnessed the transitory nature of the living arrangements of some, often due to their social, cultural and economic vulnerability, which also inhibited their continued involvement in the research.

Unfortunately, when I arrived [for a second interview], nobody answered the door. I spoke to some of the neighbours (in French) who told me that they had left the week before. I was perplexed as I had been quite sure that Bouita had been genuine. Nobody knew (or would tell me) where the family had moved to. Again, I wonder if I was being mistaken for some kind of official. I left feeling quite disheartened. Over the following weeks I kept trying to ring their phone number although this was no longer connected. I knew that these attempts to contact the family were more or less useless but I was worried about them. I'm unlikely to ever know why they left.

(Pamela's fieldwork notes)

Losing touch with some parents was particularly frustrating. We know from previous work in the area of disability and families that those whose voices we need to hear most are often the most difficult to access (Booth & Booth, 1994, 1998). As we journeyed with parents through a host of institutional settings, we were often alerted to the impact this had on the parents:

I noted that Lucy was quite different from how she had been when I had met her at home. At home, she had come across as quite feisty and

assertive. In this session with the physiotherapist, she adopted the role of
acquiescent student. She watched the physio but did not join in.

(Pamela's fieldwork notes)

The relaxed nature of parents when in hospital environments contrasted with our own. We could understand the families as institution-
alised or the healthcare setting as a regular feature of family life. As
researchers we were entering new contexts which felt unfamiliar,
strange and often uncomfortable. Yet, parents often helped make sense
of this world for us. As more time was spent in these settings, we found
ourselves more able to pick up on some of their nuances:

Most of the time (when they're not seeing a specific professional) the par-
ents and children socialise in one room. In many respects, the clinic seems
to be more about developing parental networks and contacts than anything
else. However, I also know from my contacts with parents that they are
keen that their children establish friendships with their peers so that they
can support each other through life. 'Clinics' of this kind are a first step in
establishing friendships (for both parents and children) ... The atmosphere
is mutually supportive and 'upbeat'. The medical issues are minimised or
ignored almost entirely and the professionals appear to take a peripheral
role – both in the proceedings and spatially within the room. This is quite
different from the emphasis in one-to-one interventions in which profes-
sionals take a leading role.

(Pamela's fieldwork notes)

Our growing sense of the day-to-day lives of disabled families inevitably
fed into our conversations and relationships with them. Throughout
the transcripts it is possible to view sensitivity, reciprocity, careful listening and valued interviewees. The following extracts are taken from
an interview by Emma with Kay (IV3):

Emma: I just got a sense, em, when I was here that things, that there's
a lot on your shoulders. And I know I was only here for a short while
the last time ... but I got a real sense there's a lot on your shoulders
and I was hoping that whilst we were talking this morning, you
would get a chance to tell us how bad that is for you and what's going
on. So I'm sorry to make you feel like you've been put on the spot.
Kay: Em.
Emma: We're not, I'm not, there's no judgment here at all. I just
wanted to know how things are for you.

Kay: [Pause] I don't know 'cos it's hard, but I just know how I feel about things on kind of on a day-to-day basis.

Our understandings of parents did not remain in these frozen textual accounts. Instead, through our longitudinal and ethnographic involvement, we were able to develop a far richer understanding of their lives. The extracts below from Pamela's reflections of Helen capture the broad picture obtained over time:

Helen is in her early twenties. She lives with her young son, Roberto, who has severe learning difficulties and autism. As a parent-carer, it's difficult for her to get out and most of the time she's 'cooped up' in her small house with Roberto who is hyperactive and constantly noisy. His 'special care needs' also mean that he rarely sleeps more than about 3 or 4 hours a night and once he's awake, he's immediately 'on the go' the whole time. Helen told me that she's got used to having only 3 hours sleep a night – from time to time she gets tired but it's just become 'normal'. At the end of the interview, I leave the house feeling devastated and wondering how someone of Helen's age copes with what appeared to be a multitude of restrictions and burdens . . . .

Over the months I got to know Helen, this initial impression changed radically. I realised that although Helen is acutely aware of the drawbacks of Roberto's disabilities (there is absolutely no sense that she sees the world through rose-tinted glasses), she is more than content with her 'lot' in life. Roberto is the centre of her world and when she talks about her relation with him the word that keeps cropping up is 'rewarding' ... Helen's parents who live nearby and help out with Roberto are also besotted with him.

The longitudinal work also allowed us to capture significant changes in parents' lives. Maria, in her first interview with Emma came across as having an incredible drive to communicate with her son, Luke, and a strong sense of recognising his achievements and progress. The second interview took place after Luke went through the educational statementing process (which identifies any resource needs for the child to enter mainstream education in the UK), which clearly had been a trigger point for a reassessment on Maria's part on how her son was doing and her skills as his carer.

Maria seemed to have been hit with a bolt out of the blue by the impact of seeing totally negative information about Luke down on paper, when she had up until now always emphasised the positives, the things that Luke could do, rather than what he could not do. Maria spoke about wanting to give Luke a chance in mainstream school. She had understood statementing as a process to go through to ensure support was provided that would allow Luke to participate in school life as fully and as safely as possible. However, it had meant being presented with the full weight of one professional's perspective of things Luke could not do. She seemed to have lost her normal bounce, and was much more resigned to Luke's perceived limitations, and now was saying she assumed he would have to go to a special needs school when he was older, not something she had ever suggested in the past.

The impact of the statementing process, and the words of the educational psychologist continued to have an effect on Maria through the rest of the fieldwork – even after the final interview, she was still trying to resolve the issues for her, and rebuild her previous positive approach to her son.

(Emma's fieldwork notes)

The continued presence of the research(er) also meant that parents discussed with us the ways in which their participation was changing them. Hearing how parents made use of the material for their own benefit, helped us deal with the discomfort we felt due to the time we took up. Earlier we discussed the events around Sarah and Nick's first interview. With some unease – due to the interview's length (the transcript was over 40 pages) and its content – we sent the transcript back to them. The second interview began with the opportunity for them to reflect on the transcript:

They spoke about the impact for them of being involved as being exceptionally important. In particular, having the transcript to read, and to keep, has given them a whole new perspective on their lives and how they deal with professionals. The very solidity of the transcript (its physical presence, tangibility, permanence) – their words down on paper, has proved to be a new tool in their range of ways of managing their situation. It is like they have taken ownership of their words and used them to understand more about themselves and then to move on and try alternative approaches. Sarah told me she had been reading the transcript every night, and keeps it by the bed. She explained how it had challenged her to the core, and made her rethink the way she came across to service providers. She explained she felt they had spent such a long time fighting, they expected a fight and so a fight was inevitable. Now she felt from reading the transcript, it was time to stop fighting, and start negotiating – using skills from her past experiences that she felt somehow had been forgotten under the weight of all the fighting they had been doing.

(Emma's fieldwork notes)

We were not the sole researchers in this project. Parents were active analysers of the events and stories they shared with us, and brought their analyses and its influence on their lives to us.

Parental analysis

Our theoretical agenda grew from the analysis the parents offered of what their lives implied for the position of disabled children, and the influence of societal and professionals' notions of disability in creating marginalisation. They also offered productive visions that countered common sense notions of their lives as tragedy and grief. This pointed us towards several of the key findings discussed in this book.

Lesley remained convinced, however, that life had become much easier for the whole family, especially, for Stuart, since they had realised that having autism was 'not a disaster but a completely different way of being'.

Linda does not believe that impairments are necessarily deficiencies. She explained that children with disabilities often grew up to be more loving and that autistic children are less materialistic than other kids. 'They get more pleasure being with the family or being in a quiet place in the country than they would spending money all the time ...'

Olivia praises many of the professionals she's had dealings with and for the most part she loves the Children's Centre – except for the overuse of the word 'normal' there.

(All extracts from Pamela's fieldwork notes)

Our growing involvement with families exposed us to wider disabling discourses which, in turn, increased our criticality about some of the tacit beliefs within professional and community settings. The following notes are taken from the observation of a 'parenting an autistic child' class:

As with the previous class, the emphasis was on a deficit model. Again, the approach was one of identifying difficulties. At one point, one parent said with a certain exasperation, 'Yes, but can these be overcome.' The speaker assured the parent that with expert guidance her child's difficulties would become less severe, although it was never possible to predict which children were going to respond the best. The parent stated, 'Oh, I'm glad there's some light at the end of the tunnel.' ... The speaker presented autism as an extreme form of 'normal' people's behaviour, in other words, 'we sometimes slam doors if we're frustrated'. I think this was quite useful as it places everyone 'on the spectrum', rather than simply those identified as having autism. Nevertheless, there was, as there always seems to be, a benchmark of 'normality' against which every form of behaviour is assessed. No attempt was made to question or problematise what constitutes 'normality' and achieving normality was upheld as 'the holy grail'.

(Pamela's fieldwork notes)

The close-up nature of in-depth interviewing and ethnography led us to adopt theories that were sensitive to the social, cultural and political barriers experienced by disabled families; reactive to the resistant and resilient acts of parents; and responsive to the kinds of familial, professional and community practices that enable rather than disable families. Empathy and respect inform our choice of analysis as much as the theoretical persuasions of the researcher.

Fieldwork difficulties and challenges

Any research project brings difficulties and challenges. During the research, we faced a range of expected and unexpected problems we had to deal with – not always as well as we would have liked. Below, we discuss a small sample of just some of the issues.

When working with families who did not speak English as their first language, we used interpreters (except with one family where the researcher spoke their first language). On a practical note this was something we had failed to cost for during the proposal stage; realising our error, we found funds from elsewhere in the budget to cover their cost. Interpreters were used with two families, for various reasons with greater success with one family in comparison to other. The most successful experience was the interpreter involved in our research with Corinne and Luis. She was a professional interpreter, chosen by the family because they also used her in other contexts. She seemed to be very flexible in amending her usual style of interpreting for medical and legal professionals, which she explained tended to be very formal, to the open, relatively unstructured approach taken in our ethnographic method. Her long history of working with the family helped develop trust both with us, and within the interview.

Unfortunately, in the other family where an interpreter was used, things proved to be far more difficult. Sameera requested an interpreter, but had not worked with one before; so the research team arranged an interpreter to be provided through the local NHS interpreting team. From the start, the interpreter appeared very frustrated with the open approach of questioning, and told the researcher to change the way questions were asked and time was managed after the first interview had finished. She said that Sameera should be given a set of direct questions. The lack of understanding inhibited the interview process:

> *There were a number of times when I wondered if the interpreter was omitting some of the details Sameera was sharing with us, as well as possibly not fully interpreting the way I was trying to gently probe Sameera about her situation. It took four interviews, as well as the first initial meeting, for me to start to feel I had an idea of what the family life was like, and how little support they had.*

(Emma's fieldwork notes)

The interpreter's approach undermined the relationship that was developing between the parent and the researcher. It proved impossible across the interviews with Sameera to build the kind of relationship we had had with Corinne, Luis and their interpreter. It also made it difficult for us to carry on our usual research practices. For example, interviews were usually open ended, with the parent controlling when it finished. However, when using an interpreter we were constrained by how long they were booked for. In the second interview, Sameera was discussing some harrowing details of the way her child was treated in multiple visits to hospital. In the midst of this discussion the interpreter stood up, unannounced, and said, 'I must go now for my next appointment, goodbye.' Emma did what she could to leave Sameera with some closure to the discussion and had one extra interview with her to explore some of the issues that had been raised. On reflection we should have set up our terms with the interpreter more clearly from the beginning, for example, by setting up a meeting with her to discuss our approach and the expectations we had about the way she should behave. In addition, with greater resources committed to covering the costs of interpreters, we could have booked the interpreter for extra time to ensure events such as this would not have happened.

Researching personal lives brings us into close contact with very difficult, sad and unsettling encounters. Our lives, as well as our research, have been enriched by our time with parents. Nevertheless, there were occasions when we were challenged by some of the difficulties we witnessed. Alongside the need to develop an ethical approach appropriate to the families' lives, we were conscious of the need to care also for each of us, in particular for those doing the day-to-day fieldwork. There were times when we saw or heard people at points of crisis:

> *We left the café and walked up to the car park. I helped Sharon put Aisha's pram in the car. Sharon placed Aisha, who was now sleeping, in the car seat. At first the boys were reluctant to get into the car and when they did they wouldn't stay in their seats but moved around furiously, sometimes literally crawling over the sleeping Aisha. Sharon was distressed and her calm veneer that she had previously attributed to her religious convictions had long since left her. Unable to control her sons' behaviour, she called out to them on the verge of tears 'Why do you do this to me?' As she drove out of the car park, the boys were still moving around the car in a way that was clearly dangerous and Aisha had woken up and was crying. Sharon seemed to me to be a woman who was close to breaking point.*
>
> (Pamela's fieldwork notes)

Being present on such occasions demanded a response from us; it also required a response for the researcher. Across the team, space was made to discuss encounters such as these and talk through any concerns being raised. In addition, more formal counselling services were made available for researchers to use if they wished. The most difficult challenge we faced was the death of two children during the research.

> *The house was quiet. I jumped up and down on the spot to keep warm in the November frost. A man opened the door. He knew who I was and stepped outside shutting the door behind me. He told me that they couldn't speak to me today. Their daughter had died in the night. She had gone peacefully. In time he was sure they would want to chat about their experiences. He recognised the research was important. I started to say how sorry I was. He smiled, said 'goodbye', and carefully closed the door shut behind him. I noticed he had had no shoes on.*
>
> (Dan's fieldwork notes)

The second child, Julie, died after Emma had spent time with her and her mother Elizabeth during the pre-research discussion and a first interview. Emma had already been witness to the many pressures placed upon Elizabeth, and the isolation she experienced, along with a series of disappointments over service provision and support. It was not Elizabeth, but a professional who worked with her, who told Emma of Julie's death. The professional thought it was possible that Elizabeth was part of the research, but we did not confirm either way:

> *But probably my body language and vocal timbre would have given away the shock and deep sorrow I felt at the news, because the professional continued to give me details even as I was trying to say that I could not divulge whether the family was involved in the study or not. One thing the professional was very keen to get across was that the research team should not contact Elizabeth without their approval. Still reeling from the news, and trying to regain composure, those words struck me as being highly suspect.*
>
> (Emma's fieldwork notes)

We did not feel it was the role of the professional to say whether or not we should contact Elizabeth. They were not party to the research relationship that had developed between her and Emma. Instead we felt it important that Elizabeth should be contacted:

> *But when is the 'right' time, and what is the 'right' method? At first I thought it best to leave a little time, partly to give the family a chance to deal with the initial impact of the tragedy. I also hoped there might be a time when Elizabeth would contact me herself, which would let me know when she was ready to speak about the situation to me. After a couple of weeks, Elizabeth had not been in touch and I realised it was important to let her know I know and, at least send on my condolences and let her know she could contact me if she wanted. My initial concern over the professional's apparent intention to prevent an independent researcher speaking to one of their clients had, by this time, been replaced by a simple wish to let Elizabeth know I cared and was there if she needed me.*
>
> (Emma's fieldwork notes)

After a long deliberation, it was decided that the best way to keep control in Elizabeth's hands as much as possible was to write to her and leave the next contact up to her.

> *I cared about Julie, I felt deeply saddened at the news, and I also cared about Elizabeth and had started to imagine all sorts of terrible scenarios for her now that Julie was dead. But I was also in their lives through my professional role, and never has it been quite so clear to me just how tenuous that role (of researcher) can be. I felt uncomfortable about writing the words 'call me'; perhaps this was something that sounded somehow*

insincere at the time, as though I was somehow trying to coerce her into continuing with the research. But I did not want to shut the door to Elizabeth either, so I wrote all my contact numbers down on the back of the card and hoped that she would see it and have it handy if she wanted to talk things over. She never did.

(Emma's fieldwork notes)

The events have stayed with Emma and the rest of the team. We continue to feel unease around what happened and whether there was more we could have done to reach Elizabeth. Should Emma have gone to her house or called her? At the time we felt, and continue to feel, that this would have been an imposition. There was a danger that such responses were more about providing 'closure' for the researcher than it was aimed at helping Elizabeth. It seemed the only thing we could do was hope the message was recognised for what it was; a way to communicate the deep care Emma had for Julie and for Elizabeth.

There were also issues about what to do with the data from the first interview that had been completed. Our decision has been to include the first interview in the analysis because Elizabeth and Julie's stories are important. We were saddened by, but found valuable, Elizabeth's stories as a young single mother. Others were quick to judge, and how she responded to them and cared for Julie said so much. She gave her time, while living in acutely difficult circumstances, and spoke with eloquence and honesty about her situation; to lose that from the research we felt would be another example of how she was marginalised and silenced by others.

Giving back to parents

In Fisher and Goodley (2007) we argue that while the interview may, as Birch and Miller (2000) point out, provide the opportunity for a 'therapeutic' encounter in which the research participants may reconstruct painful life events into more positive and enabling narratives, this means that the boundaries between research and therapy are inevitably blurred. While respecting issues of anonymity and confidentiality, we have been mindful of our ethical responsibilities which arise out of this situation. We have, for instance, helped some research participants to develop informal and supportive networks by enabling them to contact people in similar circumstances if all parties have expressed a desire to do so. Mothers are particularly interested in meeting other people whose children have the same impairment or label. We have also continued to provide support by making ourselves accessible by email and through telephone contact. We also feel that our ethnographic work has been helpful to many of the research participants. In some cases, mothers have told us that they consider that their children have enjoyed a higher level of care, in particular by being 'referred' more rapidly for required interventions, as a result of being accompanied to appointments by a researcher. Often, though, mothers simply comment that they feel supported by the presence of a researcher when they attend medical appointments with their children. We were also informed by a number of parents who attended dissemination events that they were happy that their stories were helping to inform understandings in this area and this might be for the greater good of all families with disabled children.

There were also a number of clear and conspicuous examples of the researchers giving back to the participants:

- Filling in the Disability Living Allowance forms for a parent whose first language was not English
- Giving all parents a leaflet about the project with helpful numbers on the back detailing local information services, disability teams, children's centres and parent groups
- Babysitting for older siblings in the waiting room while the mother met with the General Practitioner (GP)
- Driving the family to meetings and appointments – picking up the nappies from the nappy service
- With permission passing on information about services and date of the next meeting of a support group from one parent to another
- Helping with the lunch as parents got their children ready to leave the house
- Meeting for a glass of wine to discuss some other stories that a mother had remembered after the last interview
- With permission seeking out information and a potential advocate for a family who believed they were receiving discriminatory treatment from social services
- Sharing children's clothes and toys.

Inevitably, because of the close interpersonal nature of the research relationships, there were times when boundaries were blurred. Pamela recounts a story of a meeting with Sylvia:

> *We both decided to have a cup of coffee and we started to chat in a general way. Sylvia told me about a personal issue (she asked me not to include*

this in the research) and I also told her about a personal dilemma I was facing. In other words, we were exchanging information on highly private issues. We both agreed that we would not have told friends whom we had known longer. It seems that the newness of our friendship made it easier to exchange information of this kind. The fact that this information was 'exchanged' shows how balanced our relationship is and I was happy to listen to Sylvia's advice and insights. After this, the tape was turned on and an 'interview' conducted. This was quite difficult in some respects as I knew very personal things about Sylvia and would have loved to ask certain questions but couldn't because they were 'clearly out of bounds'. As far as Sylvia is concerned, there are two areas to our relationship (friendship and research) which need to be separated. I know that the interview would have been so much more interesting if I could have included the issue that she confided in me 'as a friend'. The data would have been wonderful ... I wouldn't dream of betraying her confidentiality as I am sure she would not betray mine.

Conclusions

Researching the lives of parents of disabled children calls into question the positionalities of researchers. It demands us to work empathically and carefully with participants in the implementation of empirical work but also asks testing questions about how we understand the people we work with. The relational ethics of our research, explored in this chapter, extended beyond method to the analysis stage. The analyses chapters therefore aim to conceptualise the parents in the wider structural, cultural and political contexts that they inhabit, while also providing testimonies to the resilience that they shared with us in their work on this project.

4
Unmaking Children

Janice McLaughlin and Dan Goodley

Introduction

Unmaking children refers to ways in which 'normal' narratives of childhood come apart when something about a child is read as out of place with the 'normal'. Disability contributes to the disintegration of expected narratives of childhood; it 'disrupts taken-for-granted assumptions about the mind and body' (Kelly, 2005: p. 181). Unmaking such narratives can generate regulative stories of childhood identity and potential that are assumed to be less than those of other 'normal' children; others can offer up new productive visions of what childhood can be and what futures lie ahead.

In contemporary society, due to the dynamics of governmentality discussed in Chapter 1, children are increasingly categorised into different kinds; in particular those child identities that are held up as disruptive and unruly to societal functioning – the criminal/deviant/uncontrollable child who fails to live up to societal and state expectations (Brownlie, 2001). In the UK, state mechanisms are increasing for monitoring and disciplining such disruptive children. These include Anti-Social Behaviour Orders (ASBO), curfews and electronic tagging. Disabled children occupy the disruptive child identity in two ways. First, children with labels of behavioural problems such as autistic spectrum disorder or Attention Deficit Hyperactivity Disorder (ADHD) can also find themselves with the markers of the criminal child such as the ASBO or the curfew (Brown, 2004; Koffman, 2008). The British Institute for Brain Injured Children (the BIBIC) 2006 found that a third of ASBOs had been given to children or young people with learning difficulties, ADHD, or other behavioural problems (Flanagan, 8 May 2006). These overlapping labels indicate the blurred boundaries between the criminal child and

53

the disabled child. Second, like the criminal child, the disabled child contrasts with the 'normal' child and emphasises the latter's potential productivity as the future good citizen. In an era of child categorisation, to become or be labelled disabled as a baby or infant begins to take a child down particular paths, which removes them from normal societal and state expectations. What might have been expected is taken apart and in its place is put a different set of narratives and expectations. These narratives do not predict the future for the child, nor do they contain a uniform story, instead they are full of contradictions, denials and opportunities. Such inconsistencies provide the space within which parents and children can generate alternative understandings of both current identities and future potential, which are disruptive of governing narratives of who they are.

This chapter will look at different interactions and activities that unmake the disabled child. It begins by looking at parental ways of defining the child, what influences such definitions and how they change over time. It next moves on to look at different ways in which medicalised representations and practices have the potential to 'other' the child, before going on to explore various processes within the intimate and broader community that contribute to positioning the disabled child as outside of 'normal' society. The last section explores some of the ways in which children respond to how others define them, identifying the agency children develop in relation to their own sense of self and embodiment.

Parental representations of their child

Various writers have explored ways in which parents can be complicit in the medical labelling and othering of their children. Examining the responses of parents with children with the label of ADHD, various writers, including Klasen and Goodman (2000), Singh (2004), and Bull and Whelen (2006), argue that parents actively seek medical diagnoses of their children, which confirm that their children are 'innately different from other children' (Bull & Whelen, 2006: p. 668). Parents seek comfort, abdication from blame and a promise that through a cure, the child could one day be normal. The danger is that such an approach 'reifies ADHD as an internal object that has so far not been proven to exist' (Bull and Whelen, 2006: p. 673). Other writers looking at the reasons why parents agree to medicating treatments for behavioural issues argue that they do so because they hope medication will generate a more 'normal' family life (Hansen & Hansen, 2006; McGrath, 2001; Thiruchelvam et al.,

2001; Woodgate & Degner, 2004). In our research it has been possible to identify a variety of ways in which parents are significant actors in the construction of their children as different kinds of children and members of the family. Below we explore this, along with a consideration of why parents may feel a social pressure to do so.

Most parents did not have a diagnosis during the pregnancy. Instead their expectation was that their child would be born healthy and well. Consequently, some parents struggled with the realisation that their baby or young infant was ill, or developing in ways they or others felt was problematic, or was dependent on medical interventions to stay alive. Over the first few months, when diagnoses were unclear or problems unrecognised, parents acknowledged the difficulties they had with how to think of and care for their child. Several parents talked vividly of the first few months of a screaming baby they felt they could do little for and had little support to deal with:

> But Julie, she's been so difficult from when she was born, for the first eighteen months of her life all she did was scream, manically. And she still goes for it now. I can't do anything, I can't put her down and just go and do something, she just cries. So she's just, as much as I love her, she just really gets on me nerves.
>
> (Elizabeth, IV1)

Parents openly admitted difficulties building a relationship with their child, because they did not respond like 'normal babies': 'you see other children who do respond to their parents a lot quicker, as soon as you start getting that sort of relationship there, it makes things a hell of a lot easier'. (Gill, IV1) Parents regularly compared their children with other 'normal' children:

> But whereas Chloe had been a very settled baby, Joe was just so difficult, for want of a better description, so miserable. He would basically cry twenty-four hours a day, and really scream, he was inconsolable ... he got to the age of 5 or 6 weeks when Chloe had started smiling and really interactive, there was none of that there and I really got to the stage with him, at about say 2 to 3 months, where I was getting nothing back at all other than him crying and crying and being sick ... and then he was diagnosed with his problems at about three months old, and I think again I was so wrapped in my own loss ... I used to look at him and really think, 'I could probably give you away' because, it was all one-way he didn't see us,

he didn't smile, he didn't respond, he cried, he vomited, he didn't sleep.

(Kay, IV1)

It was not easy for parents to acknowledge these feelings, and, as will be discussed later, they were not sustained over time. Nor was it a view expressed by all parents. Maria, who had had amniocentesis and knew she was going to have a Down's syndrome child before Luke was born, talked of the intense bond she had with him, which began in pregnancy and was uninterrupted by the knowledge of his label:

My relationship with Luke is I'm very, very close to him. We have a bond, right from the day he was born; in fact when I was pregnant I had a really good bond with Luke. My bond was so good with him, obviously when I was pregnant I was frightened of the unknown because I didn't know exactly what he was going to be like, but once he was born (speaks with child) it didn't matter if he had four heads and ten legs, the bond was just there immediately ... even if I hadn't have found out he had Down's syndrome when I was pregnant it still wouldn't have made a lot of difference afterwards because we've got a really good bond and it's really, really strong.

(Maria, IV1)

Woodgate and Degner (2004), looking at children with cancer, argue that families go through changes at the level of the self and subjectivity, as they incorporate illness into their understandings of identity and future. Such processes are both psycho-emotional in the explorations the individual undertakes to make sense of who they feel themselves to be in a context of disability or illness, but also socio-cultural. In any process of making sense of disability or illness, the source of dissonance it creates and the available scripts or narratives to aid the resolution of that dissonance, are embedded in the social. What we aim to work through here is how social expectations of normality and discomfort with disability are vital elements in the difficulty parents can experience when first raising a disabled baby. Moving on to reject those social expectations and discomfort, by rethinking what disability signifies, become central to developing a bond with the child and integrating the child as a full member of the family.

The emotional disquiet some parents experience can find expression in negativity directed towards the child as the source of that disquiet. Jemma (IV1) expressed frustration when she commented, 'Everything that I did 12, 14 months ago, I did with Rosa on my hip.' When Rosa was diagnosed with a visual impairment and other health problems the family as a whole was plunged into darkness as the house was adapted to block out natural light. While the mother could see the benefit for the child, nevertheless she experienced a sense of loss with light's removal (IV1); 'I love the sunshine ... last year we spent most of summer in the back room with the curtains shut.' The mother's approach to adapting family life and home to the needs of the child maintains Rosa as something different to 'normal' life. Jemma felt that Rosa would forever lack something fundamental because she could not experience certain things as she grew up (IV3): 'I cried because I thought how will I show her a rainbow? How can I tell her what an elephant is? How can I take her up into Scotland and say, "look at the view"?' It is not uncommon for sighted people, as explored by French (1993), to find it difficult to comprehend a quality of life without sight. The sense of loss maintained by such a narrative contributes to the continued preference for a 'normal' child:

> I love the normalness of Ruby [Jemma's oldest child]. [Pause] I love the fact that you can take her to see the Lion, the Witch and the Wardrobe on a Saturday afternoon; we took her to see Chitty Chitty Bang Bang and ... we were watching her half the time, watching her whole face light up ... And watching the world through Ruby's face is fantastic.
>
> (Jemma, IV3)

At the level of self, parents are expressing psycho-emotional distress, a feeling that at some level, due to the impairment, they are unable to love or bond with their child in the same way they could with their 'normal' child. This distress can contribute to the early beginnings of separating out the child from normal narratives; somehow the child is unworthy of love, or incapable of providing the interactions through which love and bonds are created. It is important to recognise this level of distress and emotional pain, which parents – mothers and fathers – articulate and experience. It is equally important to also recognise the sources, other than what is happening between child and parent, which contribute to and provide rhetorics of meaning for this distress. If we do not do this we remain trapped in existing public assumptions of grief, burden and loss as inevitable products of the impaired child.

While this argument is further discussed in Chapter 5, here we acknowledge the broader contexts which fuel such emotional difficulties.

According to popular representations of motherhood contained within idealisations of celebrity mothers, fictional representations of the good (and bad) mother and self-help guides to good parenting, mothers should form an automatic and intrinsic bond of love with their child (Douglas & Michaels, 2004; Lawler, 2000). Such discourses are embedded with norms linked to class, gender, race and ethnicity, marital status and, as we shall see, 'normal' children. While the motherly bond is said to be natural, mothers, through the numerous and ever growing parent guides now available, are also encouraged to participate from pregnancy onwards in activities, which aid the development of that bond: talking to the foetus while in the womb, playing music to it, avoiding things that may distress it, and breast feeding the child rather than bottle feed to name a few.

Equally, fathers are also being drawn in to such practices (a selection of the parenting guides for fathers include: *The Pocket Idiot's Guide to Being a New Dad* (Kelly, 2004), *You're the Daddy: From Nappy Mess to Happiness in One Year: The Art of Being a Great Dad* (Giles, 2006), *She's Had a Baby: And I'm Having a Meltdown* (Barron, 1999) and many, many others). They are encouraged to be at the ultrasound, to also talk to the foetus, and to be at the birth (usually with a video recorder). There is an expectation that parents will from the beginning – and this means pregnancy itself – love their child. We now have a name for mothers who express anything other than this natural love: post-natal depression (Mauthner, 1998). Expectations that love and natural bonds come immediately make it difficult for parents to experience anything different. It encourages a sense that there is something wrong, either in them or their child. It is therefore understandable that parents felt pain for 'failing' to live up to this expectation, and that the child and her/his disability were identified as the barrier.

Emotional distress is supported by normalising discourses of what kind of baby makes a bond possible. As the child gets older, pathological representations of disability continue to help influence ways in which parents respond. In some, but not all, parental discussions of the future, the focus was on the difficulties they saw ahead for the child and what limitations they felt were created by their disability. Angela, when reflecting on Harry's (who has the label of autistic spectrum disorder) potential future commented (IV1), 'He'll always be very dependent on adult supervision, he'll never be independent, never be totally independent … I mean hopefully things will settle down a bit but he'll always be dependent.' In response some parents wanted their children to improve and get better, in order that they might fit in with family life and broader social interactions; this trend was seen in particular among those parents whose children, like Harry, had been labelled with behavioural problems such as ADHD and autism spectrum disorder. Several parents were keen on mainstream school because they hoped that the interactions there would enable the child to learn appropriate social skills (a finding supported by Cole's research (2005)). Inclusion agendas in education are rhetorically driven by claims that they foster integration of disabled people into society. However, parents' reasons for placing their disabled children in mainstream provision are not necessarily driven by this goal. Instead it can be less about recognising diversity and more about a site where children learn to conform to norms of acceptable behaviour (Armstrong, 2005; Terzi, 2005). Such parental desires for normality also lie behind their push for children to be more capable/normal than their doctors or therapists predict. Jane, who had refused to be guided by medical advice about what autistic children could do and instead got Jack out of nappies much earlier than is expected for a child with this label, noted:

> But I really think it's made him a better person for it, he's a lot more normal if you like. We were trying to discourage him doing like the flapping hands and the pointed fingers and that. And if he gets really loud we'll say 'you know Jack you're shouting too loud and turn it down a bit'. He does take note of things like that I think because he wants to fit in, and I genuinely think he does want to fit in with other kids and what they're doing.
>
> (Jane, IV3)

Jane refused to be guided by the label. Consequently, one guideline (what it is assumed children with the label of autism can and cannot do) is replaced by another (what social norms say a child should and should not do). Parents of non-disabled children are also involved in attempts to ensure their children conform to social expectations of behaviour and attitude. However, because disabled children trouble the category of the acceptable child, this can lead their parents to work harder at trying to 'overcome' those behaviours or limitations that are assumed to be troubling. Parents appreciate that the social costs of not fitting notions of acceptable behaviour will be carried by their children. However, what we will also see later is that parents do not always seek to conform to such social expectations.

We cannot ignore that at various points and in different ways, parents could be seen as contributing to the negative unmaking of their child through expressions of failure to bond, comparisons to other 'normal children' and through parental desires to 'normalise' their child's behaviour. However, it is important to think about the reasons why this occurs (Allen, 2004; Ferguson, 2001; Green, 2004). In the same way that emotional distress, while real, can be contextualised in broader societal expectations that encourage its production. We need to explore the sense making that parents move through over time, which can contribute to the construction of difference and at other moments provide counter narratives to myths of normality, tragedy and heroic over coming.

McKeever and Miller (2004) argue that in Western society successful mothering is connected to accomplishment, producing the child whose future is somehow guaranteed by the mother's skill and expertise (what Hays (1996) calls 'intensive mothering'). Therefore, the narrative for mothers, and we would argue fathers too, of disabled children is made more complicated as the future is already read by others as no longer available. As we have already stressed, parenting is generally under a heightened gaze through increased levels of medical advice and guidance on how to raise perfect children; the more this is emphasised and wished for, the more parents of disabled children and the children themselves are constructed as failures (Landsman, 1999; Larson, 1998; Rigazio-DiGilio, 2000). Haimes (2003) argues, using a Bourdieusian framework (Bourdieu, 1977, 1996), that families may struggle to locate a child within family relations if an aspect of them does not fit. When this happens the child's broader place within society is undermined by their lack of acknowledgement within the family (McCarthy et al., 2000). Disabled children do not fit contemporary narratives of family life, contributing to the difficulties parents may face finding a space within their own family narratives for their child. Therefore, in the intricacies of day-to-day family life, from play time, to brushing teeth, to going out to the cinema, the rituals and practices around the disabled child are differentiated by the parents who look after them, constructing a sense that the child is different and has changed family life (Dowling & Dolan, 2001; Jenks, 2005).

However, this is not a static process, nor is it experienced in the same way by all parents (further explored in Chapter 5). Parents do not simply absorb broader expectations of who their child should be and act accordingly. Instead they seek to develop articulations of their relationship with their child, which is not framed around difference as lack and emotional distress. When first asked to describe Katy, Nick (Sarah and Nick, IV1) described her as 'as a pain in the neck', in the same way that his other daughter Jenny is 'a pain in the neck, Katy can equally be a pain'. Nick was not simply denying her impairment or normalising her as just the same as any other child, her disability is part of her and who she is, but rather than unmake her, it makes Katy a positive self and positive presence in the family and beyond. By the time of our third interview, when Katy was four years old, Sarah summed up their feelings about their daughter:

> I think Katy belongs to the world too. Because she's her own person, so she does belong out there in the world, and I think the world will be a horrible place without her. I really do believe that, I really, really, truly believe that the world would be a horrible place without our little girls, especially her. And she brings that bond into this house; she makes it a stronger place.
>
> (Sarah and Nick, IV3)

Recognising the child as a personality and an identity, of which disability is a part, helps parents move from just seeing and experiencing burden and resentment. Katy is now someone who contributes to the bonds that make their family, rather than someone who is outside of such bonds. Developing activities within which the child plays an equal part to others in the family can also, as Traustadóttir argues (1999), provide contexts where the child's differences are not at the centre of the interaction:

> Karen: We still try to keep him as a normal member of the family though
> David: I mean certainly the relationship when we take him out into the estate or take him out shopping, he's not treated differently to any other of the kids. We don't ask people to give him any special treatment or anything like that. Obviously, to a certain extent ...
> Karen: The medical needs ...
> David: I think now, like I say he's just the same as the other two kids, you know there's nothing, nothing different at all either in the way that we feel or the way that we act around him.
>
> (Karen and David, IV2)

Medical othering

In this section we will highlight a range of medical or pseudo medical practices and interactions, which contribute to categorisations of the child that place them outside of normal society, beginning with diagnosis.

Initial diagnosis

Disability studies has identified many problems with the ways in which medical diagnosis is often handled. This includes the failure of professionals to provide supportive contexts, the dominance of medical models of tragedy, the lack of appropriate information and the overall assumption that diagnosis is about the 'breaking of bad news' (Cunningham, 1994; Cunningham et al., 1984; Rahi et al., 2004; Speedwell et al., 2003). The parents in our study experienced many of these processes and felt the subsequent pain: from consultants who delivered the diagnosis and left the room without a word, to advice to go home and pray, to hearing the diagnosis as a message left on the home answering machine.

What we wish to focus on in this chapter are those aspects of diagnosis that contribute to unmaking the child. As Landsman (2006) and Poltorak et al. (2005) argue it is important to place diagnostic encounters in their broader narrative and cultural contexts. Landsman (2003) has identified four discursive influences on diagnosis and subsequent medical encounters, which we feel have resonance with our analysis of families' medical encounters. The first is popular culture discourses from the media and societal perceptions, which frame disability as a personal tragedy that befalls both children and families (Barnes, 1993; Hevey, 1992). The second emerges from paediatric medical culture and constructs disability as an individual pathological condition, which should be cured if at all possible (Conrad & Potter, 2000; Molloy & Vasil, 2002). The third discourse is of heroic progress; the child who overcomes her/his disability, either by sheer will or by the wonders of medicine, to walk, talk or do well at school (Barnes, 1993). Each of these narratives is based on a normalising ideology, which assumes that to be disabled is to be less than human, as 'outside the range of human acceptability' (Landsman, 2003: p. 1950). If disability is something to overcome, to stay within it is to be doomed by a condition, which frames the individual. The final discourse challenges the assumptions of the first three, by disputing the source of disability: what Landsman refers to as the social model of disability, or as we discussed in Chapter 1, critical disability studies.

Parents are active participants in diagnosis. They often seek a label for their child and participate in their own diagnostic processes. Diagnosis is often not an immediate one-off event, even if there is evidence that the child is developing or acting differently, defining the source involves a significant amount of medical uncertainty. Medical diagnosis in young children is a comparative process, made against developmental markers, which define both the normal and the distance from it (McConachie, 1995). Often there are mixed messages, generating ambiguity, from different medical practitioners. At a brain scan, before Christmas, with a different consultant than their usual one, Karen and David (IV1) were told 'Daniel wouldn't be able to do anything for himself. He would have difficulties communicating in any way, difficulties with not only learning but sitting up, walking and talking, basically to the point of never really being able to do anything.' The parents described the prognosis as 'devastating'. Then, after the Christmas holiday, they saw their regular paediatrician whose reading of the same scans was: 'so these MRI results are fairly normal then.' Different professionals interpret and approach communicating medical evidence in different kinds of ways, some give the best-case scenario, and others prefer to give the bleakest picture so that what actually develops is seen in a more positive light. All this is indicative of the uncertainty contained within the subjectivity of medicine.

When diagnosis does not occur before or at birth, but gradually comes through a reading of the child as different, the loss of normality is a gradual process. As parents and their children move through repeated diagnostic encounters it threatens to position them further and further away from initial expectations of normality. Once some kind of diagnosis is provided after repeated tests and consultations, the medical recognition it provides for parents that their child is now in the 'category of disabled' can be experienced as closing a door to the 'normal' world they once belonged to. After receiving a diagnosis, Kay described the reactions she and her partner went through:

> Where do you go? We know our baby's got brain damage now ... Do you try and get out of the house? So we ended up going to IKEA to buy Chloe a bed, I was just wandering around there like a zombie, in this little world, where everybody else was continuing in their normal world and we were in this horrible black hole.
>
> (Kay, IV1)

Genetic diagnoses in particular are complex and rarely immediate (Latimer, 2007; Latimer et al., 2006). In our study, as tests were undertaken, the parents and the child became further and further removed from the normality of having a baby. Jemma explained (IV1), 'you're trying to take it all in and digest all these big words and you think, I should just be thinking about weaning now, not having to go for ultra sound.' Surrounding family members can push for a label, something to comprehend and 'come to terms with'; doctors can become entranced by the quest for a category that defines the child, proves their professional hunches to be true, and solves the puzzle. Parents are mediating between these quests, both seeking to make sense of possible narratives offering certainty for understanding their young child, while also appreciating the potential of such quests to unmake them:

> But it's just the way people are, I think they prefer it when there's a label attached because then they can deal with it a lot easier. I mean especially the family. The latest one, a rare genetic condition, was mentioned. So they're all now, 'oh, oh I was talking to my friend the other day and I mentioned that Lauren has that condition'. And I'm like, 'no, we don't know that she has it (laughs) will you stop'. But it is we like people to be pigeonholed in a certain area and until it's actually happened they don't know how to deal with anything.
>
> (Gill, IV1)

While parents may have sought a diagnosis this does not mean that they remained happy about its implications. Instead, some parents felt that the tests, observations and appointments made it difficult to just get on with everyday family life. Waiting for medical certainty to define their child provided no solution to the challenges they faced. It also did not support the construction of versions of life and the future, which were meaningful and supportive. A removal from at least some of the medical processes was the choice some parents made. After several months of treatments to deal with Daniel's spasms, alongside appointments to establish his genetic condition, David and Karen decided to leave the naming process to the geneticists, while concentrating their energies on treatments that limited his spasms and allowed him to spend time with other children:

> David: I mean we weren't sleeping, we weren't eating properly, it was kind of everything just up in the air. And then it was one day we just said, we've got to stop this, we've got other kids ... They were noticing a difference in our moods and the way things were for us. And, it just had to be one day, we just said, right from this day forward, as long as Daniel's happy, and he's doing fine, then nothing else matters.
>
> (Karen and David, IV2)

What they realised over time was that the supposed certainty naming the condition gave was illusionary. Instead, it offered them and their child very little of value, as it was a shorthand summary few outside the genetic community were interested in or understood. In contrast, seeking that name had the potential for huge costs, disturbing their relationship with their baby, shaping the nature of that developing relationship and acting as a narrative that cloaked everything else of value within their connection to Daniel (see also Goodley & Tregaskis, 2006b).

Medicalised representations

The significance of medical records in producing constructs of the patient through their condition has been explored by writers such as Berg (1997). Such work argues that the representations of patients contained in medical records, and shaped via their structure of classification, can have a cultural currency, which patients' own voices and experiences can lack within institutional contexts (Bowker & Star, 1999). Place (2000: p. 173), in research exploring the negotiated boundaries between children's bodies and technology in intensive care units, describes observation charts as a venue where 'the facticity of the critically ill body is both ordered, externalized and merged with its representational form'. Records move through different locations and are read by different professionals, shaping the patient as a particular object. It is difficult for parents and children to escape the influence of classificatory systems. They quickly find that access to care and financial support requires defining the child by medical criteria and judgments to be found in official pro forma. Disability Living Allowance and statementing for the provision of education support, for example, require parents and professionals fill in detailed forms listing all the medical problems and limitations the child is judged to have (the role of welfare requirements in encouraging the pathological classification of disabled children is discussed further in Chapter 7). Angela (IV3) spoke of having to define her child as being 'severely mentally impaired', in order to get the level of assistance in the class room she felt he would benefit from: she commented, 'I mean nobody wants to put down that their child is severely mentally impaired but that's what you've got do.'

The significance of medical representations in framing the child as a medical object was visible via observations that took place within the study. In such observations the dominance of the medical history contained in the notes led to them, rather than the child sitting in the room, having a significant presence in the interaction. This was well illustrated in a review of Daniel held with his paediatrician and parents:

> It seemed to take a few minutes at the start of the consultation for him [the paediatrician] to gear up to Daniel's medical history and current situation, a bit of a faltering start while he looked intently through his notes. Just as David had mentioned earlier, the file was very thick – a

physical embodiment of all Daniel, and his family, had gone through over the past 12 months or so. Also noticed there were times, particularly in these first few minutes, when Karen and David were answering his questions and giving details of people involved such as who was calling round and why while the doctor had his head down as he scanned through the notes, reading letters copied into the file etc, for what felt like a few quite extensive periods ending in moments of uncomfortable silence as Karen and David finished speaking.

(Ethnographic notes)

Parents were very aware of how their child could be objectified in records and how such records could take the place of experiential evidence built up from interaction with the child. Such notes – and the testimonies of others – were privileged as evidence upon which to pass judgment:

I think the people we've had the most support from are the people who actually come to the house, and sat with us and met Jack. I mean we had two Educational Psychologists who were making decisions about him and hadn't even met him; they were basically going from what was written down in his file which I found really annoying. But they didn't see the importance of actually seeing how we lived, or meeting him as a person.

(Jane, IV2)

In other observations of professional presentations we saw children's conditions represented in ways that both stressed their abnormality and also the role of parents to do what they could to normalise their child. After listening to a talk by speech therapists to a parent group, the researcher noted: 'In each case, the autistic child was constructed as deficient and the expected role of the parent was to reflect on ways to enable their child to come as close as possible to proficiency/normality.' (Ethnographic notes)

Professionals can snap out of the objectification of children and the medical environment they work within by finding space to engage with the child in a responsive way. The ethnographic notes below provide a strong contrast to those noted above:

Throughout the consultation the doctor generally seemed very relaxed about all the things Frank was busy doing in her room, while the meeting proceeded he was entertaining himself with the jigsaw on and off, the roll of paper at the bed head, the bed itself, and the curtain at the side – something he really enjoyed getting twisted up in ... when she did speak to Frank, it was generally in a very friendly direct manner. I noticed how she also picked up on the moment when he was worried about doing something wrong and being in trouble when he had jumped on the bed and ruffled the paper. The doctor spoke to him very gently and told him it was okay, and she didn't stop him doing it again, or wrapping himself round in the curtain afterwards ... Then through the time we were there she appeared to watch how Frank played without interference or instruction, paying particular attention to how he was looking physically, and how he was interacting with Debbie and herself especially when he talked. She always spoke to him using his first name, and was familiar enough with him to remember about how much he loved trains, using his Thomas the Tank t-shirt as a prompt to help make him feel more relaxed about being there.

(Ethnographic notes)

In multiple interviews, Debbie spoke of the trust she had in this particular paediatrician, born from her ability to connect with the child and the family in a way that was grounded in encompassing knowledge of them.

Medicalised practices

Representations become powerful via the ways in which they are made real in medical practices, which continue to narrow the potential understandings of the child to a set of medical problems and failings (Place, 2000). The dominance of medical models of disability, which present the child from diagnosis onwards as a tragedy, are still present in many medical practices children experience (Imrie, 2001). Across a range of medical settings, practices and practitioners, parents found their child being treated as a particular kind of medical object due to assumptions about their disability. Maria felt that her labour had been dealt with differently because it was known she was carrying a baby with the label of Down's syndrome:

Then I felt so let down by the birth I really felt afterwards when I thought about it, I thought was it because Luke had Down's syndrome. I maybe shouldn't say this but I did feel as though was it because Luke had Down's syndrome that they were just letting me continue. You know, he's got Down's syndrome so you know, if anything happens it happens.

(Maria, IV1)

Once Luke was born the response of the nurses was to offer a private room because 'the baby has Down's'. Maria refused the offer of segregated provision and was instead happy to be with her wanted child in the general ward.

The necessity of assistive medical technologies in some children's lives is an important material marker of difference. In her second interview, Debbie discussed her hopes as Frank entered mainstream nursery. She had high expectations that the nursery would be able to cope with the medical care required due to his tracheotomy (in particular, changing tubes and dealing with blockages). However, when we undertook an observation it was clear that a different situation was occurring; the nursery staff were extremely hesitant about the technology and their responsibilities.

> Her [the nursery assistant] own concerns around her responsibility to Frank and worries about the need to be constantly vigilant meant that she hovered near to him and checked the way other children played around him with heavy emphasis on making sure no one got carried away with their playing, so sand was not chucked around. Made me wonder how conscious Frank and the other children were, how the perceived need to minimise risk and to be protecting the child also created a heavily monitored, restrictive environment around the child which might be problematic for the child's relationships to other children and sense of developing autonomy.
>
> (Ethnographic Notes)

Fear about technology, responsibilities and associated risk factors led the nursery assistants to treat Frank differently to other children. He was materially marked through the technology and their hovering response over him. The outcome was that Frank was not fully integrated in the nursery class, he was not allowed to play freely with other children and those around him were aware of the hesitation and monitoring the nursery assistants directed towards him. As Davis and Watson (2001) and Woolley et al. (2005) argue, varied social practices and cultural norms in mainstream educational settings can recreate segregation within apparently inclusionary contexts.

The presence of medical technologies and specialist support can unmake the child in school settings. However we have also seen schools operate in ways which refuse to allow the technology or the disability to define the child. After the negative experiences Debbie had in Frank's nursery, she found a totally different approach in his new school when he began in the reception class. Here his tracheotomy needs were taken on board with no fuss and no construction of Frank as different (IV3), 'All the teachers wanted to be trained in how to change a tracheotomy tube.' In the class room the assistant was not identified as his assistant, which allowed for his integration into the space. In similar ways Luke's nursery found ways to bring recognition and inclusion together via the daily routines of the mainstream nursery. All the teachers learnt Makaton and they also taught it to the other children, so that some elements of the day's activities, in particular the singing of nursery rhymes, were done in Makaton by everyone. Here the disabled child's body becomes an origin for more wide-reaching forms of support and the development of networks (Bayliss, 2006).

Over time, parents became choosier about medical interventions and appointments they felt it necessary to attend. In so doing they sought to reclaim their child and provide space for their development to occur more freely and under less regulatory scrutiny. Daniel's parents took this path and over time they felt vindicated by his development and his ability to do far more than medical professionals predicted:

> David: I've been proven exactly right to this day because, you know we were told that Daniel was basically going to be unable to do anything at all for himself. And now he sits up, he stands, he has a drink, he feeds himself, he's aware of himself, he's aware of other people. All of those things that they basically said, he's just going to lie there. And I think that's the biggest thing that we stick to them and say 'you know, you were wrong'.
>
> (Karen and David, IV3)

Any child's development follows uncertain and ambiguous paths. Medical scrutiny may seek to impose an order to development pathways which can unmake children by putting on hold relationships with others until a diagnosis is reached and by providing prognoses that have little validity as templates for who the child may become. Parents developed an increased independence in choosing which medical appointments to keep, which treatments to carry on with and which diagnostic encounters to participate in. This was strongly related to their growing realisation that medicine contained a significant amount of regulatory potential to shape their child into a particular kind of being. This notion of parental expertise and awareness is a recurring theme, which we come back to in chapters 5, 6 and 8.

Societal othering

Parents are very conscious of the ways in which those around them are factors in the othering of their children. Social responses are not just directed towards the child, they also have the potential to other the family as a whole – this latter point is developed in Chapter 8. The discourse of disability as pathology was evident when extended family rejected the child, as often proved to be the case when the child was born:

> Nick: I remember when I was little my Dad had ideas about eugenics and 'Hitler had the right idea' that sort of thing, so he's got a very strong view about handicapped people, being weak, and not needed in society ... He did come around and see her at first. And then he said something like, 'oh well you do realise you are going to have to put her in a home don't you?'
>
> (Sarah and Nick, IV1)

Extended family struggled to accept that disability was a permanent part of life; it must be something that can be heroically overcome. The only alternative is to see it as a tragedy:

> And it's difficult because, as everybody says 'oh well, well it'll be sorted, it'll be sorted' ... Bob and I have obviously spoke about it, and we now see Frank as, he's got this trachy, and he might always have this trachy, so we're far better off, he's a normal little boy who happens to have a trachy.
>
> (Debbie, IV1)

Jemma (IV1) had experienced ways in which people in broader public spaces rejected Rosa because of her difference: 'You do have people recoil away from her, or little old biddies will come up and say, "hello me little darling". And because she hasn't got the vision she doesn't interact, and then you've got to say, "oh by the way, she's visually impaired so you actually have to touch her", but then of course they're like "oh"'. Within family and social worlds, the child is positioned as different, as a troubling member, who is subsequently unmade. While parents move on from understandings of disability and their child which position them as ill-fitting to narratives of family life, other family members often continue to articulate values that identify the child as not quite right and not quite belonging.

Parents worried about the future, even when they had welcoming family and friends. While, as various disability writers have pointed out, society may find the young disabled child cute or heroic (witnessed in the voyeuristic use of disabled children in charity advertisements (Barnes, 1993; Hevey, 1992)), they are less willing to create the same social space and recognition for the disabled adolescent or adult. Maria was pleasantly surprised by the involvement of her son in social activities and relations; however she worried that as he got older that inclusion would narrow and be replaced by discrimination as the playground increasingly became a site where any form of difference (disability, race and ethnicity or sexual orientation) becomes the object of social othering and identity disputes:

> When I was pregnant with Luke if anybody had told me that he would be made so welcome I'd never have believed them ... I used to imagine this little boy that would never get invited to parties, on a down day I used to feel like that, I used to feel really down and I used to think, 'nobody'll ever invite him to parties' ... but saying that he's only five ... I think as kids get older they get cruel. Some kids do get cruel and I think it's when you get to like round about their age that's when kids start to be a bit nasty.
>
> (Maria, IV3)

In response Maria, and other parents such as Linda and Cheryl, talked about specialist schooling as their current preference for the future, in order to protect their children from bullying. There are real grounds for their concerns; one survey by Nacro (a crime reduction organisation) in 2002 suggested that disabled people are four times as likely to be violently attacked, while Scope, a British charity, found that 47 per cent of disabled people had either been the victim of physical abuse or had seen a disabled friend experience such abuse (Orr, 2008). 2007 saw two high profile cases where young men (Steven Hoskin and Brent Martin) with learning disabilities were tortured and murdered.

The artefacts and technologies, which are part of many disabled babies and children's lives, encourage those around them in school, in the family and wider community to position them as different. Therefore an aid which may help keep them alive, or give them some mobility, is also a visible marker of their difference and separation from the family:

> But now obviously she's got a tube in her stomach so they're now not sure of that, because the pump's still there. So the machinery's still

around. So … they're still thinking, 'oh she's still a sickly baby', and they just lobbed her in to that pigeon hole, right she's got the medical problem, she's sick. So they won't actually come in and look after her. I mean they're all concerned about her and they all ring up and I mean they'll pop in every now and again but even that's gone down since, as she's getting older. Because obviously she's not at that little baby cutie stage any more, so it's not where you can come and just have a cuddle, it's now she's more active so you've got to get down on your hands and knees and play and they're not sure about what they'll even do with her.

(Gill, IV1)

The significance of medical technologies in shaping the child as other, in the eyes of family and community, is apparent in how engagement with them increases as the presence of technologies reduces. Debbie noticed that the more Frank was less technologically dependent, the more the family began to treat him as 'one of them'.

But now he is getting older and he's a person in his own right, and running about and everything, he's a character, I think they're not seeing him as poor little Frank … It feels as if they're seeing him as just Frank, just another one of them, just one of the nephews, or one of the great grandchildren and just seeing that rather than the other things. But it's easier because he's not on his oxygen now he's bigger.

(IV1)

The design of assistive technologies, such as wheelchairs, is often designed to minimise their difference, in order to support the integration of disabled people into society (Levine, 2005; Watson & Woods, 2005). Several of the children had specially designed buggies, which looked like a regular slightly larger child's buggy. However, designing technology to make the disability invisible creates its own problems. Corinne, Luis and Carla were refused entry to a bus several times because they were told their buggy was too big. Rosa wore glasses to help block out the light when she was out of the house; Jemma (IV1) noted one time at the local shopping centre, a couple who walked by her and Rosa comment, 'who the hell d' they think they are, Posh and Becks?' The down side of making the technologies invisible is that the reasons for the technology are also made invisible and alongside the public recognition for the entitlements due to the child.

For parents in other studies, seeking or agreeing to medication for labels such as ADHD is influenced by attempts to contain the ways in which their children 'disturb' the operation and regulation of public space (Hansen & Hansen, 2006). Parents and other relatives felt that they should carry a card which explained the child's disability to counter such public hostility. This kind of suggestion was made most often when the child's disability was not easily read by others. Various parents talked about using a t-shirt (in one case in multiple languages) which said 'I'm not naughty, I'm autistic'. Karen and David suggested that maybe Daniel's buggy should have a flag, which indicated that he was disabled. Jemma (IV3) found that her use of a blue badge to park in disabled spaces was questioned by others: 'You can hear people whispering ... it's not obvious what her problems are unless you know her ... like I say it could be easier if I wheeled her in in a wheelchair because then, "Ah okay, she's disabled"'. David (Karen and David, IV3) felt that others look at them and assume 'they are free loaders' because they do not recognise their child's disability. Public discourses around welfare dependents and 'scroungers' were directed towards them because they were not in paid employment and because 'there's like an invisibility' to Daniel's condition. New Labour welfare policies, in areas such as incapacity benefit, housing benefit and long-term unemployment, encourage public assumptions about people unfairly living off state benefits, while good citizens are in gainful employment. Continuing on with the new right notion of welfare dependency, championed in the 1980s, New Labour is constructing a category of families who are embedded in a culture of worklessness and benefit. Some of the families in our study found that this identity was imposed on them by others in society. This reading of their position and identity encourages an identification of families with disabled children as individually responsible for their condition and ultimately undeserving of support. This has clear implications for understandings of citizenship (Dwyer, 2004), which will be further discussed in Chapter 9.

Child's sense of self

> He loves water, he absolutely loves splashing around in a bath, or the swimming pool. He likes eating ice-cream, he does painting when he's with his carer, he likes rolling in paint and he comes home with pink and green hair and painting his tummy button and things. He loves to be outside in the wind, Steven can still carry him in the backpack and he loves to be up

on Steven's back with the wind on his face and kind of
all the movement and things.

(Kay, IV3)

So far we have discussed how people around the child define, un/make
and shape their identity; what we have not explored is how children
themselves are participants in the shaping of their identity. From other
work exploring childhood we know that children have agency in the creative shaping of their identity (James, 1998; Wyness, 2006). As discussed
in Chapter 2, the focus of our study was on how parents and others
around children are influential in the construction of disabled identities;
this meant that we did not interview children during the study.
However, through the discussion with parents and observation, we can
begin to indicate ways in which children are active in constructing, from
an early age, identities sometimes shaped by the disabling processes
around them, and, at other times, in contrast to those processes.

We have discussed various markers of difference, which parents, medical actors and broader society lay out, which define the children as
other. There is some evidence from our work, particularly in later interviews, which suggests that as children develop they begin to recognise
they are being positioned as different and begin to articulate their own
self in this way (Kelly, 2005). Debbie (IV3) noted, 'He's got a thing about
being special which he's mentioned a little bit the past couple of nights.'
The ways parents respond to a child's early articulations of being different can encourage a sense that it is the medical condition, which makes
them different, securing the neat separation such categories draw
between normal and abnormal:

> Sometimes they have photos of children with disabilities come on
> TV and there's a little boy who comes on with glasses and Down's
> and I always say to Luke, 'he's like you, he's special', and now Luke'll
> look at the telly and he'll go, 'like me', and I'll say, 'yes'. So what I'm
> trying to introduce as he's getting older is to let him know that he is
> different, because as he gets older I think he needs to know that's he's
> different, that he has Down's syndrome.
>
> (Maria, IV3)

Maria also discussed ways in which Luke incorporated medical treatments and requirements into his sense of life and identity:

> I feel sorry for him in a way because he'll go to the fridge and he'll
> go (coughs) 'medicine' (coughs). I think he thinks medicine's a part

of his life, and I think it's because he takes this omega fish oils medicine as well, so I think he thinks medicine's just part of his daily life you know, it's unfortunate because it doesn't have to be.

(Maria, IV3)

However, at other times, the child can claim some agency and resistance in the playful reincorporation of medical technologies (Kelly, 2005):

Well, he's started spitting through it [Frank's tracheotomy tube] which is being discouraged, but that's just that stage isn't it – creativity. But now he is calling it 'super tube', he says, 'when we were playing football I could get my tube and I could blow that football right in the net!'

(Debbie, IV3)

An integral element in the development of a child's self occurs through the exploration of their bodies. Fun explorations of the body are constitutive of agency in the development of identity:

Corinne: Something new with Carla as well is when we are going to change her clothes, she explores her belly button, to play, she's poking it, that's new as well, she is exploring all her body, she didn't know that before. In the bath she starts to explore her body very slowly from her head down, her chest, and she just starts at the hair and goes down and down until she find her little belly button and then pokes it ... all those kind of tiny little things that I tell you, for other people maybe it's nothing, but for me, I mean for us, we get very pleased because Carla now is three years and a half and it just takes time for making all this progress.

(Corinne and Luis, IV2, via an interpreter)

Social and health care professionals such as portage workers, occupational therapists and speech and language therapist, working in the home environment tend to approach therapeutic activities through play and fun, and seek to engage with the child and the family in a form disengaged from the formality of a review taking place in the hospital. In observations of such play therapies in the home, it appeared that the child was much more of an active agent in their own right; their moods, desires and feelings influenced the direction of care and support in ways not allowed for in the hospital meetings. This came through some interviews as well, when children were positively discussed by both parents and professionals for refusing to participate in therapies. For example Debbie noted in the final interview: 'The school speech therapist was quite surprised with Frank's attitude to the home based speech therapist because he was cheeky and cocky and said, "I'm not doing that"'.

For children with the labels of ADHD or autistic spectrum disorder, any expression of individuality or fun can be read as disruptive; behaviour in others that might be read as childhood exuberance is read in them as evidence of their condition. However, some parents remained open to refusing such categories to define their child's behaviour and instead allowed it to be about creative expression and the articulation of a playful self:

> Sometimes he'll just see the sea and say, right, 'I'm just running'. He could be fully clothed with his shoes on, he'll just keep running and running, and you'll say stop, you'll think he'll stop when he gets up to his knees, but no he keeps, it's like Reggie Perin [laughs]. But then he gets so far and he turns around to look, to see whoever is running after him, and of course the person who's with him has just got to run, no time for taking shoes off, and he then thinks it's absolutely hilarious! This person running in [laughs]. I remember the first time he did it with his carer she didn't have a spare pair of jeans, she was up to her waist in the sea just stood there, and he was doubled over laughing [laughs]. So all his carers now, I say if you go to the sea, to the coast, I says take a spare pair of clothes – you'll see what I mean [laughs].
>
> (Angela, IV3)

In the same way, like other parents, parents in the study struggled with acknowledging the development of an independent self for the child, as the child's own voice developed, this was marked with both wonder and pleasure and fear and hesitation:

> And one of the things I've got a problem with is when we go to the shopping mall or something and he wants to go to the toilet, he insists he's got to go to a men's toilet. He has me on edge. But he just won't go into a woman's toilet now. I mean if you go, even if we go to the baths he wants to go to the men's bit, and I cannot let him do that because he wouldn't be able to manage to get undressed and dressed, or he'd just leave his clothes there, plus you know, that's the other thing. But he doesn't want to see himself a baby anymore, you know, and I think he's a lot more aware of like, well older boys do it,

so why can't I? He won't put arm-bands on. I think he'd rather drown than be seen with arm-bands on. So I think he's like noticing a lot more of like what other lads are doing and he's copying that.

(Jane, IV3)

Social conditions around disabled children create limiting scenarios of who they can imagine they want to be. However, they still find ways in which to express versions of who they are, which are not contained by such scenarios. It is important to recognise this level of agency, unfortunately what we see in dominant medical and welfare practices and ideologies are conditions, which are rarely conducive to such recognition. The discussion also points to the importance of bringing a discussion of the body into critical disability studies. Hughes and Paterson (1997) argue that the social model has 'cast physicality out into the discursive shadows' (1997: p. 327). In doing so it 'posits a body devoid of meaning, a dysfunctional, anatomical, corporeal mass obdurate in its resistance to signification and phenomenologically dead, without intentionality or agency' (1997: p. 329). Writers within the social model argue that bringing the body to the fore only encourages the familiar stories of tragedy and pain. However this fails to capture the significance of the body to the construction of identity and selfhood, potentially in ways that are productive. By assuming that discussion of the body necessitates talking of limitation and pathology the 'social model of disability recapitulates the biomedical "faulty machine" model of the body' (1997: p. 329). Looking here at how the children conceptualised and creatively expressed their bodies, points to a very different story about agency and selfhood, which is positive and emancipatory in potential.

Conclusion

Young, disabled children, through a variety of actors, practices and processes can become placed outside normal narratives of childhood and family. Societal and medical understandings of disability have significant influence on the unmaking of disabled children into troubling categories of difference and othering. However, the activities of parents, children themselves and some of those around them can challenge such categorisations, offering narratives of being a disabled child which integrate them within, rather than outside, family and societal life. Such alternatives are made possible by the alliances families make with those around them willing to think differently about disability. The nature of these alliances is the focus of the following chapter.

5
Productive Parental Alliances

Dan Goodley and Janice McLaughlin

Introduction

> If there is any certainty in what I say, it is that the life
> of, and life with, a special needs child is centred on
> questions both inescapable and unanswerable.
>
> (Gottlieb, 2002: p. 225)

This admission by a social researcher and parent of a disabled child starts
to convey the complex ways in which parents seek to define their lives
with their children. This chapter aims to do justice to the complexity of
parental affiliations and identities. In writing this chapter we were conscious of Read's (2000) and Ryan and Runswick Cole's (2008) points of
caution that we should not romanticise the experiences of parents of disabled children in ways that further marginalise them. There are aspects
of being a parent of a disabled child that are stressful. Contact a Family
(CAF, 2003), an organisation for the parents of disabled children, found
that 78 per cent of parents experienced stress or depression, 51 per cent
of parents had financial worries and 72 per cent of parents suffered from
tiredness and lack of sleep because of their caring commitment (see
Glendinning, 1992; Runswick Cole, 2007 for a more detailed analysis).
We also know that it is hard to separate this stress from the social and
institutional conditions within which parents raise their children.
However, we want to subvert the tendency to understand maternal and
parental feelings as inevitably tied up with bereavement, denial, sadness
and despair. As we demonstrated in Chapter 4, just as disabled children's
identities are made and unmade, so too are their parents' (Kittay, 1999b;
Tong, 2002). We aim, therefore, to explore some of the journeys undertaken by parents in their developing relationships with their children.

We start by considering some of the key elements of the distributed parent – as practitioner and ally – to explore the positions adopted by many parents of disabled children. We consider both the possibilities for complex and informed identities, while also taking a step back to consider the ways in which parental identities are governed through normative discourses and practices. After considering some of the costs involved in occupying particular subject positions, we explore in more detail the psycho-emotional experiences of parenting with a view to identify what might be seen as productive accounts of parenting.

The distributed parent

Through the readings of parents' accounts we have come to understand their identity work as something akin to deconstructing and destabilising the acts of 'parenting' and 'care'; the subjects of 'parent', 'professional' and 'child'; and the objects of 'disability' and 'impairment'. We are reminded of Stronach's (2006) point that relationships are often at their most authentic and receptive when they are under attack and have to repair themselves. The same could be said about parenting. Parents have much to say about the possibilities of inclusion and the final part of the chapter explicates some of this knowledge production in terms of productive forms of parenting.

The longitudinal method of our study has allowed us to follow parents and understand the ways in which their needs and roles shape identities overtime. It has also allowed us to access the inbetweenness of hybrid identities (Deleuze & Guattari, 1987 / 2004). Eva's first interview, for example, focused on the problems she was experiencing with inadequate housing, inaccessible buses and unbearable trips to the supermarket. By the time of her third interview, various support systems had been put in place, and Eva's particular concern on the day of the last interview was that her newly acquired, wheelchair-friendly, people carrier was still in the garage having its satellite navigation system repaired! We have seen some parents' circumstances improve, some decline, others remain fairly stable. In general, we have become increasingly aware of the stretched and expansive nature of parents' identities. The various positions that Eva, and other parents, occupy from day to day, perhaps hour to hour, highlight Traustadóttir's (1991) concept of the extended caring role of parents. On the one hand, caring can be extremely hard, tiring work that limits parents in pursuing other roles and activities. Eva was unable to return to work because of caring responsibilities for her daughter with severe brain damage and epilepsy: a factor that obviously had economic and social repercussions. On the other hand, caring can provide for more flexibility and opportunities than normally associated with the traditional parenting role. For some, their new roles as a parent and agitator became a far more fulfilling experience than the career they were forced to relinquish.

While many disabled families experience forms of exclusion, marginalisation and poverty, this does not automatically correlate with a lack of knowledge or confidence in seeking the best care possible for their children. McRuer (2002) draws upon Treichler's (1999) notion of an 'epidemiology of signification' – a comprehensive mapping and analysis of multiple meanings – to propose that people shape their own subjectivities, speak in their own voices and take control of meanings around them. Such a process is crucial, particularly when parents are thrown into the ambivalent context of parenting a disabled child: of loving a child who may well be deemed inhuman by society (Götlind, 2003). The question is, how do identities continue to get produced, embodied and performed, effectively, passionately and with social and political consequences (Bell, 1999: p. 2)? In this section we explore how new subjectivities are distributed across a number of subject positions, locations and interactions. The subject positions parents can acquire, change and refuse are multiple; here we focus on two possible identities: the professional parent and the allied parent.

In this section we take up Kagan et al.'s (1998) call to find ways of valuing the caring work of parents, by considering some of the alliances they take on in the process of parenting. Too often research on parenting a disabled child is reduced to the fixed psychological realm of coping strategies and care management. In reality, parents' identities cross various realms, including those of 'ally' and 'professional'. As we shall see, there are risks, not least in the potential for these emerging positions or performances to be subject to processes of governance.

The professional parent

> I'm involved in the system now I suppose, the hospital system, it's become such a major part of our lives that we just get on and do it. It's just a part of our lives, that's it; this is what we're used to.
>
> (Sharon, IV2)

Gabb (2005a) suggests that any analysis of parental identities must resist a simplistic mapping of parental identities onto pre-given parental categories. Instead, she asks us to consider the kinds of work that are done in the shaping of identities, by parents, through their interconnections and engagements with others. Clearly, a strong identity marker for parents emerges through a growing involvement with a host of (pseudo) professional practices. While we explore this further in Chapter 8 – in relation to the gendered nature of care – it is important to acknowledge its place here. Angela (IV1) told us, 'you're more than a parent ... you name it you've got every role to play'. Parents may mediate certain aspects of their parenting identity through professionalised discourses. We know that parents

> Occupy positions of 'reserve army' care provider or 'para – professional' in health and social care through being almost single-handedly responsible for performing skills such as physiotherapy, suctioning, urinary catheterizations, administering medicine, spoon or tube feeding, lifting and positioning.
>
> (McKeever & Miller, 2004: p. 1188)

They move constantly in and out of home, hospital, rehabilitation and community. In fact, it is their work in a variety of inpatient and outpatient settings that provide some cohesion to an otherwise often fragmented health care system (Bookman & Harrington, 2005).

The centrality of parents to maintaining the professional networks around them is not without challenges. Kay (IV1) had had direct payments in her diary every day for six months but had not got round to dealing with it. Even with her degree, marking her as 'an intelligent person', she felt that her 'personality has changed completely' by the demands placed on her. Lisa's son Eddie was in hospital for five months after his birth. During this time, her life was completely centred on the hospital. She would go home every evening and return every morning. As she put it, 'I had no life outside the hospital.' While there are clearly issues here of isolation through institutional occupation, there are also opportunities for reworking parental identities. Rapp and Ginsberg (2001) argue that parents' location in health and social care contexts may well provide opportunities for forms of professionalised cultural work:

> If you fell over, even though I have a First Aid badge, I wouldn't be any help to you. But if you were ventilated like my son is, I can help you. I can't do blood and broken limbs but I can do ventilation which terrifies a huge tranch of health professionals, let alone social care professionals. Once, a paramedic had been in my house with my

son Sam who had ventilated and couldn't cope. With me doing it, he was in safer hands.

(Tom, IV1)

Taking on the cultural attributes of professional identity can enable institutions to acknowledge the role of parents in the care of their children.

I've been through so much with Rosa [pause] you know, she's probably had more in three years, she had her op and last month, I pinned her down and gassed her! Well I didn't actually physically hold the mask but I said, 'it's alright', I said, 'I know the more she's struggling, the faster it works.' And the nurse was like, *'oh I love these professional mums'*. You know there wasn't a tear in my eye!

(Jemma, IV3, our emphasis)

Parents as purveyors of technical knowledge contrasts markedly with the identity professionals may initially attribute to parents. Larson (1998: p. 866) suggests that as professionals lose the battle to save and cure, their anger 'at the disease might spill over onto the bearer of the illness who represents medical failure', namely parents. In other writings, we have understood parents' engagement with healthcare as 'appropriation': self-fashioning professional and specialist practices as part of an ever-growing identity of carer, coordinator, advocate and supporter (Goodley, 2007a; McLaughlin & Goodley, 2008). Helen (IV1) spoke of informing her GP and a specialist consultant about what each had agreed previously about the different aspects of her son's treatment. She felt like this was akin to adopting an unpaid professional role. Similarly, Lucy (IV2) told us, 'People say to me, do you feel like a mother? And I say, "No, I feel like a full-time coordinator".' Kay (IV1) found herself managing the practice of a professional offering respite and care whose work left much to be desired:

I went down and found the bottle in the sink and the milk was a bit burnt and crusted on, and had exploded all over the microwave. I mean the microwave had been pre-set and she'd, I don't know what she'd done, but it obviously, completely over heated it. And I was thinking, 'God, has she given him boiling milk? Has she just chucked it away and hadn't said anything?' And I just thought, you know, 'She's just, she's just not trained to do this job'. We'd put up with it for 6 months, because it was the only help we'd had and we were desperate for a night's sleep, we weren't even getting that really. So we just cancelled that.

Indeed, many parents were, seemingly, more up to date about their child's care needs than many of the professionals. One consultant happily admitted to us that parents would often turn up to appointments with 'state-of-the-art' knowledge about treatment and prognosis that he was yet to hear about. Parents develop expert knowledge about their child, and there was some suggestion that this was being increasingly acknowledged by some professionals, both from the parents' own accounts and also from the focus group research with professionals:

> He [paediatrician] said himself that he's amazed how the communication is, what every single one of the professionals have said to me [is] – the communication is brilliant between me and Luke.
>
> (Maria, IV2)

> Educational psychologist: In my experience anyway a lot of parents that I've worked with had learnt an awful lot about their child's condition, but then they come up towards school as a whole new body of stuff to be learned. And some parents in my experience seem to cope by becoming absolutely expert on everything and having a far higher level of expertise than anybody that's trying to support them.
>
> (Focus Group, 1A)

Parents' incorporation of the professional subject position enables their voices to be heard in the care of their children. However, there are still times, when this position is not recognised by others. For example, Sylvia had built a positive open relationship with the professionals involved in the nursery care of her child. However, when she asked to be a member of the nursery's 'expert' panel this request was refused. Lesley (IV1) believed that professionals found it hard to accept that parents were acquiring expertise, 'I think they don't want to know about the things that we've found out', particularly when parents themselves were calling for changes of perception about who has knowledge. Similarly, for David:

> We're his parents, we're caring for him twenty-four hours a day, and we administer medication. We do all these things, yet we don't have a medical background at all ... you kind of look at these things and say well, probably out of all of the services we're more qualified than

anybody else, because you've got to do it everyday, and you're doing exactly the same as what they would.

(Karen and David, IV3)

Eva felt the wrath of a GP who believed that she had taken a step too far in terms of her pseudo-professional identity:

> I took Cindy into hospital. She'd been having loads of fits. It was just dreadful. They put her on these drugs that knocked her out. She didn't open her eyes for three days. They were just saying, 'right, we'll administer this drug again'. It stopped her fitting but wiped her out. I eventually snapped at the doctor. We spoke about the dosage. He looked again at the dosage, gave me permission to administer the drugs at home and we spoke about increasing dosage if the number of fits started to creep up. When this doctor was away on holidays, I spoke to one of his colleagues who was concerned about me being responsible for the drugs. So I carefully took her through my thinking about increasing half a ml here and there, when needed. She told me off for doing it. For increasing amounts. But when my doctor returned he said I'd done the right thing.

(Eva, IV2)

At a certain point the subject position of the professional parent hits an inability on the part of institutions to acknowledge it. This is because to do so would be to unsettle institutional boundaries and modes of practice. At the same time, parents themselves find that there are aspects of what they do and value that sit outside the professional subject position. In particular, as they seek to reimagine care and disability they find they need to explore new kinds of care and kinship networks away from the institutional priorities of professionalism. As Rapp and Ginsberg note: 'It is hardly surprising, then, that parents found identities in alliance with others outside of the professional world. On occasion, they are motivated to rewrite kinship in ways that circulate within larger discursive fields of representation and activism' (2001: pp. 540 – 1). A key element of alliance-building relates to broadening associations with others outside of the immediate home and family. This might include professionals but it also invokes significant others outside of the professions. We will return to parents' engagements with and constructions of different forms of community support in Chapter 6. Now we turn to parents' alliances with their children and the part it plays in their reconfigured understandings of disability.

The allied parent

> I think about these things. I mean my PA, wouldn't have a job if I wasn't disabled, you [the researcher] wouldn't have a job if my daughter Sarah wasn't disabled, you know, we are all dependent on each other. What's interesting for me is that this changes the value judgment that goes with the idea of dependency. If you bring an idea of everybody being dependent on each other, suddenly the value judgment starts to go out of the window because you're beginning to say, 'well actually I can't function unless these other pieces, or people are in place or situations or whatever they might be'.
>
> (Ethnographic story of Sylvia)

Such an extension is intriguing when one considers the ways in which disability is often considered to be an individual problem of the disabled person and the family. The parents represented in this study often actively sought to occupy positions of alliance with their disabled children and other parents of disabled children. Tom (IV1), for example, made the following interesting observation about the talk of his son's impairments:

> There are lots of members of my family who I have worked with, spending a lot of time listening to their worries and concerns. But, I'd much rather talk to a stranger because I'm hoping I'm contributing to some change.

Tom's clear vision of informing others outside of his immediate locality was a view shared by many parents in our research. For some, this led them into the world of the parents' movement, which we consider in more detail in Chapter 6. It is important to acknowledge here, though, the ways in which these alliances with other parents impacted upon parental identity. Lisa was an avid Internet user and spent a lot of time on a virtual community for parents of premature babies. Within this environment, she was protected from the usually inadvertent insensitivities that could characterise her interactions with other parents of non-disabled children. The tone was celebratory, all the 'premies'' (premature babies) photographs were there to be seen and among all the informal advice that was given and received there was plenty of scope for fun. This sharing of developing parental alliances was a key factor in working against social isolation (Kagan et al., 1998). Closely tied to associations with parents was a growing camaraderie and empathy with disabled children.

> I would be happy to have another autistic child. They are lovely kids. They've really taught me something. They've taught me to look at people in different ways.
>
> (Linda, IV3)

> I think ... I mean now, personally, sort of from experience obviously and seeing lots of children at different levels of ... you know ages and stuff, it seems quite awful that you can actually terminate a child ... I mean I don't ... I don't think people shouldn't because it's a personal choice, but I just think they have such quality of life.
>
> (Bernie, IV1)

> If there were a magic pill, that could 'cure' Roberto of his disabilities, I'm not at all sure that I'd want him to have it. His disabilities are part of him. If you took them away, Roberto would no longer be Roberto. He wouldn't be my child any more ... if I had another child like Roberto I wouldn't change that neither but I would like a child that was a normal child to experience a normal child, if you know what I mean, because then you've got both sides of it.
>
> (Helen, IV3)

Murray (2000) writes that a key shift in the identities of parents relates to the ways in which they may change their ideas about disability through their experiences with their own disabled children.

> You know, numbers to me remind me of when Germans killed Jews, they're not numbers they're people – and Kyle's a person. It's like hospital numbers. I hate numbers. People aren't numbers, people are people. If anybody calls you a number 'this is number Case 111' – no, I'm sorry. Kyle's a person; you speak to him as though he's a person. If you treat him 'oh isn't he lovely' this and that, no he's Kyle – just like any other kid – let him get on with it. He's not got a problem, nobody else has got a problem ... If the baby's not normal the baby's a baby. You look after whatever child you've been given. You can't just ... they're not toys in a shop window, they're not dollies – you

know what I mean? They're human beings and you have to take the rough with the smooth – don't you babes?

(Sue, IV1)

Sue's reflections hint at her growing recognition of the problems endemic with individualising discourses of disability that threaten to denigrate the subjectivities of disabled children. They also resonate with the demands of some sections of the disabled people's movement to abandon pathological labels and emphasise humanity (Goodley, 2000; Roets, 2008). This alliance with counter-hegemonic ideas of disability politics, whether or not parents are conscious of such ideas, demonstrates a willingness of parents to rework their own understandings of disability and impairment. Helen (IV3) valued the helper in her son's nursery who was also disabled. She argued that 'she's got needs herself so she understands the children's needs, she's always been disabled so she understands their needs, do you know what I mean?'. David found a stronger voice against disablism through his own relationships with his child and other disabled people:

> We did a charity gig and one of the guys was sitting there. And he says, 'Oh, is it your son that you're doing the charity thing for?' I was like 'yeah', and he says, 'Oh right can I shake your hand?' And he went like that, and he actually had a hook for a hand. And I shook his hand no problem, and I spoke to one of the guys who was in the band, and I was telling him about it and he says, 'Uggghh, you shook his hook? Ah well that's disgusting!' I says, 'Well it's like shaking his hand but he hasn't got a hand there, what's the difference? Nothing at all'. But I think there's still that kind of stigma of people looking and going, 'oh well, it's different so I've got to be frightened of it or I've got to be really careful.
>
> (Karen and David, IV3)

While David is neither formally or publicly involving himself with the politics of disability (see Campbell & Oliver, 1996), many parents like him spoke of the empathy they now had for their own disabled children and other disabled people in terms of the disabling barriers they shared. This growing understanding of disablism – gained through living with its daily realities – increased parents' sense of injustice. This aligned them with disability as a political and administrative category. This partisanship was further strengthened through fighting for their child's benefits, services and support. Many parents spoke of having to 'toughen up'; 'You have to fight for everything and you shouldn't have to fight for entitlements' (Bouita, IV1). Lucy struggled to get what Jake was entitled to:

> I don't feel as though I should be fighting for things. Everything I get, I have to fight for ... sometimes I feel like I'm scrounging ... and I'm not scrounging, I'm fighting for my baby.
>
> (extract from Lucy's life story)

Such a finding mirrors the findings of Lundeby and Tøssebro (2003: p. 2) who report:

> In our own research we have met parents saying things like: the heaviest part is not having a child with a disability, the heaviest part is how you have to *fight* the system (our emphasis).

Sue went to court to fight for Disability Living Allowance for her son. She described the atmosphere in court as formal and bureaucratic. Indignant that Kyle was being talked about as though 'he were a number', Sue pulled out a photograph of Kyle and placed it in front of the judges, demanding that they speak about him as a person. Her appeal was rejected but Sue, whom the chair of the bench described as 'vibrant', announced that she would not give up and would be back. With the help of a member of the Portage staff she made a second application that was successful. Her child, Sue explained, had given her a purpose. She was there for a reason. Kay, a trained doctor, found that having a disabled child impacted hugely on her own work. Facing disabling barriers with her child had made her look again at how she worked with her patients; 'actually being able to sit and take time with people to understand what their problems are. I really started to enjoy that' (IV1). Angela found herself increasingly broadening her own norms about appropriate behaviour through gradually accepting her 'son's ways':

> He wants his clothes off, he wants them off and you have a *right* battle, and of course the older he gets, people might tolerate, but they might start and like, look and think he shouldn't be doing that ... I often think it's quite sad really 'cause I think you know, 'what's the harm?' But it is social rules at the end of the day isn't it, what kids have to sort of fit in to.
>
> (IV3, our emphasis)

A key part of this alliance, then, appears to be associated with developing alternative conceptions of impairment (see also Fisher & Goodley, 2007; Goodley, 2007a). Angela (IV3) had taken to aligning herself with her autistic child: 'I'm a lot more satisfied in [direct payments] than I ever was with any of the agencies cos I'm in control ... that's probably the autistic bit in me!'. Sylvia described her family as: 'I'm big "crip", Sarah's little "crip" and the [disabled] cat's tiny "crip"' (IV2). From these alliances and generation of alternative meanings emerge alternative ways of being. Lesley had had mixed experiences with health and social care services. She felt that the ethos underpinning the delivery of services was based too heavily around normative modes of communication. 'Stuart doesn't have speech', she explained, 'but he does communicate in different ways. He uses a different language to us, but I think we have to learn his language as much as he should have to learn ours.' She felt that autism was simply 'an alternative way of being' (extract from life story). For Lesley, her alliance with her autistic son raised real questions about curative discourses of disability. She asks:

> Why would you want to get rid of it [autism] anyway because I think some of the experiences that we've had with Stuart are just amazing and very humanising really. I mean some of the things he's able to tell us, I really think that some adults would be struggling to find the words for that and the fact that we've worked very hard together to always find a way of understanding each other, it's very enriching. Nobody in the services has told us anything about this at all; we've had to find out this for ourselves.
>
> (IV2)

A parental identity that works with disabled children involves an acceptance of diversity and difference. Tom spoke about the workshops he had started to offer to parents and professionals that addressed disability issues:

> I use a slide when I'm presenting saying, 'I'm going to give my son the label that will help you understand him more and understand who he is' and I put a slide up and it's called Sam – Monkey Boy, because that's what we call him at home, you know, 'you're a monkey', he is, he's five years old and he's so funny. He's non-verbal, has very limited physical movement ability below his shoulders – but he's just ... a tease.
>
> (Tom, IV1)

This recoding of disability underpins parents' demands for their children's identities to be valued and their rights to be acknowledged. This allegiance is sometimes ignored in the disability studies literature. As Ryan and Runswick Cole (2008) argue, mothers of disabled children are more than allies to their disabled children, as they experience directly, and by proxy, many of the discriminatory practices and attitudes their disabled children face. Alongside these difficulties, though, are productive possibilities:

> We shouldn't have a boring life, that's for sure [laughs]. I'll never have the chance to sit down and think, 'oh I'm dead bored' [laughs]. The same with the people who work with these kids, I mean, I cannot believe that they'll ever have a boring day at work, no day will ever be the same as the one before it.
>
> (Angela, IV3)

The identities being created here differ markedly with previous literature that has over-emphasised parental identities as tragic, in denial or burdened.

The governed parent

> No matter how much you read or how much you work in this area, you could never understand how profound it is, the loss that you experience going through it ... And people just don't see, the support isn't there ... it's just trying to get people to understand how kind of damaged and devastated you are as a person when this happens, but then the expectation that you'll suddenly become super-woman or super-dad, and take on physiotherapy, thousands of hospital appointments, and do all of this stuff as well as that, it just doesn't, it's an equation that just doesn't work.
>
> (Kay, IV1)

As Foucault (1982, 1991) argued, there are prices to be paid in the process of occupying a particular subject and the related subjectivities. In particular, parents' encounters with professionals – especially those of mothers – often draw them into broader social and political formations of what it means to be a 'good parent' or 'good mother'. Early intervention strategies on the part of professionals in the lives of families are far from neutral (Jones, 1999). While intervention ensures provision of services – at times some of it life saving – it also introduces normalising practices that separate the 'normal' from the 'special', threatening to place the disabled family under the spotlight of professional assessment and surveillance. Many of the parents we spoke to signal the pervasive nature of governance: where professional and institutional input leads to setting normative agendas and expectations. The term 'parenting support', in particular, describes the method by which parents are encouraged to reflect on and regulate their performance, through reference to 'expert' advice and training. Rose (1999: p. 192) points out 'such moralizing ethicopolitics incites a "will to govern" which imposes no limits on itself.' Below (see Table 5.1) we provide some pen portraits of experiences described by parents and elaborate on their relationship with the processes of governance.

The first thing we want to say about these pen portraits is that we are not suggesting professionals are in any way consciously attempting to disempower parents. Nor are we suggesting that parents are, in some way, passively conforming to the expectations of others. Indeed, pen portrait eight might be viewed as an example where together a professional and parent reject the governing presence of assumptions about the continued self-sacrifice of mothering. However, in general, these pen portraits highlight the imagined, unconscious, indirect constrictions and mechanisms of power associated with the governance of parents of disabled children. Bio-power, professional discourse and the naturalisation of the 'normal' are key characteristics of what Rose has termed the 'psy-complex' (see 1979, 1985, 1989): the growth of a human industry engaged in understanding, treating and therefore governing human subjectivity. Parents of disabled children occupy a particular place in this complex (see also Goodley & Tregaskis, 2006a). A number of key elements of this disempowering and alienating process occur. First, constructions, expectations and standards associated with *parental competence* cut across the pen portraits. Booth and Booth's work (1994, 1998) on disabled families indicates heightened expectations and standards required of parents: in terms of the tidiness of the home, psychological maturity (often assessed in terms of attachment theory), parental capacity (measured against seemingly unreachable standards of parenting) and the prevalence (or absence) of risk. A failure to meet these standards and parents are likely to face sanctions: at worse the removal of their children (see McConnell & Llewellyn, 1998). Second, a couple of the pen portraits reveal gendered expectations around parental competence. For Woodward and Emmison (2001) matching 'appropriate' clothing and personal appearance are strategies widely

Table 5.1   Governing the Parent: Nine Pen Portraits

1. Sylvia made sure that she got up at the 'crack of dawn' to tidy the house in preparation for the health visitor 'assessing the suitability' of the home. She wanted it just right.

2. A physiotherapist discussed with the researcher a parent's 'struggles with controlling her weight'. They confided, 'They are bound to affect how she looks after her child'.

3. A professional had told Lesley she must fit locks on internal doors to prevent Stuart from 'going where he shouldn't'.

4. Mags was encouraged by the nurses in the special care baby unit to leave her child for a while 'to get some fresh air'. They were worried about the 'attachment problems' that might result from her spending too much time with Gerry. She had to 'let go'. Mags had had experiences of a couple of units and they differed in their approach She had been allowed to bath Gerry at the first unit but in the second, she was told, 'oh no, he shouldn't be having baths yet'.

5. A number of mothers told us about feeling an intense pressure to dress their children up in the nicest clothes possible for hospital appointments so as to curb any possible inference that they were incapable of looking after their children.

6. Angela described how she adopted a business-like demeanour for professional appointments, including wearing a suit, carrying a briefcase and consciously altering her speech pattern to neutralise her local accent.

7. Sharon joked, 'I didn't have time for my postnatal depression' because she had to demonstrate to others she was capable of being a parent.

8. Cheryl had initially felt that she could not ask for respite care to 'just' go to the post office because it seemed too trivial. She spoke of the relief she felt when a health visitor encouraged her to employ a support worker to sit with her son for an hour while Cheryl took a bath.

9. Sharon had been visited by Sure Start workers. She had been peeling onions when they arrived and answered the door with tears streaming down her face. The Sure Start people had left saying they would call at a more convenient time. In due course, they alerted the Social Services and shortly afterwards a social worker had visited the family. This had incensed Sharon as she had not requested support from Social Services. She wondered if it was because she had appeared distressed during the Sure Start visit.

expected of and adopted by women in public spheres in order to manage their relations with others (see also Tannen, 2006). Similar strategies also appear to be applied to their children. These pen portraits indicate that discourses of femininity, parenting and professional ethics are often bound together (Thomas, 1997, 1999b). Parents, particularly mothers, have to quickly learn how to perform parenting in ways that are in keeping with the implicit expectations of the professional gaze. They govern themselves.

Third, these stories reignite our interest in a key contradiction associated with caring for a disabled child. In previous analyses of parenting, Larson's (1998) work on the parenting paradox has been hugely influential (McLaughlin, 2005; Trute & Heibert-Murphy, 2002). The paradox is understood as the management of internal tensions of opposing forces between:

- Loving the child as he or she is while also wanting to erase the disability;
- Dealing with incurability while pursuing solutions;
- Maintaining hopefulness for the child's future while being given negative information and battling one's own fears (Larson, 1998: p. 865).

This approach adopts a medical sociology approach to the study of disability through its focus on biographic disruption, an attention to the maintenance of a 'stable self' in the face of disabling adversity and the splitting of disabled/ill and non-disabled/healthy life worlds (see Thomas, 2007 for a critical discussion of this approach). Parenting, specifically maternal work, is seen as constantly under threat of 'crashing' as a consequence of these tensions. In order to maintain some form of order, mothers internally strive to maintain a 'tenuous hopefulness' through promoting an extension of maternal skills that work towards a hopeful life trajectory for the mother and her child (Larson, 1998: p. 865). Mothers create a 'positive bias' and regain a sense of control through fuelling their 'optimism in maternal work' (ibid.). While this analysis has been useful – and might help to explain some of the identity work undertaken by parents and children explored in this and the previous chapter – the work with our parents suggests that the paradox goes far beyond internal conflicts associated with tragedy, disability and poor prognosis. Parenting a disabled child is not simply a case of dealing with the paradox of loving a child you want to cure. Larson's paradox is in danger of reducing the identity work of parents into a balancing act of accepting difference while pursuing normality. This paradox fails to understand the complexities of the ways in which parents are governed.

While parents are expected to take control of the care of their disabled children, and to clearly demonstrate their abilities to do so, there are also expectations that they will submit to the authorities of medicine, management and cure. While parents are expected to be rational and autonomous, they are also expected to conform to the expertise of professional knowledge. Parents might find themselves overly protective but also emphasising their child's 'normal place in the family' (David and Karen, IV1). Moreover, while parents are expected to be functioning neoliberal subjects (pliant workers and productive citizens), their children are often deemed to be the very opposite (passive recipients of expert care as subjects who lack the competencies to act as responsible citizens). Caught up in such contradictory positions, parents are acutely aware of the limits of their citizenship, aware that they are free only to govern themselves in ways that fit with these clashing contradictions. Parenting is linked to constructions of competence, citizenship and dis/ability. Expectations of accountable forms of performativity reflect wider neoliberal constructions of the citizen endemic within current health, social and educational policy (see for example Dwyer, 2000, 2004; Harris, 2007). Neoliberalism places the onus on the adult citizen to have the capacity to make decisions from which they take full social and economic responsibility. Simultaneously, the citizen is made more accountable for his or her own actions, they are expected to engage in performativity and a growing industry of associated professionals provides training, monitoring and assessment.

Our research has allowed us to observe a variety of parenting interventions including Parent craft classes adopted by Portage workers, Sure Start interventions in poor communities and parenting workshops for parents of children with autism. While, undoubtedly, these interventions aim to tackle lack of information and social inclusion, we wonder to what extent they draw upon particular conceptualisations of parent and family. We also wonder about the types of governance that are being produced. The push by New Labour to promote parenting skills often targets families from poor areas of the community. As we have argued elsewhere (Fisher & Goodley, 2007), the related policies and practices create a particular type of citizen who fits with the neoliberal subject of the market: rational, skilled, responsible and ready for work. Sylvia, a disabled mother, felt particularly alienated by some services because of her lack of fit as a disabled person with this autonomous model of the parent. She did not fit the non-disabled ideal. In contrast, she felt incredibly patronised by professionals who, she felt, assumed that she needed training in parenting skills:

Dear Pamela

...

I see the professionals as a welcome part of 'our' team. And I think the system they are part of, ensures they see themselves as the professional experts that I, as the mother, should kind of bow down too. I see the relationship between us and the professionals as a healthy interdependence, where all parties are equal and therefore all people and views are respected and valued. This immediately sets me up for potential conflict as the system tries to make us dependant by design. I think some mainstream teachers, especially perhaps the older ones, are being almost forced into adapting to integration in the classroom ... I am seriously considering home schooling. I don't want my daughter 'statemented' [the process for disabled kids in UK schools] i.e.: labelled big time. I'm not sure how many children who are statemented make it into Uni. My guess would be very few. Sarah may well not have the intellectual capacity to even think about the option of Uni, but my opinion is that I want her education to open doors, not close them. I am extremely fearful that the present 'professional led tick box ethos' is a process that will close far more doors than it is supposed to open, whilst at all times covering the backs of the professionals who process it in relation to which ever child. Ok, I'm a cynic. But there is plenty of evidence to make being wary a sensible approach in order to be at least one step ahead, as necessary.
Regards,
Sylvia
'Stupidity is NOT a disability. Park elsewhere!'

(Email received from Sylvia)

The private lives of parents continue to be made public even in their own homes, particularly through early professional interventions such as appointments of midwives, health visitors and Portage workers (home based pre-school education). As Gabb (2005b) notes, while the home is seemingly a place to escape disciplinary practices that regulate our bodies in everyday life, the public world does not begin and end at the front door. For example, Sylvia objected to the paperwork of assessment required by Portage workers used to assess the development of her child's skills and behaviours. Sharon was visited by a trainee social worker who expressed concern at the absence of one of her disabled son from school. He had recently been absent from school in order to assist with the caring of his disabled sister Aisha. The situation, however, was in hand, and Sharon and the school were cooperating on this issue. How parents reconcile these powerful processes of governance remains a key question, one that we take up in the next section.

The psycho-emotional aspects of parenting

> Karen: There are no formal qualifications of being a parent, let alone of being a parent of a child that has special needs.
>
> (Karen and David, IV3)

In this section we consider in more depth the psycho-emotional experiences of parents against the backdrop developed above of the shifting nature of the parental subject and the governed parenting paradox. In this chapter we focus on the affective worlds of parents as they, with others, make sense of parenting and disability. We consider some aspects of the psycho-emotional lives of parents of disabled babies with a view to not only understand the impacts of disablism but also the resistant strategies that they develop in their constructions of self. The registers of the emotive and psyche are always embodied, political and shifting. Parenting a (disabled) child can be tiring, distressing, upsetting and heartbreaking. It can also be rewarding, affirming, enjoyable and heart-warming. We heard all of these emotions in the accounts of parents even during the shortest of conversations. Parenting is always full of contradictions and uncertainties. However, we are mindful of governance and socio-political constructions of disability that infiltrate the psycho-emotional lives of disabled families. As Gabb (2004) indicates, while emotions are felt by individuals, they gain their meaning through culture. Clearly, any consideration of the psycho-emotional will necessarily invoke a consideration of the wider communities and environments inhabited by families. In Chapter 6 we examine in more depth the meaning of community.

Managing difficult and spoilt identities

> You get that all the time, people stare, people comment, or people ... I would rather people said to me, 'What's wrong?' rather than just stare and then you can hear them as soon as you walk past, [whisper sounds].
>
> (Jemma, IV1 and IV3)

Previous work in the area of disabled families has illuminated the emotionality of parenting. In their phenomenological study, Kearney and Griffin (2001) found that while parents spoke of anguish and sorrow they also spoke of hope, love, strength and joy. Similarly, Lindblad et al.'s (2007) study produced the themes of being gratified by experiences of the child as having a natural place in relation with others and being provided a room for sorrow and joy. At the same time, psycho-emotional responses to disablism can be more productive – not least through the occupation of alliances and the shifting nature of the human subject described earlier in this chapter.

> When Danny was first born ... I wanted to get pregnant again as soon as possible because I felt that I hadn't got the baby I wanted. Now, I'm not so much in a hurry to have another child because I do really enjoy him. It's taken me a while to get here but now I am at that stage, I want to carry on enjoying him. Another child might change that.
>
> (Rebecca's story)

The oppressed/resistant nature of the psycho-emotional raises interesting questions about the types of subjectivity that are formed by parents of disabled children and how we as social researchers can understand such complexity. Clearly, there are aspects here of a normalising of the self which can be explained in terms of the governance of disabled families outlined above. The disabled activist Mason (1992: p. 27) captures this very powerfully when she argues that disabled people:

> harbour inside ourselves the pain and the memories, the fears and the confusions, the negative self images and the low expectations, turning them into weapons with which to re-injure ourselves, every day of our lives.

Marks (1999: p. 619) understands these as psychical defences which are always intimately bound up with social structures and embodied differences. These troubling views of disability and impairment are captured in Elizabeth's (IV1) disclosure:

> I just know, a lot of people seem to just be able to accept their disabled child, the people who I've met. They don't seem to have any real problem, they're just, the people I've met do seem to be completely devoted and I'm just not. It sounds awful but I can't. I can't resign

myself to, to just looking after Julie for the rest of me life 'cos it's not what I ever wanted … It's not that I resent her, I just really resent the situation. It's not her fault … Well, it's not my fault either … I'm always there for her and I do everything she needs doing, but, I think because I know I'm gonna be doing it for so long I just can't, I don't know, I don't always em, I don't always take pleasure [laughs] in looking after her. I don't know what else to say.

Kay (IV1) similarly found aspects of parenting difficult, particularly in the early days. She described how it was all one way:

He didn't see us, he didn't smile, he didn't respond, he cried, he vomited, he didn't sleep … there was nothing in it for me, and I didn't even feel like a mother, I just felt like I had this really difficult baby to care for … My relationship with Joe has definitely changed gradually over time and now I just, I love him to bits and the fear of anything happening to him is terrible. And I think if I didn't, I think if I didn't feel like I do now I would find it difficult to talk about how I did feel at the beginning. I hated myself for the way I felt. I felt like the worst, most selfish, horrible mother in the world. I hated myself.

We can read Kay's account as psychologically renegotiating normative expectations in order to reach an attitude and affect that accentuates the positive elements of her child. While this is not the place to heavily invest these analyses with psychological theories that respond to resistant repositionings, parents' accounts clearly point to a need to start taking seriously psychological and psychoanalytic engagements with disablism, the normative and governance. Such analyses must resist psychologising the experiences of parents and, instead, put them in their psycho-social, political and cultural place (see Goodley, forthcoming). What is clear is that the emotional life of parenting goes way beyond Larson's paradox. Parents do not simply convey loving a child they would like to be normal. We hear about the material realities of caring for a child alongside the affective consequences of long-held pathological discourses of disabled children *and* governing discourses of normality. David spoke of the emotional exhaustion he felt in the early days: 'It just eats away and eats away and eats away until you get to a point where you just end up losing your temper and shouting at them and things like that' (Karen and David, IV3). When one of the research teams spoke to Sue, she was suffering from a summer cold. 'Oh, I can't be ill, though', she explained, 'because then I can't do my stuff for Kyle'.

Processes of self-surveillance may further magnify these material bases of emotion. Parents often felt that they had to limit their public displays of emotion or vulnerability. Jemma (IV3) felt anxious when she cried during a meeting with a teacher in school because she did not want to come across as a 'neurotic mother'. In this sense she regulated her emotions. The mothering expectations we discussed in Chapter 4, we can now think of as a form of governance (Shelton & Johnson, 2006), with the power to embed a set of expectations against which mothers are judged:

> I find a lot of the people involved with my daughter's care ... expect you just to be totally devoted to your disabled child and just to be in the house whenever they want to call around, or, not forget appointments, and, be like utterly organised ... quite often feel like I can't do what's right by Julie because I'm too, because of me emotions and stuff and the way I feel about her. And because of her, her lack of co-operation with me as far as doing her physio' and stuff's concerned, I feel like almost as though she would be better off sort of institutionalised with professional people looking after.
>
> (Elizabeth, IV1)

A key element of the psycho-emotional is the relational. David told us that for a long time both he and his partner had been thinking about particular issues associated with medical intervention with their child but had not mentioned it to one another for fear of upsetting one another (Karen and David, IV1). Jennifer and William had attended many professional appointments together. While they found this mutual support helpful this had also led to resentment on the part of William who had felt ignored by professionals and his wife (a point developed in Chapter 8). We discussed earlier in this chapter the ways in which parents manoeuvred themselves into particular identity positions. There are, however, psycho-emotional costs to such work. Parents who challenge parenting norms – either vocally or through their actions – place themselves at risk in terms of others' views of their parenting capacity. Law (2007: p. 71) suggests that, should a parent question the wisdom of dominant parenting and professional discourses then they are more likely to find themselves questioned and evaluated as being 'good' or 'bad' parents. For example, Sylvia's position as a disabled person appeared to be equated with problem parenting. Sylvia is a wheelchair user and she felt during the period when she was in hospital having her baby that her suitability as a parent was constantly being questioned. At one point she started to doubt that she would ever be able to take her daughter home. In the extract below from her life story, Sylvia recalls a conversation with a nurse who told her:

> 'Oh I rang your Health Visitor' and I said 'Why?' and she said, 'Well you're disabled what do you expect'. I burst into tears, because it was my worst nightmare that somebody was judging my parenting ... and it was beginning ... and I just thought, 'I've got to let go of Sarah because they're not going to ever let me bring her home'.

One day after an appointment at the Sheffield Children's Hospital, Sylvia, Sarah, her PA and a researcher were leaving through an automatic door when a little boy pointed to Sarah and asked his Mum, 'What's wrong with her?'. Sylvia and the researcher exchanged glances but nothing was said. Disablism was not limited to professional interactions nor directed just at Sylvia. For many parents, the difference associated with their children heightened their social visibility as a family and invited the gaze of others. Waiting for appointments could be a nightmare. Sharon's disabled son with Tourette's syndrome was 'kicking off' big style in the waiting room and the consultant was running almost two hours late. He kept throwing himself onto the floor and a certain amount of tutting was audible. She left him there and watched as people stepped over him from time to time. Thomas (1999b) and Reeve (2002, 2007) have suggested that some of the most effective forms of disability oppression are to be found in the stares, reactions and responses of others. Sylvia, herself a disabled mother of a disabled child, was acutely aware of such oppression. After being the victim of an attempted mugging, Sylvia was interviewed by a police officer who told her that he thought that the crime was particularly offensive, as it had been carried out 'on someone like you'.

> My depression ... I did have it before but it is a reaction and I guess there are other contributory factors like the fact that I don't have a partner and I'm doing it all by myself and ... it goes on, you know, there's lots of different bits and bobs, not having much money and that kind of thing, living in an inaccessible house, living in an external community environment that is very different to where I feel comfortable – it feels quite hostile out there, you know, different things happen.
>
> (Sylvia, IV1)

Fortunately, for parents, managing these difficult aspects of parenting led them to find productive positive forms of identity work and it is to this that we now turn.

Productive psycho-emotional life

> You see, I can't keep chasing the normal. I mean I've done so much to try and make my son normal but I can't keep that up ... I need to accept him in the ways that he is and just enjoy them and him. I must stop pressurising myself.
>
> (Rebecca, extract from her life story)

Selves can be understood as continually constituted and emergent (Kondo, 1990). They are also contingent on relationships with others and unconscious notions of what selves should be. Productive psycho-emotional activity appeared to reside in negotiating the meaning of parenting *with* the child. Lesley (IV1) suggested that opening up dialogue with her disabled son allowed for the setting of expectations, 'Stuart understands that we're doing our best ... and while it's not going to be perfect, we're doing our best to help him. If we show that we care about understanding what he's feeling, he can accept more in terms of things not being "right"'. Affective aspects of parenting are captured well by Rebecca (from her life story) where she reflects:

> I wanted to have an intense relationship with my child ... with all Andy's difficulties; it's certainly what I've got. In the end maybe I got the child I wanted.

Jemma felt that her daughter Rosa had encouraged her not to be as opinionated as she was used to being and 'take people at face value, and think, literally what they are is what they are' (IV1). This gives a very different view of the psycho-emotional life of parents to a prevalent perspective in the literature, identified by Grant (2005), which views parenting uncertainty as a necessary engagement with stress and coping (see Lazarus & Folkman, 1984; Taanila et al., 2002). While a number of writers have suggested that it is not caring for a disabled child that causes the stress, but the processes which the families have to go through accessing provision (Cole, 2004; Murray & Penman, 2000). Dale (1996) argues that it might be more helpful to view some of the experiences of parents in terms of uncertainty. Similarly, Gabb (2005a) describes this as a dislocation of identities. Bernie (IV1), for example, felt that the early stages of parenting were like 'a sort of limbo period ... I mean I don't think I let myself get too close to her at that point, cared for her and everything'. But these moments of limbo need not necessarily be unproductive. Often, in these moments of uncertainty we might find exciting ways of viewing and acting with the world. Angela (IV1) summarised her life with her disabled child as one of constant surprises:

> It's never boring, always lively, sometimes not the lively type that you would like and other times when it's absolutely hilarious, and other times you're just about pulling your hair out and just think I just cannot cope anymore, but you do, and you get up and get on with it.

For Lindblad et al. (2007) a recurring theme for parents of disabled children was being enabled to live an eased and spontaneous daily life. While parents such as Angela (IV2) worried about what might happen to their children when they became 'dependent adults', other parents' reflections hinted at different conceptualisations of the present and future.

> I am coping. I do one thing at a time, one day at a time. I do not make huge plans, I don't expect certain things. If we overcome a hurdle then great but there will be something else around the corner.
>
> (Cheryl, IV3)

Jennifer and William did not like hearing about the development achievements of other Down's syndrome children. While they recognised it was well intended, they didn't want to compare Robert to other children; they just wanted to enjoy *him*. David and Karen shared these views:

> David: I mean we actually went into the doctors and said to them we don't want to know what you're thinking, what you're investigating ... we had been given so many different diagnoses, no one could agree ... we said if Daniel's happy, and he's doing as well as he can every day, then that's all we, we really need to know.
> ...
> Karen: I don't think we look too, that too far ahead into the future, I think most things we just try to take on a daily basis, and deal with information as it comes because you can look at the future and say, because there's so many different scenarios because we have nothing

concrete, it's like well, it could be when he's five year old he could be like running around or he could be in a wheelchair or he could have no, still no recognition of who anyone is. So I think at the moment it's pointless trying to look
David: We're in limbo ...
Karen: Most of the time it's a waiting game, isn't it?
(David and Karen, first extract from IV3 and second from IV1)

Contemporary western parents are often expected by others to play a pivotal role in enhancing their children's 'futurity': their anticipated value, productivity and well-being as adult citizens (McKeever & Miller, 2004). But, parents also, may well have a tolerance for ambiguity, disorder and uncertainty because these are requirements of child-care. Larson (1998) suggests that parents simply learn to embrace the paradox as a tenuous emotional compromise. Our research places stronger emphasis on parental forms of resistance that go beyond compromise. As we have argued elsewhere (Goodley, 2007a; McLaughlin & Goodley, 2008), parents engage in sophisticated meaning-making practices which range from embracing the certainties of knowledge provided by institutions such as medicine and education through to the more uncertain and ongoing terrains of parenting, love, care and nurture. For some, parenting is a process of becoming that is intimately tied to uncertainty. Often, in the related literature, uncertain parents are presented as being in denial or lacking the awareness to 'properly' accept their children. In contrast, a number of parents have reminded us that uncertainty may promote openness to new ideas and locations: a way out of the parenting paradox. For the feminist philosopher Braidotti (1994, 2006) subjectivities of the twenty-first century are fundamentally nomadic in their quality. This refers to the kind of critical consciousness that resists settling into simplistic, often professionally owned arenas of thought and behaviour. Nomads, instead, find themselves in different locations and lands (Bayliss, 2006; Goodley & Roets, 2008; Roets, 2008).

I have this booklet written by the mother of a special needs child. It's called Welcome to Holland. She talks about the wonderful dreams we attach to pregnancy, birth and having the child and likens it to going on a journey to Italy. It's what you've always dreamt of, you get on the plane and you're all excited. And then you get on this plane after a couple of hours later or whatever, you've now landed in Holland. And you were expecting this fantastic place, Italy, and you're just so disappointed. But if you look carefully and do let go of Italy you'll see the beauty that's in Holland, the beautiful tulips, and the canals. It will have certain things Italy may never have. You'll meet people that you wouldn't meet if you were going to Italy. And you might not get Italian wine but, hey, they've got some really good beer in Holland.

(Rebecca, IV2)

This notion of parenting as a journey into and within particular locations and communities raises questions about the quality of relationships. Birkett (2000: p. 190 cited in Russell, 2003: p. 144), reflects on learning of the diagnosis of cerebral palsy for her daughter:

From that moment my life diverged from the way of lists. It was as if I had been following some roughly mapped route and suddenly the car swerved wildly and I began to plough through terrain I had never dared venture into ... I could no longer imagine what lay ahead.

We should be careful, however, not to presume these journeys are the stuff of car crashes. Instead, we remain committed to capturing some of the complex identity work of parents. Lauritzen (1989: p. 31) draws attention to the new romanticism which attempts to rekindle a moral opposition to the competitive model of moral relations dominant in the marketplace and in most contemporary (male) moral philosophy. This emphasises intimacy, nurture and affection. Hence, when the self is defined in relation to others, a concern for relationships rather than for rights may well be a productive outgrowth (ibid. p. 36). Becoming might, then, allow a way out of the pincer-like grips of governance and the pathologies of dominant parental discourses.

Conclusion

In this chapter we have demonstrated some of the identity work of parents, through various subject positions, under the conditions of governance, with a host of psycho-emotional response. The transformation of emotional and relational life can foster networks of activism and community engagement (Rapp and Ginsberg, 2001). It is to these networks we now turn.

6
Community Practices

Dan Goodley and Janice McLaughlin

Introduction

This chapter explores the different ways in which parents and their disabled children populate community contexts, including distant and close networks of support, friendships, virtual networks, the extended family, leisure spaces and institutions. Communities are understood as complex and shifting phenomena that parents respond to and, in many ways, create. Families live within these changing communities and institutional settings and find them both supportive and marginalising. To this end, the chapter defines and understands the notion of community through reference to concepts of negotiation, citizen, spatial location and belonging.

What is community?

> But yes, I want a life, I'm twenty-four, I'm allowed to
> have a life, its normal. But you know they want, it
> seems to me as though they expect you to be com-
> pletely devoted. I should be in the house all day every-
> day, doing what physio' I can with my daughter, and
> getting her in a good routine, and taking her off to all
> these groups and you know, like all these special needs
> groups ... But to be honest with you, I find that I would
> rather spend my time hanging round my friends, just
> take her to the local playgroup.
>
> (Elizabeth, IV1)

Elizabeth's frank reflections capture some of the complex ways in which we relate to community and the different senses of what it might mean.

Russell (2003) adopts the work of Bronfenbrenner (1977) to understand different levels of community participation. These include the microsystem (e.g. how conceptions of a child's psychological development are played out within the family); the mesosystem (e.g. friendships, family support; access to services and professionals); the exosystem (e.g. local and national service networks) and the macrosystem (e.g. social values bestowed upon disabled children). Community spans home, education, work and leisure and includes friends, families, neighbourhoods and (inter) national contexts. For Ledwith (2006), who adopts the work of Freire (1972, 1998) community hints at a network that denotes a sense of belonging, a shared culture and history, made up of distributed skills with an economic base, that provide resources which may or may not be accessed by members. But communities are also heterogeneous. Crucially, they are sometimes in conflict. Indeed, for many families, the wider community may be experienced as exclusionary. It calls upon parents, then, to create new forms of community within which they can participate in ways that value them and their disabled children. Community might relate to a sense of belonging in which we assess the extent to which we feel nested and accepted by the values and practices of a given culture or group (Sarason, 1974). In sketching out the complex debates associated with community belonging, and following Bell (1999), we can highlight a number of overlapping elements:

- There is not just *being* but also *longing*: an affective/emotional dimension – which will pull at the very heart of the psycho-emotional experiences of parenting alluded to in previous chapters;
- Belonging can be considered to be an achievement, a performance and an ongoing one at that – so that the communities we occupy, and our performative responses to them, will change and morph over a given period of time;
- Communities have histories to them – some of which are more inclusive than others;
- Communities provide possibilities for the makings of diasporic belonging – so that individuals spread from one community into another.

A key element of community participation for disabled families involves their relationships with professionals. In Chapter 7 we will explore the constitution, makings, demands and challenges of professionals and professional practice. Clearly, though, it is impossible to separate professional interventions from other community practices.

Not only are professionals key members of communities but also their interactions with parents and children will often have a huge bearing on the ways in which parents experience other aspects of family, work and community life. For example, the inflexibility of health services to organise appointments at times before or after the normal working day, hugely impacts upon parents' work commitments (Kagan et al., 1998). Moreover, the extent to which informal and formal support networks interact – such as family and friends, voluntary organisations and statutory services – allow or prevent parents from caring in ways that support the community involvement of their children (see Wolfensdale, 2002). We will leave a more detailed analysis of professionals for later. In this chapter we turn to other ways in which communities are constituted, understood and populated.

Community participation: Friends, family and (how to be) parents

> Our experience – with its pain, vigilance and hard work – has heightened our senses when it comes to our child. We are TIGER MOTHERS! Ever watchful, ever ready, tireless to protect, provide, defend. Sometimes we sense others are wary of us. They feel – and fear – the great power within us, the burning fire in our eyes.
>
> (An email from one of the parents represented in this study)

> You know, but it would be nice just to, I don't know; just get a break, that's all I want. Some adult company. I don't want much ...
>
> (Jemma, IV1).

A common thread of research in the area of disability and families relates to the coping strategies of parents. For example, Taanila et al. (2002) identified strategies that included developed forms of information, acceptance of the child, family co-operation and social support, optimistic attitudes, good family cohesion, good communication and shared parenting of housework and childcare. In contrast, Ryan and Runswick Cole (2008) offer 'combat' as an alternative to 'coping'. They argue that parents (especially mothers) of disabled children start off as worriers and become warriors. Crucial to both these positions are the relationships forged with friends, family and other parents. The quality of these relationships plays a huge part in coping or combat. In this section we explore some of these experiences, from the everyday need for adult friendship to the politicised identity of the parent group. On route we also briefly look at the impact of online support.

Family and friends: negotiating values and acceptance

> Steven's family are very close, my family never have been and I think I hoped in the early days that this would be, somehow things would magically change and this would bring us all together. But I mean that only happens in films.
>
> (Kay, IV1)

As we noted in Chapter 1, following Vanobbergen et al. (2006), the parent, child and family are involved in ongoing negotiations about the form and scope of their participation in communities. The negotiation model does not, however, denote a power-free act of agency. Negotiation implies the possibility of conflict and contestation. Moreover, negotiation inevitably transmits preferred ways of family living or, as we explored in Chapter 5, ways of being and governance into the household. In this sense the family and community are not distinct entities. Many elements of the wider community flow into and inform the constitution of the family. The family is an ideological tactic, a pool of public policy and an ideal in which people are supposed to live (Sherratt & Hughes, 2002). It is also a relational context in which members, especially parents, negotiate expectations, ideological constructions and power formations. The family is one institution at the heart of ordering people's lives and is consistently being reconstituted. Work done in the domestic site of the family flows back out into parents' interface with the community. Families are becoming more diverse. Less and less families stay together in the same neighbourhood. There are blended forms of childcare including, for example, nursery provision and the informal care of grandparents (see Mooney et al., 2002). Such shifts heighten the need for negotiation over caring networks.

For some parents their extended family were noticeable via their absence from the family's life:

> My brother has a birthday for his daughter in July and I'm supposed to be her godmother but they didn't invite us along and I think it's because of Jack's condition because they don't like it.
>
> (Jane, IV1)

Seeing their child rejected by those around them was extremely painful for parents, this often led them to reject existing kinship ties that were unwilling to recognise their child as a full member. When extended family were involved this could also bring tension and conflict. There was often a collision of different understandings of disability, good parenting and ideas of what was 'best' for the child. Not surprisingly, perhaps, some of the parents in our study acknowledged tensions with their own parents about parenting standards. Sometimes this led to conflicts between different generations:

> But like, other people, even like my mother-in-law was like really [pause], me mother-in-law's had seven kids and she was 'oh well you should be doing this with her and you should be doing that, and the other.'
>
> (Elizabeth, IV1)

Parents found themselves having to carefully juggle the well-meant, but ultimately contradictory, comments of family members:

> Karen: In the beginning we did actually have to have a few words with them because, when we first found out about Daniel's condition we either had two, two schools of thought didn't we?
> David: It was either, 'Oh, everything's gonna work out perfectly fine and everything'll be great, and keep happy,' and
> Karen: 'He'll get better'
> David: 'He'll get better; oh it'll not be as bad as that.' And we were trying to get the message through, no; we know exactly what's gonna happen. And then you would get the side where it would be like, 'Oh I just don't know how you're coping. Eeh it's so terrible. Eeh it's such a burden.' Which just made it worse, so much more worse because we were on the borderline of coping, and every time somebody mentioned that, you were thinking well, ugh [sighs and laughs].
> Karen: You know, they'll say 'how d'you cope?' and you're like, well you've just got to.
> David: Well it's not a case of choosing!
>
> (IV1)

Extended families were able to place boundaries around how far they would go in providing help. Quite often these limits were created by discomfort around disability. A real anxiety for Lucy was that when she tube-fed her son Jake, there was always a possibility of food entering his lungs. On one occasion, she had difficulty feeding Jake on a Friday evening. The health visitors worked from nine to five, so there was literally nowhere to seek advice until Monday morning. Her mother and sister were not around to offer support. 'They don't like to tube-feed Jake', Lucy explained, so she was forced to ring intensive care. Some forms of extended family support were blocked by policy formations. Helen's mother, for example, was an experienced child minder and only too happy to look after Roberto. This would enable Helen to spend more time at work. However, the only way that Roberto's grandmother could look after her was if she was paid. Current policy at that time prevented the financing of formal childcare provided by a family carer. For Angela (IV1), the way she viewed her child's needs meant that she felt unable to negotiate support with others close to her:

> I have other friends and relatives but on the whole, like my child is very active and I'm very wary of leaving him with anybody who I don't think could cope or wouldn't keep an eye on him as much as I think he needed. So, we are quite limited as to who I would feel more at rest with them looking after him. And plus, as he's getting bigger and stronger you've got to take that into consideration as well.
>
> (Angela, IV1)

While the inclusion of extended family members in caring practices could raise issues, it is also clear that such inclusion does have the potential to create broader networks of caring practitioners. This can provide much needed respite and practical help:

> David: Her mam, her mam looked after the kids overnight, and then they went down to see their aunty down in Newcastle for a couple of hours and it gave us just, well for the first time about, a night and a bit of a day just to have some time to ourselves and it was lovely. We didn't do anything special, just walked around the shops, not having to worry about pushing kids and pushchairs and things like that.
>
> (Karen and David, IV1)

> When you've had a baby, any help's fine. I mean I was ... it was fantastic ... I mean the support from family and friends was absolutely brilliant, because obviously when it was winter, taking her out and stuff, and people would take her sister up to school. And ... the next door neighbours were very supportive taking Jessica to nursery and things ... And I mean I suppose my parents ... and my mum,

you know, I think my mum she came up and my father-in-law came up and my brother came up. Yeah, in some ways it was like a holiday.

(Bernie, IV2)

This kind of support by the extended family required negotiating the distribution of specialist skills and sharing of technical knowledge:

My parents were coming up at different times ... her dad learned how to work the tube feeding, her dad's mum learned how to do it, my mum and dad, my sister – because they were going to be all those people that were going to be my network of people that were going to help me look after her. At the time I was living at my parents, I wasn't with her dad, so I mean they had to ... well they wanted to but they had to learn how to do it.

(Eva, IV1)

When families are responsive they provide belonging and the fostering of strong, inclusive, accepting relationships. Over a 100 family members and friends attended Robert's christening (Jennifer and William's son). They spoke often about how fortunate Robert was to be growing up with a large social network to support him. Their numerous friends have children of the same age as Robert who 'will look out for him – he's going to be fine'. Helen's dad lived nearby and helped out with her son, who was equally besotted with his granddad.

My own Dad and my son, because they have that time together on their own. I mean my Dad, he comes and, he says 'Is my little lad coming now?' Do you know what I mean, and he crawls up to him and he's 'mmm ...' so you can tell he's happy to see him.

(Helen, IV2)

Helen told us that her mother was hoping to change her job from ward assistant to a role in which she could work with children with special care needs. Through life with their children, parents and, in this case, grandparents, acquire new understandings and skills that they want to pass on to others. In contrast, for some parents, their social isolation and dependency on professionals left them feeling helpless and alone. Extensive informal/formal social networks can greatly influence the community participation of disabled families (Taanila et al., 2002). This can include input from siblings, grandparents or friends. Of course, the family can sometimes become slightly claustrophobic:

> Karen: It was nice to have the family there, to have people to talk to and that but, like you say it was almost too much 'cause sometimes they would be knocking on the door and you'd be just like, I can't be bothered because they would be, they would come around every single day.
>
> (Karen and David, IV3)

For this reason Karen and David were pleased to obtain a house move that took them slightly away from extended family; from where they were able to exert more control over the extent to which they would be involved in their lives and care of Daniel.

The role of siblings in the negotiated care networks around disabled children receives significant public sympathy and media coverage:

> I do feel guilty and sorry for Sian because I tend to be quite a strict parent, I'll not let her get away with things, and yet she sees Harry getting away with throwing things down or pulling the wall paper off or, or hitting people and all that, now there's no way I'd let her get away with things like that. And she must think at the end of the day, yes, she's well aware that he's autistic and what it entails, but it must get to her thinking he gets away with things and he obviously gets a heck of a lot more attention than she does, but I mean we always try and get her to have special times, like tonight she starts her first swimming lesson, she's at stage 3 now, little things like that.
>
> (Angela, IV1)

There were many challenging experiences for non-disabled siblings. Being informed that a brother or sister was ill can be very difficult to come to terms with; 'I think it was hard for her, she was really .... she really felt it very much, because she's a very sensitive girl' (Bernie, IV1). Angela (IV1, IV2 and IV3) and Maria (IV2) talked of their daughters not having friends around to the family home because of how their disabled siblings behaved. In the process, the discomfort others feel around a disabled child, closes down the community networks of their siblings too. Elizabeth (IV1) spoke of her guilt as she recalled the numerous nights her non-disabled son was kept awake by the cries of his disabled sister. David (Karen and David, IV1) acknowledged that he did not have as much time to spend with 'the other two kids'. Interestingly, during reflections later in the interview, David saw this as a potential space for reworking family activities for more shared times together.

David: I think the other two … aren't as close to Daniel as we would, we would hope they would be. But that's something, that, we've obviously got to try, I think by doing things as a family together, that's going to be a lot easier for them to come together.

Hence while much of the research in this area re-presents the disabled child as burden to their non-disabled siblings, our findings support more recent work which attends to the positive contributions of the disabled child to the lives of their non-disabled brothers and sisters (Connors & Stalker, 2003; Priestley, 2001, 2003; Shah, 2005; Shah et al., 2004). Families clearly spend time working out their shape and character:

Emma: How does Sian react to all of this, do you think?

Angela: I think she just takes it all in her stride, she worries about him a lot, more than like, another nine year old should have to worry, and [pause] she's always like, she's watching him in the garden, and watching him when we go out and all that, I don't think, it doesn't bother her, other people's reactions to Harry. She's more concerned with Harry. But I think that while she has grown up with Harry, she's never known any different, she was the younger one. So, it seems hard on her now but probably when she grows up she'll be a much stronger person than your average little girl or teenager or whatever. [Pause] And she'll be a lot more understanding I think than a lot of other kids her age, so. [Pause] Even the teachers at school, well the last school, and the school have commented on how patient she seems to be.

(Angela, IV3)

This resonates with the findings of Hames (1998) who found that non-disabled children often developed sophisticated ways of understanding their disabled siblings, including imitation, copying parental forms of love and working through means of support.

Alongside these family dynamics were accounts of friendship. For some of the parents we spoke to, having a disabled child had threatened long-term friendships. Jemma (IV1) remarked, 'I mean I have had friends that I've known for 20 years and I haven't seen them for dust'. She continues:

I've got a friend who, she's actually my daughter Ruby's godmother, and we've been friends since I was thirteen, so you're talking about

18 years now since then, and if she comes here now, she'll come down, the last time she was here it was my daughter's birthday and she actually just pushed a card through the door. I saw her in the village on Sunday, but they don't come and knock at the door. And if she does come, she stands in the doorway and I'll say 'do you want a cu', 'no, no, y' see, I can't stay', she can't stay, I feel like she can't sit down in my house, you know I feel like I don't know if she thinks she's contagious.

(IV1)

Elizabeth also felt tensions with old friends but this was connected with wider expectations (and issues of governance explored in the previous chapter):

Yeah, there's a lot of times I don't want to take her out with us, lot of times I just won't go out. I mean I get asked to go places quite a lot, and I'm like, ah, it's pointless, my daughter will just scream. So it's like, my friends ask us to go out, you know, just to go for a walk, or even just to go somewhere, and I'm like, oh she'll just scream and there's no point, or go into town, and I'll try desperately to get her watched so I can go to town without her, but just like can't half the time.

(IV1)

Having a disabled child appeared to push some parents to the periphery of friendship groups. Where once they might have considered themselves as core members their new status as parents of disabled children called into question their legitimate membership (Avis et al., 2002; Lave & Wenger, 1991; Tobbell & Lawthom, 2005; Wenger, 1998). For Elizabeth, a general lack of support from her friends and families led to social isolation:

I really resent the fact that I've been kind of landed like out of my two children, I've been landed with looking after the most difficult one [her non-disabled son lived with her ex-partner for much of the time]. And I don't get any help, not really. My little brother will baby sit for us occasionally, I can occasionally get a baby-sitter. But her dad, her dad doesn't help at all with her, I mean he doesn't, he doesn't even normally see her because I pick my son up from school during term time, drop him back up at school. And my mam doesn't help, and I did get a respite carer, it was good couple of month ago, but she's just packed in now and there's no one else to do it again.

So I've been waiting three years for respite, got it, and then she's not, she's not doing it anymore, there's no one else to do it .... But no one ever offered to help though, you know, and you've got this manic-screaming child, no one ever turns round and says, 'oh d'you want us to take her for a night so you can have some sleep?' And still no one does.

(IV1)

Kay (IV1) managed to maintain friendships though this was not without challenges:

I've got a group of very close school-friends who I've known since I was probably eleven, a young teenager, and we were all pregnant with our first baby around the same time, and then pregnant with the second one around the same time. And they all had healthy children and obviously I didn't. Em, but we used to meet up every week, and because I'd known them so long, although it was hard seeing their babies every week, it was good in a way because I couldn't shut myself off and pretend Joe was ok. It was very hard seeing their babies make progress and Joe just wasn't, but it meant I had to deal with it, I couldn't bury my head in the sand, and also I could talk to them really, really well.

A key element of community participation appears to reside in the mediation of relationships in the family, with children and friends, by parents. In light of these varying experiences of friendships and family it is perhaps no wonder that parents seek support and relationships from similar others and it to this that we now turn.

The online community: actual value in the virtual?

Blackburn and Read (2005) collected the accounts of parents of disabled babies who were keen Internet users. Participants reported using it for a range of purposes, directly or indirectly related to the care and upbringing of their disabled children, with a common vision being the maintenance of a reasonable quality of life. Useful information and services were not the only outcomes. For some users the Internet kept them in touch with family, friends and other parents, allowed a space to purse leisure activities and provided necessary shopping opportunities.

These findings were highlighted, to some extent, in our research with parents. The Internet was something to be plugged into when required. During a hospital meeting, rushing from one department to another, Eva pulled out her mobile phone and called up an Internet link to clarify the meaning of a clinical term used by a consultant. She then quizzed the nurse at the next appointment why this term had been used. Eva demonstrated her rights as a knowledgeable recipient of medical intervention partly through her informed position developed through a relationship with the Internet. Other parents spoke of the affective register of Internet participation. Sylvia (IV2) portrayed her participation in an online parent community as a chance to chat with some of 'the best friends she had ever met'. Others referred to the online community as a place to visit, from time to time, when required. Cheryl (IV3) saw the online community not solely in terms of active participation. She gained just as much in terms of accessing information and a sense of belonging as a 'lurker' rather than a 'contributor'. The parents' accounts support the findings of Siddiquee and Kagan (2006) whose study of online community involvement found a number of key outcomes including (1) maintaining links and re-building networks, facilitating resettlement and integration; (2) facilitating the maintenance and development of personal identities and fostering psychological empowerment; and (3) the development of social identity and community narratives, and collective consciousness. Indeed, a growing consideration for the development of parent and disability groups lies in critically assessing the extent to which online communities provide possibilities not only for accessing information (Kagan et al., 1998) but also for new forms of social movements and disability politics (Brownlow & O'Dell, 2002, 2006). For example, Granic and Lamey (2000: p. 94) argue that the Internet is 'a self-organising system' that has the potential to 'catalyse major shifts in the cognitive styles and beliefs of its interactants'.

There are, however, clear questions to be raised about the quality and form of knowledge available to parents on the Internet. Are sites promoting medical or social models of disability? Is the Internet a tool for the promulgation of pathological discourses or more positive alternatives? Whose agendas are being promoted? Borrowing from Colebrook (2006), to what extent does the virtual nature of the Internet reflect the discourses of disabling society, which view disability as deficit and impairment as illness? Dixon-Woods (2001) has argued, in an analysis of patient-information leaflets, that dominant discourses tend to privilege bio-medical forms of information and adopt a one-way model of communication. Ong-Dean (2005) suggests that advice books and Internet sites for parents of disabled children draw on assumptions that favour disability claims made by white, degree-educated and upper-income parents. Brown (1997) develops this point further to suggest that the contemporaneous self-help culture in which we live, and its associated texts, militate against, rather than support, the development of positive articulations of the self precisely because they are so closely bound together with notions of 'stress' and 'coping'. Readers find themselves not only lacking in terms of the model of the coping subject presented in these texts (which they are supposed to aspire to) but also inevitably start to use these understandings to assess (and govern) their own ways of being. Consequently, readers never match up to (but find themselves using) the unattainable ideal of the coping, informed and knowledgeable subject portrayed in self-help texts.

On a more productive note, we could argue that the constantly shifting nature of knowledge through the Internet might well prevent certain ideas from gaining foundational authority. Karen and David set up a website to share their experiences with other parents; this was initially very important to them because their child had a rare condition, so reaching out to parents with similar experiences meant reaching out internationally. Here parents may well develop forms of intellect and subjectivity that are constantly in the process of review and development.

> Karen: But we do have a place on the message boards where if you want to let off steam, you know you can go and have your bit to say about doctors and you know the care and things like that. And it, it's been the case of, people who've read the information and have come back have said, 'it, it's good to find this is what we can expect because nobody has given us this kind of information.'
>
> (David and Karen, IV1)

Interestingly, Karen and David told us that they had lost interest in the Internet by the time we met up for our third interview. Elsewhere we have discussed how parents vary in their use of the Internet as a space for support and debate (Clavering & McLaughlin, 2007a). Some use it constantly and consistently, others find that their involvement trails off and they use it only intermittently. Internet participation illuminates other practices associated with information gathering and the interpellation of parents' identities. Cheryl (IV2) contrasts her experience as a passive subject of research (as she is often approached by medical and social researchers to participate in research studies) with her role as an investigator actively researching aspects of her child's impairment, needs, services and available resources (sometimes via the Internet). In its most positive light, the Internet might well be seen as providing the very resources associated with a community as defined by Ledwith

(2006); hinting at networks, denoting a (temporary/occasional) sense of belonging, a shared culture and history, made up of distributed skills that provides resources which may or may not be accessed by members. This fits with Rapp and Ginsberg's (2001) view of electronic media as neighbourhoods for the creation of mediated kinship through which normalised notions of family life are reassessed. The Internet might be a sole support for an otherwise isolated family:

> I found up to about pre-school age quite difficult because I was on my own at the house and me and my husband really had to do what we thought was best for her. We read a lot but other than that we didn't know what we were doing.
>
> (Josie, IV1)

Parent groups: differing typologies and interests

> Karen: We did have a bit of a run in with Dr Bootle.
> David: Yeah. That was the one who told us to pray.
> Karen: Yeah.
> David: The one who said that he would pray rather than ...
> Interviewer: Give support?
> Karen: Yeah, advised us against support groups. Erm, said he didn't, didn't believe in going to support groups and basically said ...
> David: Then started asking about our beliefs and stuff ... so he said, 'but Jesus said I was the way!' and I was like, whoa [laughs].
> Karen: I think he did notice after a short period of time because the atmosphere changed in the office because I, I don't have a problem with anybody in their religious beliefs at all, but I don't like people forcing their's on me. And the way that we were feeling was we actually went to see him with regards to our son's *medical* health as opposed to you know some kind of theological help.
>
> (Karen and David, IV2, our emphasis)

Many of the parents represented in our study had involvement with parent groups. This aspect of community participation denotes parents' engagement with civil society. These groups have grown despite the opposition of others, including professionals and disabled people's organisations, whose own ambitions are seen at odds with those of parents. Groups differ in their philosophy, affiliation and aims. Speaking generally, rather than specifically naming the affiliations of the parents represented in our study, it is possible to identify different types of group. Two frameworks are helpful here. The first is offered by Hughes (2007) in his distinction between 'biological citizens' and 'social model stalwarts'. The former, he suggests, refers to those organisations whose remit focuses around the treatment, rehabilitation and, sometimes, cure of a specific condition or impairment. This would include those parent groups that are brought together under a specific call for a cure for a disabling condition or research into the genetic basis of impairment. This is captured in Helen's account:

> The National Autistic Society are good ... they've given me some cards that say 'he's got autism' ... Yeah. If anybody says anything or ... and it's got a number on if they've got any questions. And it says that they can't talk and they can't interact and stuff like that so.
>
> (Helen, IV3)

The latter type identified by Hughes relates more closely to campaigning organisations of disabled people whose concerns are less with impairment and more with the disabling conditions of society. A number of parent groups would share this commitment, for example, in their campaigns for inclusive education for disabled children in mainstream school settings.

A second framework for understanding the typology of parent groups is provided by People First of Washington State (1984) – a self-advocacy group of adults with learning disabilities – who distinguish between a variety of organisational locations including service-based groups in health and social care contexts and coalition groups affiliated with other campaigning disability groups formed outside of professional or explicitly political organisations. Parent groups represented in this study could be viewed as emerging from these different locations including professional settings (e.g. parent groups linked to a specialist nursery), activist contexts (e.g. a disabled parents' network) and independent groups (e.g. local parent groups set up by the parents themselves who offer a regular coffee morning to parents with disabled children). Nevertheless, these typologies capture only some of the nuances of the civil society occupied and constituted by parents. Parent groups' aims and activities often blur distinctions. Every Disabled Child

Matters and Parents with Attitude are campaigning organisations with clear affiliations with organisations of disabled people. They could also, to some extent, be viewed as 'social model stalwarts' though they also blur independent and coalition typologies. The National Autistic Society, MENCAP and Down Syndrome Association blend the 'coalition' type of campaigning for the inclusion and acceptance of disabled children alongside the 'service' focus associated with the promotion of information on services for parents and professionals. They complicate matters further because they appear to embrace the aspirations of the biological citizen and the social model stalwart; take for example the following extract from the National Autistic Society:

> The vision of Research Autism is a world where those on the autistic spectrum are able to realise their full potential and where they and their families are able to enjoy a good quality of life. This is achieved by understanding, preventing or overcoming the disabling effects of autism and related conditions and by applying the most timely and effective therapeutic and remedial interventions.
>   (http://www.nas.org.uk/nas/jsp/polopoly.jsp?d=1290&a=10468)

Furthermore, the ways in which parents use groups will alter how they are perceived. To what extent is membership of a parent group one of consumer or campaigner? What makes a parent group radical or conservative? To what extent are these groups gendered? Feminist critiques have drawn attention to the ways in which women are over-represented in parent groups (Hanson & Pratt, 1995). Here parent groups provide possibilities for an engagement with social mobility within and across households and this is particularly important to mothers:

> Since women are traditionally concerned with home and family and community, they're the first to recognise threats to them and to act on those threats ... men are more integrated into the system that creates the threats, and that since women have been excluded from that system historically, they have less to lose them in fighting for it.
>   (Witte Garland, 1988, p. xii, cited in Ledwith, 2006: p. 50).

This does, however, raise questions about the place of fathers in the parents' movement. A number of dads that we spoke to felt marginalised by parent groups, because they tended to be dominated by mothers. Tong (2002: p. 209) argues that while many parent groups can empower their members with knowledge, skills and affirmation, many of them have a tendency to promote personal adjustment instead of social reform. Similar arguments have been made about some factions of other new social movements including self-advocacy of people with learning difficulties (Goodley, 2000), parent-school initiatives (Vincent, 2000) and carers groups (Abel, 1991).

In our study we came across a number of parent groups with different institutional and discursive foundations, blurring a host of group types identified by Hughes (2007) and People First of Washington (1984). Some seemed more geared towards personal reform. A mothers' coffee morning does not, at first glance, seem the most politicised of gatherings. However, to dismiss a personalised agenda ignores the potential of a group to act as a catalyst for the development of ideas and practices that promote well-being through accessing and creating new communities: a key aim of community participation (Nelson & Prilleltensky, 2004; Rappaport, 1977; Reason & Heron, 1995):

> I went to a support group meeting ... we had an evening meeting that someone set up and that was at the Sports Centre but only four of us turned up which was a shame, but it was the usual four and so we still got on and had a good chat. And we've become more like friends now, it's not just a case of going and getting things off your chest about autism, it's 'how are you, what have you been doing and ... you know you're forming friendships with people.
>
> (Cheryl, IV2)

This sharing of lives is clearly important in light of the governance experienced by many parents (discussed in Chapter 5). Parents are all too aware of the ironies of engaging with what might be understood as a new social movement:

> You shouldn't have to ... shouldn't have to be a powerful group of parents, you should have, like these are the rights for your child.
>
> (Angela, IV3)

Cheryl returned time and time again in her interviews to the significance of the parent support group. When the group folded she described this as 'losing a limb' (IV2). Many of the parents we spoke to were involved in setting up and preserving groups.

> We both like going, it's sociable because you're sat at home, and it's a bit like being sat at home on your rowing machine or your

treadmill on your own, and the difference between going to the gym and doing it. It's more motivating, and I've met other mums there who I get on really well, who've been through the similar mill, who have equally horrible stories. And we've got a lot of support from each other. And I just wish somebody had told us about that rather than this random chance finding it.

(Kay, IV1)

In light of the psycho-emotional experiences of parents encountered in the last chapter it is not surprising to hear of what Ledwith (2006) terms the emotional life of communities. Questions are raised about values, mutuality and empathy. Hustedde and King (2002: p. 340) suggest that in order to understand a community we must attempt to make sense of its 'soul', which is present 'when non-dominant cultures and people speak their value judgments (emotions) of compassion, forgiveness, and hope amidst despair'. Hope translates into the collective reworking of the wider disabling community. Elizabeth particularly valued a special session of the local cinema, organised by the local parents group:

I can take my daughter to the cinema without worrying about the noise she's making. There's so many other snuffly, screaming kids there it just doesn't make any difference.

(IV1)

Bouita spoke of the benefits of dropping in to a nursery run by parents of disabled children:

That's like a mingle for the kids. They mix and we talk … and they just play … We'd like to see more of that. You can take them there and get together with children and everything like that. They love that.

(IV1)

Parents feel included because of a shared acceptance of difference. Other parents spoke of the mutuality of relationships with other parents in similar circumstances:

Isn't it funny how our circle of friends has now shifted? It's people, I mean some of them, like I say they're fantastic, we've still got the same friends but a lot of our new friends are friends that we've met like Jackie and Adam with Isobel, in the same situation as us. And our friendship tends to be at a different level now. It's not going out and having drinks, it's just the phoning up and the support that we get off each other.

(Jemma, IV1)

Here friendship brings with it further layers of reciprocity and commonality and these layers do not simply reside in the parent group. Parents found allies from other parents of disabled children that they bumped into, time and time again, before hospital appointments, outside the school and at the shops. These transient communities allowed for opportunities to catch up as well as share knowledge about new initiatives and services. These alliances would extend to strangers. Jemma (IV1) recounted the tale of seeing a mother of a child with a similar impairment to her own:

I tried me damnedest to find her, to accidentally bump into her, just to speak to her 'cos her little one was wearing glasses. I never actually found her. I was gutted; I don't know what I would have said to her if I bumped into her.

She also agonised about acknowledging another parents' experiences whose child also had visible signs of cancer treatment; 'I thought, I hope she doesn't think I'm staring because her child had no hair. I was staring because I *knew*' (IV1, our emphasis). It is possible to view these encounters as similar to those of community activists. Lucy (IV2) is driven by a sense of isolation from other parents, particularly those with 'normal children'. For Eva (IV1), giving up paid work to care for her child placed her parental labour firmly at the centre of attempts to create a supportive home and neighbourhood. This became her job. Helen (IV2) conceptualises a key point of her parental role as developing not just friendships but also 'allies and comrades'. The 'parent group' is therefore not just a complex entity that resists attempts to categorise it but is also a shifting paradoxical phenomenon at the nexus of self, family, home and community. It can create alliances that are enabling or constraining, it can sustain, yet also constrain:

Yeah, because you're stuck in a room full of, and a lot of the mothers, I try and kind of look after myself still, but a lot of the mothers you can see they've just got so little energy, and they've just let themselves go, and they don't care about how they look ... they're just kind of all frumpy and can't be bothered with themselves, and you're sitting in a room full of other disabled kids and I just find it really depressing. It's like, why should I be like pushed off, it's like segregated, oh there, now you've got a disabled child so you have to go over here and hang around with all these other people with disabled children. And that's just not what I want … it is useful in a way, meeting other parents with disabled kids, 'cos you do find out more stuff. 'Cos obviously like different people have had to, that's how I found about having to fight the education authority.

(Elizabeth, IV1)

The various formations of parent groups provide opportunities for rethinking the rights of groups historically marginalised from civil society. Consequently, this promotes questions about the realities, artefacts and elements of citizenship. This is taken up further in Chapter 9.

Community exile? Of supermarkets, nurseries and schools

Clearly parent groups provide access to support environments that many parents find useful, but what about the wider community? For Oldenburg (1999) most people develop in three key areas of social and political life: the home, the office and the community hangout. Across and within these locations are a whole host of community settings. Disability studies analyses have illuminated dominant forms of disablism in the community – connected to social, material and cultural life – which are experienced by disabled families as exclusion from mainstream life, work, education, leisure and welfare (Riddell & Watson, 2003). Families find themselves on the outskirts of everyday contexts such as nurseries, schools, parent groups and workplaces. We will consider some of the ways in which they tackle this peripheral membership. Parents not only access aspects of the community, they are also implicated in its *construction*. Pretty et al. (2002: p. 106) urge us to consider the ways in which everyday community experiences with neighbours, shopkeepers, workmates and other 'ordinary' community members might provide possibilities for positive psychological outcomes. In this section we consider three areas of community life that threaten to expel disabled children and their parents, develop analytical takes on these areas and consider possibilities for resistance.

Schools and Nurseries: Homo sacer?

> How's school going to be? How's society going to react? Will he be picked on in mainstream school? Sometimes, I'm scared of the future. I'm scared of society, of how they'll treat him.
>
> (Lucy, IV1)

> They [other parents] want their kids to have good role models ... it is a concern a lot of parents have. They worry I suppose that they'll get ... the ones that are better will be dragged down.
>
> (Sue, IV1)

> He came back with somebody's, another pair of shoes on, his shoes were absolutely soaking wet, his clothes, different set of clothes on, now his clothes were in the bag not a mark on them and I then thought, hang on, Wednesday, they've been swimming, he's been in the pool with all his clothes on, they haven't kept a hold of him.
>
> (Angela, IV1)

Any discussion of education and disabled children will inevitably invoke debates associated with inclusive and special schooling. For Azzopardi (2005) the last ten years, particularly in the UK, has seen inclusion become a cliché: a well-worn, ubiquitous term that fails to address a myriad of exclusionary practices that exist behind the legislative push for the acceptance of disabled children in mainstream schools. Various practices such as the Index for Inclusion are now part and parcel of school assessment. The anticipatory duties of schools to provide an inclusive setting came into force in September 2005. More and more disabled children are entering mainstream schooling. But still, parents continue to speak about struggling to include their children in schools and nurseries:

> I changed her playgroup because the playgroup she was at, they were quite precious over her, even though it was mixed ability, they did take special needs kids, they were kind of shooing all the other kids away from her.
>
> (Elizabeth, IV1)

My Duncan is ... how do you put it? Wild. I used to go along to this nursery with him when he was little boy. It was held in my local library. There was a woman taking the register, a sort of committee and a list of rules as long as your arm. It was very cliquey. During coffee break, I was told by one of the other mothers that during coffee break 'we like the children to sit quietly at the table over there'. Then during singsong time, all the kids were expected to sit cross-legged on the floor. Totally not Duncan's place!

(Cheryl, IV2)

Lesley confided in the researcher that she would prefer to have her son Stuart receive home-based Portage support than have him attend a mainstream toddler group. She said that it would be painful for her if other parents commented on Stuart's slightly delayed development in ways that contrasted with his contemporaries.

Numerous parental stories raised questions about the inclusion of disabled children. Some disabled children were not invited to the birthday parties of their non-disabled peers from the nursery and school. We heard accounts of petitions to school objecting to the inclusion of a disabled child whose behaviour was considered to be 'too disruptive for the normal children'. Parents reported feeling excluded by close-knit groups of parents in the playground. Accounts show the difficulties disabled children face in joining in with their non-disabled peers because of the presence of an assigned adult teaching assistant. Why do some parents continue to talk of their children facing consistent forms of exclusion and rejection even in a culture that apparently (at least legislatively) has embraced some of the tenets of inclusion?

A powerful theoretical explanation is provided by Reeve (2007) who has recently extended her work on the psycho-emotional aspects of disablement by drawing on the work of Agamben, specifically his notion of *homo sacer*. Homo sacer, 'the sacred man', refers to a figure of Roman human law where the person is banned from the city or polis and is excluded from all civil rights. She/he is defined in law as an exile: so the law not only excludes but also denies. Reeve (2007: pp. 1–2) argues, quoting Agamben (1998: p. 8), that homo sacer is someone 'who may be killed and yet not sacrificed'. She continues:

'He who has been banned is not, in fact, simply set outside the law and made indifferent to it but rather *abandoned* by it, that is, exposed and threatened on the threshold in which life and law, outside and inside, become indistinguishable.' (Agamben, 1998: p. 28, italics in original) This zone of indistinction represents a state of exception in which homo sacer is bare life, zoē, stripped of political rights and located outside the polis (city); in other words homo sacer has biological life, but that life has no political significance.

Reeve suggests that such a concept resonates with the experiences of disabled people in the contemporary climate of anti-discrimination disability legislation. She points to an example of a wheelchair user being forced to choose the goods lift to access a shop. Here the shop owners conform to the requirements of the 1995 Disability Discrimination Act. However, they fail in terms of broader forms of inclusion in everyday life by subjecting the wheelchair user to the indignities of accessing the shop via the 'back door'. The wheelchair user is synonymous with the delivery of goods.

Similarly, in our research, parents of disabled children report examples of their children – who are 'included' in nurseries and school at least in person – being stripped of humanity by precious others, their status and impact on other children being questioned, prevented from connecting with other children as parents shoo them away. According to Reeve (2007: p. 4),

> Disabled people find themselves dependent on the goodwill of the service providers because, like homo sacer, they cannot rely on the law to fully protect them by ensuring that adjustments made to the environment restore independence *and* dignity and self-esteem to disabled people.

In terms of schooling as a key aspect of community involvement and social development, disabled children occupy the position of homo sacer:

- A place outside of the playground, classroom and friendship groups (the polis);
- A presence in the nursery or school but one exiled from the normative activities of children;
- A biological life (bare life) denied any political significance in the educational institution.

On a more productive note, we were informed by parents of attempts to challenge the peripheral status of their children. Indeed, educational professionals and parents were often grappling with forms of institutional accommodation. Kay (IV1) struggled to find the words to capture the significance of the support of nursery teachers who were prepared to administer medication if her child had a seizure:

> And a lot of people would be, if you did that at a mainstream school they would run a mile [as indeed Frank's nursery did as discussed in Chapter 4], but ... they were even prepared to do that and I was so lucky. That, that was it, about the nursery, the top and bottom of it.
>
> (Kay, IV1)

And Cheryl's experience of the 'cliquey nursery' reported above did not dissuade her from making subtle attempts to include her son:

> During singsong time, all the kids were expected to sit cross-legged on the floor. Totally not Duncan's place! You know that you and your child are not up to doing that sort of thing. But, if you choose to give up at the first hurdle – thinking he just won't fit in – then you've given up. So we persevered. And when he was ... well, 'being Duncan', I didn't get involved, I just let if fly over me and I'm thinking, 'no, I'm not letting that do us'. And so he went on. And they watched. And they watched.
>
> (Cheryl, IV2)

Sylvia's email reports with trepidation on finding a mainstream nursery for her daughter:

> I have checked it out with other people and they know of people whose kids go there and 'Aye, it's Ok', which of course makes me feel that my gut reaction is probably right. We visited last week and stayed for about 2 hours +. They seem very positive about Sarah and disability in general ... I know her disability takes up so much time at this point in her life, but if I never tried to go 'integrated' I would never forgive myself. I must give her that opportunity. I am becoming aware that she probably has some learning disabilities, but at the same time, that doesn't mean she's unintelligent or not interested in what's going on around her. It seems to be quite complex. So that's exciting! (I think).
> Love Sylvia x 'Great spirits will always encounter opposition from mediocre minds' – Albert Einstein

We followed up Sylvia's experiences with the nursery to see if her hunches were correct. Sylvia's daughter Sarah has difficulties with co-ordination and dexterity. When she eats, her plate tends to slide all over the table. To avoid this, Sylvia always uses a place mat. Instead of simply supplying Sarah with a place mat, the staff in the nursery provided all the children with one. The special was made general. Parents consistently find themselves negotiating with others the meanings attached to their children in order to challenge the prohibition of disabled children from educational institutions. This emotional, intellectual and political labour of parents continues in other community settings.

Supermarkets and shops: disabling geographies

Emma: Do you take Harry quite often into the shops?

Angela: Oh yeah, I, well, I think he's part of the family you've gotta get on with life and yes it is difficult for us at times but so what, we've just gotta get on with it and if he does things to other people and its just one of those things. Like a few weeks ago he was going off it going round Tescos and got a bottle of sauce and threw that in the middle of the fridges. Got something else threw that in the middle of the meat. Got a load of the old packages and like reached over from one of the workers trolleys put it in a woman's trolley. Then he'd been eating a French stick again, hollowed out the middle took a look at the cashier on the next aisle along, mustn't have liked the look of him and got it and stotted it off his head. And again I didn't explain I just said, 'Eeeh you don't want this do you' and just got it and put it back in the trolley and carried on putting my shopping away (laughing) so they probably think its not the child who's got the problem it's the mother (laughing). I did see him a few days later I think he was a cashier or something and there was one of the lads was helping pack the trolley who knew Harry and I says, 'Oh well you'll remember Harry from the other day' and he looked a bit sheepish. I says, 'Well Harry was the one that threw his French stick at you'. 'He goes oh, oh yeah' (laughs) and then I think he'd twigged as to the reason as why Harry, well not the reason but could understand it more why he'd had this French stick stotted off his nut (laughs). It always seems to be French sticks (laughs) it was hollow anyway couldn't have hurt.

(Angela, IV2)

Kitchin (1998) argues that the geographies of disabled people are so closely connected to those of non-disabled people that disabled people are either spatially excluded or have to 'pass' themselves off as suitable occupants of those spaces. Chapter 4 explored aspects of this through discussion of the social othering of disabled children; here we aim to explore this more broadly through a consideration of how families as a whole are subject to pressures to 'pass' in order to have a space within social spheres.

Karen speculated about what the neighbours might say about her carrying her child. 'They're probably saying, "Oh, she's carrying the bairn into the car", and not even thought twice about the fact that I'm always carrying the baby into the car you know. And I half expect for one of the days for somebody to say, "You've gotta let that bairn walk!"' (Karen and David, IV3). Jane (IV3) was very conscious of encouraging her son to act as normally as possible. This meant reminding him to lower the volume of his voice and discouraging him from 'doing the flapping hands and the pointed fingers'. Consequently, some disabled children may be encouraged, wherever possible, to minimise their differences in order to fit with geographical norms to ease their family's movement through public space. Other times call for an active, often subtle, re-engagement with and resettling of the environment. The making of environments and the social actors or objects within, play a crucial role in what Imrie (2000: p. 9) describes as 'the constitution and transformation of the subject: the various interpolations and practices through which individual subjectivities are constituted'. Similarly:

> The experience of environments depends on one's existential – phenomenological stance to it, the organisation of materiality, as well as one's sensual experience of it (and on being able to imagine sensual alternatives, more comfortable ways of organising materiality).
>
> (Freund, 2001: p. 689)

Parents and their disabled children highlight the struggles for belonging to place. This links into a point we made earlier, appropriated from Bell (1999), that belonging can be understood as an achievement, a performance that changes and morphs over a given period of time, in and out of different locations. For Allan (1999) and Runswick Cole (2007) when disabled families enter social contexts they expose their lives to public scrutiny. This then renders them vulnerable to assessment of others who will make judgments about how 'well-adjusted' or 'dysfunctional' they appear to be:

> We were in Tescos a while ago now. And my son had a paddy because there weren't any cookies. I strapped him in and I said 'Come on, if you're not going to walk nicely you can sit in the pushchair' so he was in the chair and he was kicking and fidgeting and testing all the

boundaries. And this man came up to him and went 'you stop that' and I went 'you get off my son' and I shouted at him in this shop and I was like 'get off him' and I nearly swore and everything, and it was like a complete stranger goes up to you and touches your son, telling him off like that – no, no, no. I don't go up to my friend's children and say 'don't do that'.

(Cheryl, IV2)

Because she used to cry the whole time, I used to get really bad reactions from the general public. I'd walk along with the pram and I've got this little bundle screaming like mad, she was always bright red, she's going, 'huh', 'ca' like couldn't breathe properly. And other people would like tut and shake their heads, and, 'ehh that poor bairn', and I still get ... all that, 'ah she's not well, oh, she's hungry', people offering us a lot of *disguised* advice.

(Elizabeth, IV1, our emphasis)

Both these accounts illuminate Imrie's (2000) notion of the constitution of the subject – or the management of public selves – in particular geographies of supermarkets, shops and town centres. These 'spatialities of disability' (Kitchin, 1998) mediate the ways in which disabled children and their families are allowed and expected to inhabit space in normative ways. Expectations of functioning are reflected in the social organisation of community spaces. Occupants directly or indirectly shape the ways in which families plot a course through these environments. Families experience this organisation of their space and time in the ways they are viewed by others such as tourist attraction, object of ridicule and socially disruptive (see also Clavering & McLaughlin, 2007a). Fortunately, the mediation of space provides possibilities for contestation. The subject is also open to transformation. Elizabeth found more sympathetic public reactions when her child's impairment was more visible:

Because before that [the tube feeding] she just looked like this tiny little baby who was screaming and her mother wasn't doing anything about it, but then when she had her tube on, people started behaving differently again. It was like people kind of whispering and looking.

(Elizabeth, IV1)

As discussed in Chapter 4, technology can become a signifier of disability, in some ways providing legitimation (as it does here), in other contexts a marker of difference. For Angela (IV3), even the 'outing' of her son's impairment was not enough in her attempts to smoothly navigate social spaces, on a visit to their local café. Harry had a specific chair he always used, on arrival they found a woman sitting there and Harry responded by kicking and screaming:

> This little old woman in her Sunday best and with a little hat on there, went to sit down with her hot chocolate and the cream on the top, and we were just about to sit down in the one next to it, but Harry must have thought no that's my seat, I'm going there. Anyway he went and he kicked the table, nearly spilled her thing, screamed and flung himself on the floor, so anybody normal could have seen that there wasn't something quite right with Harry. Anyway this woman goes, 'What on earth is going on there? What's up with him?' and I explained that he's severely autistic, he has severe learning difficulties, he can't help it. 'Oh', she says, 'well, can't you keep him under control?' And I'm afraid, on this, about the only occasion I snapped, and I thought it's like waving a red flag to a bull, so I said, 'can't you keep your big fat gob under control? Unless you know what you're talking about keep it shut', and then I called her a wizened old bag or something and stormed out with Harry.
>
> (Angela, IV3)

The accounts of parents hint at the work they do with others, sometimes strangers, in order to refashion what is understood to be normal in a social space. The way they challenge strangers resonates with the account of the feminist scholar Kittay (2006: pp. 104–7), herself a mother of a young disabled woman:

> We refused the pity of those that could not understand, and we refused the attempts of others to sanctify us, to call us 'remarkable' or 'saintly' ... to accept the view that what is normal is fixed and cannot be altered is itself problematic. If we can love and accept our children, if our norms are malleable, they why should we suppose that others cannot? ... The community we forge with our child can be enlarged and love need not be out of reach.

Following McRuer (2002), Guter and Killarky (2004), Sherry (2004a), Whitney (2006) and Overboe (2007), we could argue that parents of disabled children 'queer' (hetero) normative and disablist spaces precisely because they have to. Passing, as Hemmings (1999) argues in the context of lesbian and bisexual subjectivities, can undermine the normative powers of public spaces and interactions. Blurring into the backgrounds of community settings is impossible, as a lesbian mother said of her own family in Gabb (2005b), 'Trying to hide our family is like hiding an elephant'. To continue their work as activists and allies to their children, detailed in Chapter 5, parents explore social spaces that accommodated disability and diversity. Parents with kids whose behaviours might be seen as too challenging for normative community settings found acceptance in loud and chaotic places – such as the 'Land of the Golden M' identified by Ryan (2005a). Fast food restaurants can provide the perfect foil for a 'disruptive child' whose differences are subsumed by the noise and behaviour of a group of teenagers. A number of parents expressed their relief in finding aspects of the community that invited difference and diversity because 'people don't do odd, do they?' (Ryan, 2005b). Away from the chaotic, families also find places of calm and solitude:

> Whenever you take him it's all new and interesting. I mean we've got a friend who lives on a farm in Boston. I mean I can let him out of the trailer tent and I can sit and I can watch him and he'll go and feed ducks.
>
> (Sue IV1)

> I always tend to go in on a Monday morning after I have dropped her sister off at school so it's nice and quiet, she's normally got the shop to herself, she can have an explore. The girls are used to her, more so because she has to go, she has to sit on their knee, and of course she recognises the uniforms.
>
> (Jemma, IV1)

Freund (2001: p. 699) refers to these social spaces as 'enclaves' or safe spaces, in which people are not only physically safe, but exist in ways that affirm their bodily and psychological senses of self. However, they are also marginalised spaces. The geographical elements of the community are not simply about spatial location: they are at the core of what it means to belong and to be included.

Conclusions: Parents as community activists

> Because love is an act of courage, not of fear, love is commitment to others.
>
> (Freire, 1998: p. 68)

Following on from the previous chapter's analysis of the distributed parent, this chapter has demonstrated the ways in which parents' engagements with others have the potential to constitute new forms of community development. Their achievements are remarkable in light of the work they face in challenging subtle forms of exclusion and destabilising disabling geographies. Drawing on Ledwith (2006) it is possible to view parents' community engagement in terms of five specific elements of community activism. First, some of the parent groups situate their aims and philosophies within an analysis of ideology and structural power. Parents peel away the discursive layers of disablism. Second, parents appear to promote forms of critical education that question existing realities. They (re)negotiate roles, meanings and values with family, friends and strangers. Third, they challenge a culture of silence that exists around the exclusion of their disabled children through active participation in mainstream contexts and interactions with other parents. Fourth, this allows possibilities for developing community groups that are grounded in values of equality and the practice of social justice. Trust, reciprocity, respect, dignity and empathy are in evidence in the accounts of parents when they talk of the benefits of being with other disabled families. Fifth, community participation appears to have a number of outcomes (learning, justice, action) that address various organisational partnerships through the subtle reshaping of disablist geographies. In this way, then, parents attempt to articulate the aims of a caring, safe, creative, healthy and citizens' based community. An interesting point of departure for future analyses of community and disabled families would be to explore the ways in which parents and significant others connect with cultural, political, social and economic issues through the sharing of everyday life experiences. Here the work of Freire (1972, 1998) would provide an analytical framework for considering processes such as *conscientisation* (where understanding is located in experience and forms the basis of collective action), *dialogue* (through the sharing and collection of stories); *denunciation* (to develop better strategies for naming and analysing new understandings of oppressions) and *annunciation* (to find new forms of action to unite us in mutual struggle). What starts with their children and families ends up with a wider engagement with the community at large.

7
Professional, Institutional and Ethical Practices

Janice McLaughlin and Dan Goodley

Introduction

In Chapter 1 we highlighted the criticisms that have been made by disability studies and others, of the dominance of professional authority over the lives of disabled people. Changes in both society and government regulation, over several decades, have sought to undermine such authority and replace it with different models of how welfare organisations should operate and work with service users. In this chapter we explore professional responses to such changes. A number of key areas are looked at in the chapter: societal mistrust of professional authority, the introduction of practices associated with 'new public management' (NPM), the implementation of standardisation via evidence-based practices and, finally, changes derived from the introduction of consumer choice into welfare rhetoric. Overall, what we seek to do is to understand how professionals discursively frame their role and the changes they see, and how they are part of the institutional governance of disabled families. In places, we contrast this to parents' views. In addition, we consider what kind of professional ethics may be a suitable way to work with parents in a context of seeking to enable parents and children to be partners in decision making, which are yet to be fully incorporated into the policy directives currently emerging from government. Our argument is that there are ways professionals can work with parents that can create a space for partnership and such practices need to be incorporated into both articulations of professional identity and also acknowledged within the institutional contexts of professional activity.

Changing contexts of professional authority

For much of the twentieth century, professional bodies and individuals, particularly in areas such as medicine and law, were able to exercise considerable autonomy over their practice based on the assumption (which they promoted) that they held the expertise within which to judge what was best. Self-regulation via bodies such as the British Medical Association (BMA) symbolise the right and power some professional organisations have been able to create over their practice and field of activity. However, models of self-regulation and professional autonomy are now under question, as both citizens and government question the right of professional bodies to both self-police and make decisions about those they work with, without external scrutiny and audit. This questioning, particularly by government, has introduced new modes of management over professionals, which radically change how they work and how their relationships with service users are scrutinised. Below we highlight just some of those changes.

Public scepticism

The societal shift, supported by various scandals that have seen professionals and public sector organisations fail in their duty of care, is a greater scepticism about whether professionals and their organisations have the interests of service users at the centre of their practice. In light of such scepticism self-regulation has lost its social legitimacy (Groenewegen, 2006). Self-regulating bodies, such as the BMA, have been criticised for being more interested in the protection of professionals rather than their regulation. In the aftermath of the problems in Alder Hey, when tissues and organs were collected from deceased babies without the consent of their parents, we have seen patient groups express significant opposition to professional power and self-regulation. The failure to look after and provide for children has been a particular area of significance, symbolised by the Climbié inquiry in 2003 (Laming, 2003). At the same time, from as far back as the 1960s, different publics (we are drawing here from critical public engagement literature, which uses the phrase 'publics' to emphasise the multiplicity of voices and positions within the category of the 'public' (Wakeford, 2002)), often through the influence of advocacy and patient groups, have sought to have a greater say in the services they use and are more willing to question the presumed authority of others to make decisions on their behalf (Crompton, 1990; Dingwell & Lewis, 1983). As Foster and Wilding note:

> In the 1970s and 1980s ... a critique of the position, roles and functions of welfare professions developed. The historically taken-for-granted assumptions about the professions fitted less easily with a more plural, less deferential, more educated and more critical society.
>
> (2000: p. 144)

The influence of disability groups, in the UK and other countries, in creating a more critical and questioning context for professional practice, cannot be underestimated (Barnes, 1992; Dreidger, 1989; Morris, 1993b).

New public management (NPM)

During the same period, multiple governments have sought to restructure the institutional power and position of professionals, in particular within the public sector of health and social care. The changes represent different ways in which professionals work with each other, with managers and with service users (James, 2005). A key aspect of change has been the introduction of new patterns of management, often put under the rubric of NPM, which seek to introduce a culture of audit, contract and management surveillance (Ackroyd et al., 2007; Dean, 1999; Germov, 2005; McLaughlin et al., 2002). It is worth noting that the category of NPM can disguise important variations in newer managerial perspectives and practices; it also does not always make clear the continuity of well established practices that date back to the formation of the modern welfare state during the post World War two consensus. However, for the purpose of this chapter we will use NPM to signify changes in management, which place greater emphasis on audit and contractual processes as a way to manage the relationships between welfare organisations, between professionals and between organisations and service users. Webb (1999) suggests that these changes in approach affect the underpinning culture of welfare and professional practice. Welfare services are now

> increasingly managed by cost-limited, output-driven, 'enabling' organisations in a network of contractual service relationships ... The principle of equity is being eroded in favour of selectivity in provision

and the ethos of professional self-regulation in a high trust, state-funded framework has been replaced by low-trust centralised financial control and quasi-market regulation as part of an overall transition from a 'welfare' to a 'workfare' state.

(p. 753)

As part of these shifts we have seen the introduction of internal markets into the NHS, separation of commissioning and provision of services, budgetary devolution from local authorities to individual schools, individual GPs, and Hospital Trusts and Primary Care Trusts (Ferlie et al., 1996).

Although these changes began under the Conservative government, the core ethos has been left in place under New Labour (Jordan, 2001; Webb, 1999). In particular, the current government is continuing to push the right of individual organisations to control their own budgets and the benefits of separating provision from commissioning (DOH, 1997). Indeed this process has increased within education and healthcare through the inclusion of private sector organisations in the building and running of schools and hospitals via Private Finance Initiative (PFI) schemes (Hebson et al., 2003; Petratos, 2005).

Evidence-based practice

At the same time Labour has also introduced various policies into the NHS that seek to modernise treatment and management. Much of the ethos behind this is encapsulated in *The NHS Plan* (DOH, 2000) and *The New NHS: Modern, Dependable* (DOH, 1997). Central to the modernisation agenda is the notion of evidence-based practice, which has become a dominant rhetoric and practice within health and social care (Fitzgerald et al., 2003; Timmermans & Berg, 2003). Evidence-based practice seeks to embed all decision making in gold standard evidence (usually equated with randomised control trials), in order to achieve greater standardisation of care, with professionals being led by evidence rather than by individual whim or experience. In both health and social care, organisations have been set up to standardise practice and treatment: National Institute of Clinical Excellence (NICE) in the case of the NHS and Social Care Institute for Excellence (SCIE) in social care (Long et al., 2006; Shaw et al., 2006). An additional element of the standardisation strategy is the creation of National Service Frameworks for areas such as chronic illness and health inequality. The frameworks lay out guidelines, outcome measures and targets to be met by services across England and Wales.

The welfare consumer

At the same time service users have become consumers of health and social care, in theory, with the right to pick and choose the services they will use (Harris, 1999; Newman & Vidler, 2006). Along with the language of consumerism has come the language of partnership, where government policies in areas such as the Patients' Charter, the NHS Plan and the National Standard Frameworks all talk of the need to involve service users in decisions about their support (DOH, 1991, 1997). Consumerism is supposed to replace the passive patient of traditional professional authority with an active agent with specific rights to have options provided to them and access to notes and documentation about them. Patient and user groups are now highly visible and back up individual consumer choice, with organised scrutiny of both welfare organisations and professionals (Barnes, 1999). For example, the Department of Health now funds an organisation called INVOLVE (http://www.invo.org.uk/), which promotes public participation in NHS, public health and social research. The new organisational structures set up by the current government, such as Children's Trusts and NHS Foundation Trusts are required to have representatives of the communities they serve on their executive boards and to engage in regular public consultations. Consumerism can be seen as one response to disability movement calls for disabled people to have a say over the kinds of support and treatment they receive. In particular, Direct Payments and Disability Living Allowance (DLA), although they can be criticised for problems in how they are operationalised, as we shall see later in this chapter, seek to provide disabled people with greater independence, choice and say over the services they use (Pearson, 2000; Spandler, 2004).

Policy changes in the area of disabled families all include new patterns of professional regulation, new methods of standardising practice via evidence-based practice, and echo the service user as consumer rhetoric. For example, *Children's Trusts*, the *Children Act* (2004), the *Health and Social Care Act* (2001) and the *Health Act* (1999) all use NPM mechanisms for implementing audit and contractual arrangements; the *National Service Framework for Children, Young People and Maternity Services* is geared towards evidence-based practice as a tool to standardising practice, while *Every Child Matters* (Department for Education and Skills, 2003, 2004a, b) addresses the consumer agenda by advocating a partnership model with parents. Each of these areas, in different and, at times conflicting ways, potentially undermines traditional models of authority for professionals. This is either by producing greater transparency and accountability in their practice or by taking away scope for variability in their practice or by insisting greater consideration of the views of parents (and occasionally children) in the judgments they make.

Therefore, the picture for professionals working in children services is of multilayered changes, which require new ways of working with service users; new ways of cataloguing and representing their work through the demands of NPM and evidence-based practice; and new ways of working with each other as the children-led agenda compels them to bridge the traditional boundaries of health and social care. How do professionals make sense of this? Do they consider change to be positive or negative, threatening or enabling? Using our focus group data, we will now explore this at two levels. First, the descriptive: how professionals describe change and whether they consider it to be good or bad. Second, what these descriptions tell us about how professionals use rhetorical devices in the construction of identity. By first looking at NPM and evidence-based practice, before moving on to public scepticism and welfare consumerism, we will look at how professionals (and parents) responded to and conceptualised these changes. It is worth noting that in the discussion below we focus on areas of consensus that emerged in the focus groups; in other writings we highlight differences in professional perspectives that emerged in the group discussions (Clavering & McLaughlin, 2007b).

The threat of instrumentality

The professionals we spoke to were keen to critique practices associated with NPM and evidence-based practice as barriers to effective care. The professionals often talked about the encroachment of practices linked to both, which were imposed on them by management. This was visibly displayed when community paediatric nurses turned up to a focus group wearing nurse uniforms. In a change to Trust policy, from that morning community staff were required to wear a uniform. Later we gathered, the policy was aimed at giving a 'standard look' for all Trust staff across different contexts. This clearly angered both the nurses and others they worked with. The professionals were strongly against the policy, they felt that families would not like the change and that it threatened the relationship they had with them, which incorporated some level of familiarity and informality. It challenged their role and identity and placed them more strictly within a formal hierarchy, in comparison to others who were not in uniform.

The professionals argued that NPM and evidence-based practice restricted their relationship with parents. One prominent example raised was the DLA, which necessitated the production of minute levels of detail about the 'burden' of caring for a disabled child in order to qualify for support:

> We go into detail about how dreadful their life is and their quality of life and how depressing it is, and how impossible it is to cope and nobody actually really wants to think about that, they just sort of get on and live it. You don't want to go into details of 'how many minutes does it take to do', 'how many times a day do you have to'.
>
> (Focus Group, 1A)

NPM requirements for accurate and medically validated measurement of time and activity clash with professional values of empathy and support for parents. It emphasises their roles as cataloguers of impairment and the limitations children face. It associates their practice with pathological understandings of disability. Professionals wanted the space to engage with parents at an individual level, which could capture broader aspects of their lives, which were not just about what they and their children could not do. They argued that this kind of knowledge and relationship was unsuitable, or at least invisible, to the world of questionnaires and management language. The intricacies of supportive relations and activities were not always easily translated into performance indicators as demanded by NPM:

> I think though when you're giving support to families you can never definitively say that we caused this to happen ... you might say, 'well this boy went to a sibling group and then his behaviour changed'. I can't scientifically prove that that was the consequence but the two things are together ... I work with Early Years Support Services, I do a lot of work with them and this is one area we're really struggling with at the moment, the idea of evaluating .... How do you estimate what the impact of what you've actually done is? Particularly in a climate when government wants our statistics.
>
> (Focus Group, 3A)

Professionals felt it important to indicate how their role was distant from management imperatives and practice, which they argued undermined their ability to do their job:

> I have a frustration with other providers and commissioners who don't always seem to recognise need by identifying from the ground

level, and dismiss that and then we have to cope with the parents' anxiety about not having the services they need.

(Focus Group, 1B)

When asked what the key function of their role was, the common response was to focus on care and relationships with parents:

the difference that you feel you can make when you're working with parents, you can offer support and you do feel that you're able sometimes to make their lives a little bit easier.

(Focus Group, 1B)

The argument of the professionals was that the way they engaged with parents was difficult to represent within the performance criteria of NPM and difficult to actually carry out within the standardised approach of evidence-based practice. However, it is those aspects which sit outside NPM and evidence-based practice, which lay at the centre of how they defined their professional practice. They talked of wanting to work with families holistically, rather than simply focus on the provision of equipment and responding to particular medical needs. Anything that got in the way of the direct caring relationship they had with parents was articulated as a threat. Their arguments make a case for the maintenance of established professional values of care and response, which they felt was neglected in instrumental approaches to management and audit.

Metaphors of being on the front line, working at ground level, were continuously used by professionals, both as a reasonable reflection of where they work, and also as a reminder that they discursively align themselves with parents against a wider institutional system that they view as flawed by NPM and evidence-based practice. The arguments of the focus group professionals echo much in the academic critique of NPM, in particular the articulation of a separation between care-led professional practice and audit-led management initiatives. Much of the research exploring the implications of NPM and evidence-based practice presents a world of competing and conflicting cultures; as drives for financial efficiency and instrumental rationality threaten professional values of trust, human response and care (Allen, 2000; Germov, 2005; Gregory & Holloway, 2005; Le Grand, 2003; McLaughlin, 2004; Newman & Nutley, 2003). NPM and evidence-based practice undermine values of care and responsiveness and replaces them with 'budgets and performance measurement' (Webb, 1999: p. 754). In the process, the role of the professional is marginalised and replaced by 'flexible, routinized, and standardized models of work organisation' born from 'NPM-compatible labour processes' (Baines, 2004: p. 268). Where ever NPM or evidence-based practice is found, the same critique emerges of the suppression of professional values in favour of the 'enhanced rationalisation' (Germov, 2005: p. 737) of audit, contracts and performance management:

> The colonization of professional activity by managerial discourse has produced a context where professional activity is defined by a series of managerial imperatives and trust; formerly, this was the product of intimate social activity, but is now shaped through techniques based on distrust, such as audits and quality monitoring.
>
> (Gilbert, 2005: p. 461)

Standardisation, as envisioned in evidence-based practice, is at odds with professional values of responsiveness, which sit at the core of professional modes of practice (Timmermans & Berg, 2003):

> The standardization of social services delivery abstracts the lived-in realities of individuals and communities, replacing multi-service, holistic approaches with narrowly calibrated ones to diverse problems and issues. In public sector and large non-profit agencies, paper- and computer-based standardized forms, record keeping and assessments have replaced the informal interactions and assessments of the past.
>
> (Baines, 2004: p. 277)

If we look at data from our work with parents, we find similar criticisms of such practices in their lives. Audit driven management cultures produce paperwork, which parents, as well as social workers, must manage:

> Sarah: ... red tape bureaucracy, form-filling, sometimes does take precedence over *life*, or just living.
>
> (Sarah and Nick, IV3, our emphasis)

Form-filling is hardly new to social services, the bureaucracy of welfare and its ability to instrumentalise need, care and individuals is well established (Fraser, 1989). However, within NPM practices there is a level of micro collection of data meant to represent life, which is distinctive and, in part, made possible by the new possibilities of collection and audit within management information systems (McLaughlin & Webster, 1998).

For example the DLA, as highlighted above, asks parents, across 52 pages, to go into extensive detail about their child, solely focused on the medical condition and what limitations the child faces. To give a sense of what the parents face, the areas they are asked to respond to are listed here: it begins by asking them to categorise their child according to particular medical categories of disability, before going on to ask them to detail:

- How far the child is able to walk outside
- How often they find it difficult to walk outside
- Who needs to be with them when they attempt to walk outside
- Who generally 'keeps an eye' on the child
- How delayed their development is
- Difficulties they have waking up and getting out of bed
- Difficulties they have washing and cleaning
- Difficulties they have dressing
- What help they need to go to the toilet
- What difficulties they have communicating with others
- What difficulties they have eating and drinking
- What medication the child takes and how much help is needed to administer it
- What therapies the child has
- What medical equipment the child needs
- What blackouts, fits or 'something like this' the child experiences
- What the child's mental health status is
- What difficulties there are with the child's movement and mobility
- What difficulties the child has when in bed
- What help the child needs when they go out in the day or night time
- What time the child spends in hospital or care home.

In each category parents are asked to stipulate how many days of the week the child finds each activity difficult and how many minutes each activity takes. It is no surprise that parents (and many professionals) found the DLA form a complex task, but also one that they found literally exhausting in the intimate scrutiny it demanded of their child's difficulties:

> His DLA's up for renewal again, so I usually start about six months beforehand, and start writing a diary, and I'll get in touch with Disability North and get one of their advisors, she'll go through filling

the forms out for us, because if you put one word that's wrong it'll have consequences.

(Angela, IV3)

NPM pursues the detailed collection of information about people in order to set detailed criteria against which to judge what support people have an entitlement to receive. Such criteria are meant to replace professional individual judgment and therefore allow for greater standardisation of provision across services. However, in the push towards rationalising and standardising services, irrationality creeps in via the criteria's inability to respond to the possibility that human need does not easily fit into such fixed categories and criteria. Various examples were provided of management criteria replacing human judgment on the part of service provision. Luke, Maria's child, appeared caught in a Catch 22 where the same professionals who said he would benefit from occupational health, were also saying that he could not receive it because his disability was not included in those conditions that allowed for a referral. Maria's response was to look into paying for private provision of the therapy recommended and denied by social services. This points to another aim of such criteria apart from standardisation: the creation of criteria that aids the rationing of care and the increased role of service users in the provision of support.

If we follow Jane through a discussion that took place in her first interview, regarding her various attempts to get her son accepted into a mainstream educational environment, at each point we see instrumentalist, budget driven decisions, marginalising both her and her son. The first stage in getting provision put in place within a school or nursery is the educational statement produced by an educational psychologist, which will outline what is needed to enable the child to be supported in a mainstream context. Like other parents, Jane felt that the assessment process produced a representation of Jack she could barely recognise, and was driven by records of other assessments, rather than an engagement with him:

Because they're office-based [education authority] and they don't know the individuals, but they're treating you very much like a number, a name and number, and they don't really think of what you're going through, and that you are emotional. You know, as well as trying to get the best out of it for him, you're also probably, you're emotions are up and down all the time, even throughout the day because you just, you don't know what's happening next.

(IV1)

As the process progressed she attempted to participate, trying to find out when case discussion meetings would be happening: 'on two occasions I phoned up and said, "I believe you've just been discussing my son this morning, can you tell us what's happening". And the first thing both times they said was, "How did you know the meeting was today?"' While partnerships with parents may be on the agenda, decision-making continues to be done at a distance from families, via both the criteria used to make decisions and the lack of space provided for families to participate in the shaping of such criteria and decisions.

Once the statement was agreed there was little scope for Jane to ensure that what was provided was appropriate for Jack, because a distance continued to exist between a broad understanding of what kinds of support he required and recognition of him as a child with rights. It was agreed that a taxi would pick him up for school, but Jane wanted to meet the taxi driver before Jack was picked up:

> I'd asked if he could meet the driver, and she goes, 'Oh, why?' And I said, 'Well, because he's five years old and I'm not going to let him go off on his first day with anybody'. That could be absolutely anybody turning up at the door and saying, 'I'm the driver who's taking Jack to school', I know it's a bit far-fetched, but, he needs to know because he's not going to go off with a complete stranger. But they don't seem to think of practicalities, you know like treating them like they're human, they just seem to just sort of pack them off.
>
> (IV1)

Jack was accepted into a mainstream school, but Jane continued to find a context where Jack was far from welcome and included. The resource-driven approach to services, and the greater emphasis on budget control within schools, can position the disabled child as costly and inconvenient to target setting and the performance criteria of academic excellence. The devolution of budget decisions to schools, and the increased power of head teachers to make decisions about enrolment leave local educational authorities with little power to enforce inclusion within schools unwilling to provide the space, resources and culture:

> It was like Jack was this complete hassle; he was a drain on their resource. We got into more and more meetings, the head teacher started saying, 'Oh, the money that this has cost me, and it's a massive drain on resources'. And I got sick to death of hearing about the school budget. So straight away you're feeling really awful that

you're taking up the budget, it's made to feel like a huge pot of money, for somebody to look after your child ... You feel like you're stuck in the middle because the local education authority have got this manual of what ideally should happen and then the school is just off on their own agenda doing whatever they want.

(IV1)

Across the views of professionals and parents, we get a shared concern with the instrumentality of management and institutional practices associated with NPM and evidence-based practice. This shared agenda presents professionals and parents on the same side, wishing to retain a model of professional practice associated with empathy and recognition rather than criteria and scrutiny. However, there are various reasons for suggesting caution about this representation of where alliances and shared values lie. This caution can be addressed by returning to the two other areas of change affecting professional authority: public scepticism and welfare consumerism.

Public scepticism and welfare consumerism

The argument that NPM and evidence-based practice means that professional values of care and trust are being replaced by values of instrumentality and standardisation needs to be complicated in a number of ways. First, while change is directed towards greater financial accountability, the changes also reflect the greater public scepticism about whether professionals do act in caring ways, and are best left to their own devices to monitor themselves. There is a public drive to see greater accountability placed on professionals, because the values of trust and professional care are not enough to ensure an equitable and appropriate service. Financial audit may not be the only way to increase surveillance of professional activity, but the concept that professionals could be left to their own regulation carries little public legitimacy.

Professional critiques of NPM robbing them of their holistic and caring values need to sit alongside accounts of service users, which document the abuses of power they have experienced when unable to question the services they receive. The professional articulations of a model of professional care, weakened by NPM, excludes the other elements of professional practice, which service users have become increasingly unwilling to accept; namely the presumed authority professionals assume they have to know what is the right thing for those they are supporting. As Pinder et al. (2005) argue we do not live in an era where publics are willing to hand over all say to paternalistic professionals who know best. Instead we live 'in an era troubled by revelations of professional misconduct' (2005: p. 762). Professionals may seek to and believe they are working within ethical values and personal commitments to their work (Freidson, 2001; Hoggett et al., 2006). However, this does not mean that, from the users' perspective, this is what they receive.

From the experiences of the families in the study it is clear that there are interactions with professionals that owe much more to notions of professional authority and paternalism than either managerial regulation or responsive care (Chevannes, 2002; Davis et al., 1997; Rummery & Glendinning, 1999). What they also provide testimony to is the current limits to consumerism as a reasonable reflection of the rights service users can properly exercise within the welfare arena. Parents often talked of the lack of negotiation or transparency, which surrounded the support that professionals put in place. Instead they often felt that their perspectives and knowledge were ignored or unacknowledged in decision making. In such contexts, instead of partnership rhetoric what was seen was suspicion and mistrust between parents and professionals. This lack of trust was a product of both individual behaviour on the part of the professional and wider institutional processes, which left the parents distanced from decisions being made about them and their children. Parents responded to professionals as both organisational actors with constraints on what they could do, but also as individuals who they expected to do what they could and maintain a level of human response and honesty in their interactions.

The parents provided varied examples of the assertion of professional authority at the cost of them playing a role in deciding the services they would receive:

I feel it is too much hassle when I ask for help, they don't listen, and nothing happens ... they offered to help by taking my son to school ... however this just did not work for me ... He didn't want to be seen to be different from the other children, and I was worried about potentially losing contact with the school. This contact is really important to know how my child is doing, and what is going on in school, and it is a good time to be with my son, a chance to bond with him and talk to him outside the home. So, because this was not suitable to our family, they would not give me the sort of support I wanted, and no alternative was offered. They did not take into account my needs.

(Sameera, IV1, via an interpreter)

For Sameera it was very clear that she was not being positioned as a consumer, instead, as a non-English speaking immigrant she was being positioned as someone who should be happy about whatever was offered: 'In business the customer is always right but in hospital, the professionals are always right.' (Sameera IV1, via an interpreter)

Instead of a model of consumer power we see the randomness of what individual professionals will do to support families, across both health and social care, and the continued potential for professionals to have power over those they are 'supporting':

> I thought the special needs health visitor wasn't doing her job, that there were a lot of parents out there that needed more help ... And they were more or less playing god, and they shouldn't be doing this, they should be helping everybody .... I got taken into hospital and they told me that I was anaemic and I was down on the bottom, I was worn out. Now she [the special needs health visitor] knew all this ... She never picked the phone up and asked how was Luke? How was I coping? Because I'd been poorly, nothing, not one message.
>
> (Maria, IV3)

Professionals are still in a position to exert power, which is far away from any notion either of consumer choice or of genuine partnership. Corinne and Luis had been waiting to get offered new housing from their local housing authority. Eventually a council house was offered, which they did not believe was appropriate to their needs. From the perspective of their housing authority, as refugees and the parents of a disabled child, the rights of the consumer were not rights they should be able to exercise:

> Corinne: The [housing] officer said, 'but anyway you cannot choose, you have no choice'. I replied, 'What I was told is that once you get the documents, the permission to stay in this country we could choose the accommodation we are going to go to, why we cannot choose now?' ... they say, 'but the thing is that you don't have the choice because you need to leave this accommodation very quickly'. I said, to her, 'but that's not my fault, because you wait for about one year looking for another accommodation for me.' From her mouth was only saying, 'you have no choice, you have no choice, you must do it'.
>
> (Corinne and Luis, IV2, via an interpreter)

There were many reasons why the house offered was not acceptable, not least because Corinne and Luis had begun to find a home and a sense of community where they were now living and did not wish to move out of that community into an unknown area away from the friends they had made, the GP surgery they used, and the supermarkets they could afford. While the professional did not believe consumer rights were applicable to Corinne and Luis, they did not agree, refusing to accept they had no choice and refusing to accept the substandard housing the social worker attempted to impose. Through the support of an occupational therapist, the parents were eventually able to arrange suitable accommodation within which they have become comfortable, feeling for the first time that they now have a home.

The ability of professionals to restrict the scope of consumer rights on offer for parents such as Sameera or Corinne and Luis points to the broader debate about the applicability of consumer rhetoric to the context of welfare and the danger that some, rather than others, will be given the space and have the resources required to exercise consumer choice (Barnes & Mercer, 2005; Boyte, 2005; Kremer, 2006; Priestley, 2000).

Building partnership via performance management

The continued operation of professional models of authority over parents refutes the notion that the problem with NPM and evidence-based practice is that it replaces values of care and responsiveness with values of managerialism and standardisation. However, in part, due to the influence of greater public scepticism regarding professional authority, some professionals are beginning to reflect critically on the continued presence of such authority within their relations with service users. Professional organisations and the education and training of new professionals are also seeking to move away from notions of power over in favour of partnership. However, an examination of these developments is outside the scope of this chapter. What we would like to consider are some interesting ideas from professionals in our focus groups on how to encourage models of partnership with disabled families and the role they gave NPM and evidence-based practice in that goal.

Professionals in the focus groups acknowledged that some of their practices (and colleagues) continued to exert authority over parents in ways that had been unaffected by changes brought about by NPM, evidence-based practice or consumerism. In a move away from such approaches, at least rhetorically, the professionals spoke of wishing to develop new models of relationship with parents less tied by traditional understandings of the role of the professional. They wanted users to be active participants, rather than passive receivers, of care and support. While, still intent on presenting their role as a caring one, this was not without a reflexive acknowledgement of the need to include service users in the provision they receive. In particular, they argued that they did wish to move beyond the paternalism of 'we know best' and instead embrace a model of uncertainty, which recognised the contingency of what they knew and what they could do. Trust is something professionals should earn with parents, rather than assume that parents will implicitly have for them due to their role and status. At first glance we would think that this kind of cultural change away from professional power to partnership is incompatible with NPM and evidence-based practice values of monitoring and surveillance. However, things are not so straightforward.

The biggest barrier professionals identified in bringing to reality the new ideas about partnership between services and parents was managerial apathy and institutional intransigence. Without a cultural change in how both managers and professionals work, proper change would be difficult to sustain. Changes in cultural values and perspectives require an environment where they are allowed to thrive. Without such contexts, the wish to work differently could be broken down. What is significant is that in the context of the vulnerability of cultural change, professionals sought managerial and structural support for the changes they wanted to introduce. Without drawing on these supports, cultural change could not work its way up the organisational hierarchy; in relation to increasing partnership working with parents, one respondent noted: 'I think it was *organic*, but it's only the change in *structure* that has allowed things to happen' (Focus Group 3B, our emphasis).

The tools associated with NPM re-entered the picture as useful elements of securing change. Focus group participants argued that partnerships with parents will be aided by requiring it within the performance indicators of NPM and the requirement to produce evidence of impact:

> but actually building in systems in the management structures that have parent representation and not just tokenistic parent representation, it's in the legislation that you have to actively involve and demonstrate in part of the performance measures for the organisation to how they are going to be rated, how they are involving public and patients in their service development is now going to be part of the rating, so it is starting to be part of the targets.
>
> (Focus Group, 3B)

The legal imperatives and political agenda, which the current government are putting behind parent involvement are important measures to
enforce change. They are setting targets and priorities managers cannot
ignore. For example the National Services Framework for children will
prescribe how organisations should take the Every Child Matters agenda
seriously:

> you are building those things into your service and investing in chil-
> dren awards; we used to have investing in people awards, now we've
> got investing in children awards, there are lots of incentives to serv-
> ices to really make it be working out.
>
> (Focus Group, 3B)

While they recognised there would be a danger in relying on performance indicators, in particular that change would not be real, instead just
a tick box on a form, they argued, 'Parents are not going to put up with
being treated in a tokenistic way ... they've wanted this so long they
will not put up with it' (Focus Group, 3B).

The professionals' support of NPM and evidence-based practice-type
strategies as a force of generating change indicates that to see these policy directives as completely in opposition to professional interests, as
writers discussed earlier such as Webb (1999) and Gilbert (2005) claim,
is inappropriate. Professionals themselves are involved in the implementation and development of these practices (Charles-Jones et al.,
2003; Farrell & Morris, 2003; Germov, 2005). In our focus groups, cultural discourses around care and empathy, and managerial discourses
around performance management targets and evidence, were not constructed as opposing values or demands in all instances. The cultural
shifts around parent partnership and inclusion were instead presented
as made possible through these managerial directives that could be used
to force through those cultural changes:

> There is so much incentive for people to actually get it right, I
> mean, if you think about the joint area review process, you're a
> parent with a child with a disability, I'm a manager, I know that
> the inspectors are going to come and talk to you about your expe-
> rience ... That is a huge incentive for me to please you rather than
> please this school and that organisation and that body, because
> they are going to be asked, so there's a huge investment in getting
> it right for you.
>
> (Focus Group, 3B)

How can we understand the adoption of NPM and evidence-based practice as drivers of positive change by professionals usually associated with arguing that they are sources of instrumentality? We would suggest that whether professionals situate these kinds of practices as either a source for good or bad is related to what kinds of rhetorical claim they wish to make about their professional identity and role. We cannot look at how professionals discuss change as empirical observations of a new reality (Artaraz, 2006; Freidson, 1994; Hanlon, 1998). This is because they are also interpretative responses, which enable change to be incorporated into professional identity and, where necessary, new boundaries to be drawn (McLaughlin & Webster, 1998; Reed, 1996). So at some points NPM and evidence-based practice are articulated as the antithesis to a set of professional practices viewed as important to defend. While at other points they are articulated as positive forces for change, which can direct others to adopt the same values and practices seen as important to defend. By proposing they can be conceptualised as rhetorical resources, we can reposition them as tools in the construction of professional identity and meaning within institutional relations. Both the challenge some professionals mount against NPM and evidence-based practice, and the equal use made of them as things that can be positive, are opportunities to articulate professional values and norms.

Reflexive professional ethics

At the level of both practice and rhetoric, we saw in the focus groups, acknowledgement of the limitations to support and care that parents receive. From the perspective of the professionals the culprit in this is often institutional contexts and limitations, alongside the inability of some individual professionals to respond to the new social worlds emerging. However, is this enough to explain the varied experiences of parents in the responses they receive from professionals? Is the refusal to accept a child into a mainstream school or the damning assessment of an educational psychologist a product of policy, rules or individual professional actions? What scope is there for professionals to act differently? Is there an element of using budgets as an excuse not to engage with inclusion as a valued part of school culture and purpose? As organisational actors, professionals are both constrained by the policies that surround them, while also provided with a creative space within which to alter, reshape, work with or against such policies. Attributing problems as 'it's the policy not me', or 'it's the form not me', can act to legitimate a failure to engage, or as a smoke screen against individual accountability for action.

The parents do not tell a uniform story about their experiences with professionals and institutions: not all schools refuse to welcome their child; not all experiences of statementing lead to them feeling their child is pathologised; and not all attempts to get support are rejected. What the following experiences, as well as others discussed in previous chapters, indicate is the possibility of responsiveness in the ways in which professionals respond, which suggest that they can act in ways not solely determined by the institutional processes they are embedded in. In such instances we see a model closer to the notion of partnership rhetorically promised in new government agendas; what is significant is that partnership often emerges in attempts to work around institutional practices.

Some professionals are able to create a relationship with the children they care for, which moves past forms and labels in order to capture the broader person they are working with. The difference this makes is clear to parents:

> When he was at nursery at the School the teacher and the nursery nurse there were brilliant but they both left within about a month of each other for one reason or another, and the two that they replaced them with just didn't have time for Jack at all, I think they just thought he was a naughty boy. He couldn't do anything so what was the point in him being there … if we went to his school review meetings they virtually rattled off a list of things that he couldn't do and never said a thing about anything that he could … but in this [new] school they just seem to have really small goals and they're all achievable, you know rather than setting things like, he's got to be able to sit on the carpet for forty minutes, there's no need for him to be able to do that but his reading skills are above average for his age which is great.
>
> (Jane, IV1)

Jack's current teachers developed an approach to learning that began with him, rather than abstract criteria or easily acquired assumptions about his inabilities. This kind of approach builds from time taken to listen to both children and their parents; respecting the knowledge they have of what works for them, what fosters their quality of life and what is fun. This relates to notions of productive pedagogies which attempt to create the relational and contextual conditions necessary to value diverse learners and the input of parents as key advocates (see Goodley, 2007b; Lingard et al., 2003). Professionals able to work in this way became a source of trust and enabling care:

> I wanted a wheelchair for Joe when he was about two and a half, and there's this stupid rule apparently, you're not allowed one until you're three, and she [her physiotherapist] said, 'well we're not supposed to, explain to me why you need one'. So I showed her what Joe was like in our normal pushchair, hanging out the side. And she said, 'fine, I can understand that, I can't promise anything but I'll see what I can do'. She went away and then got back in touch, 'Well, you're not really meant to have it but I've got you one, and here it is', and it was great, fabulous.
>
> (Kay, IV2)

The professionals who most often stood out for parents were those who seemed able to move past protocol and job descriptions, to provide intuitive and responsive care:

> She knew Frank, she actually came to our home twice, to see Frank and then we'd been to the clinic a few times, and when we were in hospital over Christmas she *knew* Frank, she knew what we could deal with as a family, because she'd met us a couple of times.
>
> (Debbie, IV1, our emphasis)

Direct payments are expected to enable parents to make choices for themselves. However, parents beginning to use direct payments sometimes found that when they approached agencies the assumption of professional decision making continued, while other agencies acknowledged the new right of parents to purchase services for their child. When Sarah and Nick approached two care agencies about providing support they wanted to use their direct payments for, they were asked to get their social worker to contact the agency to discuss the matter. At the third agency – the one they eventually went with – the response instead was:

> Sarah: 'What disability does your daughter have, how many members of the family are there?' I said, 'we've got three children, there's my husband and myself'. She talked about us, she didn't mention the social worker ... I suddenly felt like, as if somebody was listening ... She took the time to come from out of town to here, to have a look

at the situation, to find out what our family required and things like that. And that made a world of difference to us.

(Sarah and Nick, IV2)

Parents are aware that within the same institutional processes professionals can respond in different ways. Through these contrasting experiences they recognise the forms of interaction that make something akin to partnership possible:

I mean we've got support through parent partnership ... When we went to school review meetings it was like having a close friend, not a professional sitting there helping you, backing you up.

(Jane, IV2)

What a partnership also suggests is that the child is involved too and is not just supported by the professional, but instead is also someone who enriches the professional's life:

Those people that are involved with her from week-to-week, especially they get the benefits from it, [pause] as Lauren gets benefits from them, they get it in return. [Pause] So you can tell at once that she recognises and knows and loves.

(Gill, IV2)

As individuals, professionals can make a difference in their way of working, respecting, indeed caring, for families:

Previously we had a very bad experience with the social worker a year and a half ago when Ali was first ill, since then any improvement or help has come from the new social worker, which proves for us that different people can make a difference, and one social worker can help, while others will not. It shows us how people can make a difference, and that it's not always the policies/system that stops you getting support.

(Sameera IV1, via an interpreter)

The concern then is how to conceptualise this different kind of practice and understand what makes it possible within institutions. Is it just about the individual and how the individual can make a difference?

And a good example of that would be our social worker, and I really didn't take to her at all at first. But I think, and over time we've actually got a good relationship now and I think what's it's been is she's actually a very caring person that's conscientious in her job, and cares about the family she works for. But her hands are tied if she can't offer them any services. Then I've got the opposite with somebody like the portage woman that I've moaned on about [laughs]. She actually had a valuable function to perform you know in terms of bringing toys and things that were useful to Joe so it was actually useful to us but it ended up becoming a really bad service because of her personality.

(Kay, IV3)

There is a case for saying that individual practice does matter. If we acknowledge the emotive aspects of both the work for professionals and the care for the families, then it is impossible to ignore the interpersonal significance of the relationship that emerges between parent, professional and child. Whatever the institutional limitations to the contexts within which people work, there is a role for individual response and for acknowledging the care that professionals can develop in spite of institutional contexts. This is important because it refuses to let professionals off the hook as individuals and instead places them as societal actors with shared responsibility to provide appropriate and adequate care. It also signals that alongside the discursive construction of professional identity we have discussed, there are social practices, however framed discursively, which are experienced by parents as qualitatively different, making them feel valued, enabled and listened to. While some of that is about the provision of things, of resources, it is not only about that, it is also about the development of patterns of relationship, listening, engagement, understanding, which can form the basis of respect, trust and partnership.

However, alongside it is important to see such individual instances of enabling provision for families as about something more than individuals who happen to care. The danger is of dissolving the identification of such good practice into heroic stories of the noble professional. This can easily fall into either a familiar story of the paternal care provider, or a gendered discourse of the essentially caring professional. What we are exploring here is *professional ethics*, a process that professionals cannot escape, for they are 'actively practicing ethicists who reflect on ethical principles and put them into use' (Pols, 2006: p. 425). As they do so, we can identify what moral values we wish individual professionals to develop, which are respectful of parents and children, are enabling in practice, and conducive of partnership building and trust. Our assertion is that while its implementation does require the commitment of individual actors, it cannot be answered solely at the individual level. It is not just about the individual, because moral problems and solutions do not occur in the abstract, except in philosophical writing; moral dilemmas 'can only be evaluated in the world the way it is' (Jennings, 2000: p. 130). As Kälvemark et al. (2004) argue, the ethical dilemmas professionals face are often the result of a disjunction between what they wish to do, what they believe to be the right thing to do, and what they can do according to the resources available and the rules that institutionally surround them (Raines, 2000; Robins, 2001). We would also add it cannot be left up to individual professionals because ascertaining what is the right thing to do, as opposed to simply what the professional wishes to do, is not something they can do in isolation: it calls for partnership with those they are working with, both other professionals, but crucially families as well.

This moves us towards considering ethical practice as being a deliberative and negotiated activity, one that cannot be predetermined, but instead involves what Pols calls 'contextual reflexivity' (2006: p. 426). Pols argues that contextual reflexivity involves professionals working with those they support to define what is good care in the contexts within which they practice. From professional practices that parents highlighted as providing enabling care, we see such reflexivity in action, as patterns of engagement that were useful to the family, were embedded in knowledge of them and which expressed value and recognition. It is not just up to individual professionals to provide this form of practice; if such approaches are culturally valued within institutional settings, articulated within discourses of what encompasses professional identity, made visible in templates of what makes a good professional and explored within training and education, then they become visible markers from within which to judge the ethical efficacy of both individual professionals and the institutions within which they practice.

Conclusion

Management practices that seek to standardise, instrumentalise and monitor the support parents receive are embedded in services such as DLA and educational statements. Both professionals and parents have seen the services they are involved in changed by the requirements of a contract and managerial culture that appears to have little scope for recognition and negotiation. At the same time other shifts towards partnership and consumer rights are compromised by both managerial culture and continued professional models of authority and paternalism. However, through the experiences of parents we can glimpse a model of professional practice, which finds a space to allow for negotiation and recognition, despite institutional structures. It refuses both managerialism and paternalism as the model for how families should be supported. It represents a form of professional ethics, which envisions partnership as a product of intimate knowledge, respect and contingency in the modes of care, which work for different families. It is not enough to celebrate individual professionals who, from the perspective of families, practice such a form of ethical support, instead it needs to be seen as an equal, if not superior, value to already existing articulations of professional role and made visible within the institutions of welfare provision.

8
The Gender Dynamics, Transformative Potential and Boundaries of Care

Janice McLaughlin and Dan Goodley

Introduction

In Chapter 1 we highlighted feminist work on the gendered division of labour, particularly, within the home. Feminists in the 1980s attributed the dominance of women in the caring role to societal constructions of gender and family role, and identified these constructions as a major barrier to women's full participation in the public sphere (Baldwin & Twigg, 1991; Finch & Groves, 1983; Graham, 1983; Land, 1978). Recent empirical work examining caring responsibilities within the home has raised the possibility that the gendered division of labour, in part due to the efforts of feminisms, is no longer as significant (Baxter, 1992; Lupton & Barclay, 1997; Sullivan, 2000; Ungerson, 2000). The last census in 2001 appeared to indicate that men and women are providing similar levels of unpaid care within families (ONS, 2007); while, women, including women with children, are entering and staying in employment in greater numbers than ever seen before. A growing percentage of households with children are co-habiting families and their patterns of caring responsibility suggest a greater level of equal sharing than found in married couples (ONS, 2007).

However, the statistics paint a mixed picture. Further analysis of the census data indicates that when men care, and who they care for, is different from women; the greatest prevalence of men taking on caring responsibilities occurs in later life, when looking after an ill spouse (ONS, 2007). While mothers are present in employment, they continue to be paid significantly less than men, in part because they are over represented in part-time work (one in three women in the UK work part time (Burchell et al., 2007), in lower paid sectors of the economy (Walker et al., 2001)). Sociologists acknowledge that something is changing within the division of labour within families, but it is not a clear-cut reduction in the significance of gender to who cares and for whom (Lewis, 2002, 2007). Feminists argue that social conditions, gender norms and welfare policies continue to create traditional demarcations of gender roles within the home, including in families living apart (Charles, 2000; McKie et al., 2002; O'Brien, 2007). McKie et al. argue that women continue to 'live out the contradictions of their identification and preoccupation with both care and their paid work in their daily activities' (2002: p. 913). In addition, Traustadóttir (1991, 1995) argues that when a child is disabled any equalities of care responsibility can quickly disappear as the more intensive care is still directed towards women.

Summarising the broad range of care debates both within and outside feminism is beyond the chapter. What this chapter does seek to do is to draw from feminist ideas in order to explore the social significance of the patterns of care discussed by parents. This will allow us to consider three important factors in the dynamics of care, which are present within families with disabled children. First, the gendering of such care practices; second, the transformative potential of care; and, finally, the boundaries of care. However, before doing so it is important to consider the criticisms of feminist work raised by disability writers in Chapter 1.

As already highlighted, disability studies' unease with feminist analyses of care is particularly concerned with feminists' sole concern for those who care, rather than those who are cared for (Begum, 1992; Keith & Morris, 1995; Morris, 1993a). In addition, feminists have done little to challenge some of the pathological meanings associated with care as either an act of charity or of burden (Begum, 1990). However, in this chapter we will draw from feminist work in order to consider the contexts that frame particular activities as care. While Skeggs (1997) (one of the key contemporary feminist writers who explores care subjectivities) fails to examine care from the perspective of anyone but the carer, usefully she highlights how the contexts within which individuals are involved in caring activities frame and influence what is seen as care, how care is performed and how it is received. Processes of both self-regulation and agency within gendered and class boundaries influence the patterns of care women enact and how they and others read it as part of their identity as women, mothers and workers. Therefore exploring the social, cultural and political contexts within which care occurs is important to understanding its significance (Kittay, 1999a). This is vital within debates about disability, it provides for a deeper appreciation of the significance of the support provided by carers and assistants for disabled people. It also allows for a broader understanding of the relations, experiences, engagement, interdependences and politics involved in caring activities (Watson et al., 2004). It creates a space to recognise the agency and identity of disabled people within caring roles, pushing towards a position that blurs the notion that there are those who care and those who are cared for (Fine & Glendinning, 2005; Lloyd, 2000, 2003). As the census data discussed above shows, a large number of people who report care responsibilities also have their own health problems, which require care and support.

Gendered division of care

As we explore the gender dynamics at play within the lives of the parents and their children, it is important to consider the influence the dynamics identified play on the creation of subjectivity and what contexts help shape that influence.

'Am I going be a carer for the rest of my life?' (Jane, IV1)

Within our research we were unsurprised to find the gendered division of labour prominent in families. Mothers described themselves as the prime carer in all cases apart from three (where both parents described the care responsibilities as joint). In nine families the woman was on her own raising her children. Some of these lone parent families were the result of a divorce or separation that occurred after the birth or diagnosis of the disabled child. According to Mauldon (1992) divorce is more likely among parents of disabled children. In the majority of these cases the divorced or separated father played little role. Where he did continue to play a role, this was often in relation to the care of non-disabled children. In the most extreme case of this, Elizabeth's non-disabled child Mack lived with the father who refused to interact with his disabled child Julie. In those families where both parents were present raising the child, there was evidence of fathers playing caring roles, but core responsibility was in most cases the mother's:

> So I still feel like the responsibility lies on me. I'm also the one that pre-empts things happening or worrying about things, whereas I think John's life's a lot easier and he just like drifts along blissfully unaware of everything that's going on around him.
>
> (Jane, IV3)

This section will explore how the balance of responsibilities between mothers and fathers develops.

Finch and Mason (1993) identified various processes that feed into the drift of care responsibilities towards women. Myths of motherhood present the skills women develop raising their child as inherent and assume that men neither have nor can develop them (Douglas & Michaels, 2004; Johnston & Swanson, 2006). The prominence of women in care then emphasises their 'natural aptitude' and creates different relationships between mother and child and others in the family, including the father. This process appears particularly marked in the care of disabled children. When mothers are asked to provide key roles in the day-to-day treatments and therapies for their child, this is based on their presumed inherent ability to care and absorb additional tasks into that role. Over time this becomes part of the processes that consolidate the gendered division of care. The expertise mothers develop in treatment and supporting the child leads them to continue to be seen as the obvious carers for their child, which excludes others from participating in those activities (also discussed in Chapter 5). A visible distance emerges between the mother and child and the father who can be in the wings removed from the intricacy and intensity of the caring activities:

> Jim hasn't got a clue! ... I think it's just because he's not here. I manage fine. Jim would struggle if it was down to him but it's not, so we're fine. It is hard work but then now I think it is part of me, because now I get the carer's allowance, I think I'm being paid to do this, this is my job ... I've taken that stance on it, this is my job to look after Luke. You know it isn't his fault he's like this. But then sometimes when I'm feeling really, really down and fed-up and you know I think well, it's not my fault he's like this either.
>
> (Maria, IV1)

Over time families can try to work to reduce the gap, but it can be difficult to resolve the skills gap that appears between the mother and the others involved in caring for the child:

> I think everybody just gets on with it now, because he's communicating so well, they are just getting on with it. They've copied all the sign books, they've all got the signing books and different things, and they probably don't use the Makaton as much as I do, [to Frank] 'but even daddy doesn't, does he? Daddy's been given a task of learning more about Makaton with you this week hasn't he?'
>
> (Debbie, IV2)

One of the reasons it is difficult to close the skills gap, is because it is supported by wider gender ideologies that create the notion that women are naturally better at these forms of care and skill (O'Brien, 2007; Orme, 2001). When mothers argue that fathers could not take responsibility, or are too distant from caring activities to know what to do, they are reconfirming such gender ideologies.

These same gender ideologies frame notions of the 'sole carer' and caring intimacy in such a way that they can make invisible the roles fathers can and do play within the overall caring dynamic around the child. Jack's father worked both full time for the council and part time as a taxi driver. However, John's engagement with his son followed him into the public sphere as he freely spoke about him to passengers and sought advice from anyone with similar experience or who worked in the area:

> And he only does the taxi'ing at the weekends, he's forever coming in, I don't know how many people that he talks to about Jack, but anybody who's got anything to do with special needs or autism, or special schools, he seems to talk to them, and he says he gets a lot out of that.
>
> (Jane, IV1)

However, while most fathers are not completely absent from care, for the majority of families, across the range of family type from married, cohabiting to sole parent, a familiar pattern remains across the fieldwork and time. The types of care activities fathers are more likely to participate in are those with fun value such as going to the football or playing with the child, the more day-to-day labour around feeding, cleaning etc. often remain (with exceptions discussed further on) within the woman's role. What we most often had within the research was cases of men *participating* in some of the care, while women remained *responsible* for the provision of care (McKie et al., 2002).

Paid work

The significance of care responsibilities meant that mothers struggled to return to work after the realisation that their child was disabled. Lone mothers found this the most difficult; during the study only one lone mother (Helen), with the support of her parents who looked after her child while she worked in a shop at the weekend, returned to work at all. While lone mothers reflected positively about the intensity of their caring role with their child/ren, this was not without a sense of

isolation and loss over other parts of themselves, which they sometimes struggled to develop because of the demands created by being a
sole parent. For the other mothers who went back to work, for all bar
one this was to part time work, with little or no opportunity for career
progression. The priority was now fitting work into the care responsibilities they felt were theirs:

> They're definitely going to cut jobs anyway at work ... so, in some
> ways I'd be quite happy if I could get a good package, just going and
> working completely around the children, working a couple of
> evenings a week in Tescos or something, but at least it'll be fitting in
> around the kids and that's what I'd probably prefer to do. Though it
> means giving up my career ... I mean career wise, mine's stopped
> anyway because I cannot do the kind of job that I should.
>
> (Jane, IV3)

A return to work did not always lead to any change in the division of
care responsibilities within the family:

> It still is me who is the lead person. I've organised the nursery, I've
> made sure that everything is in place, that the training's there, that
> his bag's ready and I've done all of that ... Bob is fantastic with him,
> but it is me who takes the lead on, on all of that.
>
> (Debbie, IV2)

Work had to fit in with continued care responsibilities. Flexible employment was often sought, during the evening, or term time. Nevertheless,
while managing paid work and care was difficult, they did not want to
give work up: 'work is important to me it's, it's that bit where you switch
off, you can get into something else'. (Debbie, IV3) Work was a signal to
them and to others that they had a life and identity beyond being their
child's carer:

> So it is now a reality, my mindset is now getting back into a work ori-
> entation, and not just the *caring* role that I've had, for the last fifteen
> months, it's now more right, it's starting to get my life more back on
> track and not Lauren encompassing it all.
>
> (Gill, IV2, our emphasis)

Work can provide satisfaction and respite that may negate some of the
social isolation associated with parenting a disabled child (see Lewis et al.

(2000a)). Mothers considered work to be an important part of their personal and social lives, but felt stymied by a number of barriers. Tong (2002), who refers to parents, particularly mothers, as 'dependency workers', found that support was lacking in terms of little flexitime or job share opportunities, an absence of family friendly policies and little to no on-site childcare (see also Lewis et al. (2000)). These findings were supported by the accounts of parents in this study. Cheryl reported having to use up her dinner hour to take her child from one nursery to another due to lack of spaces for full day provision. One of Sharon's ambitions was to get childcare provided in hospitals so that she could drop her oldest child off before keeping an appointment with the consultant for the youngest. Indeed the lack of childcare provision had threatened to make Sharon's child miss an important operation. Given the potential for work to provide a relief from the challenges of being a carer, particularly a 'sole carer', it is important that employers and service providers think creatively about what they can do to make work possible for parents of disabled children.

Alongside work, other activities were sought and found that were not about caring for the child. Parents, mostly mothers, talked of the half-an-hour shop or going to the gym as a momentary escape. Karen had joined a drumming group during the study, while David, who was equally involved in their child's care, was a member of a band. Paid work and other activities that were done without the presence of the child were defined by parents as respite care; Sarah (IV1) noted, 'If I want respite I've got to go to college ... in order to get respite from the kids or to give Nick a break.' However, the challenges of balancing different activities, for example combining education, work and caring responsibilities was rarely easy (while extremely important) for parents:

> David: The College, they have been really, really fantastic, if I have an appointment they have been understanding. As Karen was saying, its juggling you know.
>
> (Karen and David, IV1)

These different quotes point to the importance of seeking out alternative forums of community participation, as discussed in Chapter 6. For example Kagan (1997) stresses the importance of family-friendly policies, such as flexitime and job share, childcare provision that is accessible to all disabled children and greater appreciation among service providers that parents are not always available during the day.

Changes to the division of labour

It would be a mistake to present the gender division of labour as completely static. Over time the division of labour within families did change in ways that highlight the micro spaces and processes, which can create subtle changes in gendered patterns within families. Such subtle changes are important for considering what factors can contribute to creating different patterns of care, and for recognising both what creates rigidity and what enables flexibility in care patterns. In the one case where the mother returned to full time work, in education, this triggered a need to reconsider the division of labour within the family. The negotiations within the family were influenced by the fact that Gill could earn more than her husband:

> I'll be going back to work and I won't be here for Lauren as many hours in the day. So at the moment I'm in two minds of trying to make a decision of whether do I go back to the same job, or do I look for another job which is fewer hours but obviously less pay? And I'm the main wage earner. So that's sort of the position that we're in. Because obviously it's going to come as a shock to her system and there's no way in my job that you can actually start going back part time just to get used to it and then go full time ... So that's the only thing for the future, dealing with how it's best to keep everybody happy.
>
> (Gill, IV1)

While Gill challenges the gender division by being the main earner and eventually choosing to go back to full time work, gendered patterns of care remain in her concern to ensure that what is worked out will 'keep everybody happy'. The gendered division is also maintained by the role the grandmother took in filling the gap in the childcare needs created by Gill's return to work. Indeed it became clear in the second interview that the grandmother was taking a greater role in the provision of care for the child than the father (who also worked full time, involving long hours). However, things subtly changed again when in later observations of the child's home therapy visits the father was playing an increased role. From the discussion between the father and the support worker it was clear that he was also playing a role in the ongoing care of the child:

> Sam [father] said how it was very different last week when they couldn't get Lauren to do anything, she was just not in the mood,

but today she was much more into it all ... Sam laughs and said if I'd
seen her last week, 'it was an embarrassment'. Francis [grandmother]
said, 'She wasn't having any of it last week'. Sam spoke about how
much she has come on since her heart operation, and that having
the second operation on her stomach has also helped.

(Ethnographic notes)

In other families we saw changing patterns of work and care over time.
In the first interview Jane was working part time, while the father, John,
worked two jobs. In the second interview Jane discussed how they were
reconsidering the pattern of work and care they had in place in order to
have greater flexibility over the care of both their children. Someone
would have to change their work and it was decided that it would be the
father who would change to only taxi work due to the flexibility in
hours this allowed. For another family, a new pregnancy encouraged a
greater emphasis on the father providing the major caring role, in this
case the physical tasks moved to being provided by the father:

And especially since I've been pregnant, I mean there was some
days, and even now really with having Daisy, I feel like I hardly see
Joe, because Stephen tends to get him ready in the mornings,
because he needs lifting and handling and I'm still not meant to be
lifting until six months after I've had her ... Stephen tends to get
him ready when he comes in from school at night. It depends who's
here if Stephen's working, he tends to do a lot of stuff with him in
the evening and lift him in and out of the bath, and get him ready,
put him to bed, and I feel, although I'm in the house and physically
in the same place, I hardly spend any time with him. But Stephen's
taken on a much more active role, and he's doing much more and
he's much closer to him as well, and I can see that now which is
nice. So we've kind of swapped over a bit, whereas I guess when Joe
was little, there were days when he probably didn't do anything
with him at all.

(Kay, IV2)

The changing caring roles also contributed to Stephen reducing his
hours at work.

As mentioned earlier three families had developed, or maintained
from the beginning, a division of labour, which blurred gendered patterns of care far more significantly than we saw within other families
across the lifetime of the project. Karen and David had sought from the

beginning for both to be involved in all aspects of their son's care. In the first interview Karen was a full time carer, while David studied and played an active role in Daniel's care, with support from his college. Later, in reflection of Daniel's needs, their other children and to provide space for the mother to do other things, the father gave up his studies. They made significant efforts to ensure that both attended medical appointments:

> David: Because right from the outset we've always gone to the appointments together, we've always ensured that we've both been there whenever there's a decision to be made about Daniel's medication; we've both sat down and spoke about it.
>
> (Karen and David, IV1)

However, their joint care for their son was frustrated by systems and practices around them, which assumed the mother would be the main carer:

> David: At the moment I know with carer's allowance and things like that, Karen claims it because she cares for Daniel. But on the other hand I do just as much caring for Daniel as well. It tends to be a case of, certainly from a Benefit side of things, they tend to say it's just one person looking after the child. I've made a choice where I want to be involved just as much as what Karen does. But I think it's because there's still that kind of stereotype of the woman looking after the children, that I've certainly had experience before where I'm pushed out to the side and it's like, 'Oh well we're speaking to the primary care-giver'.
>
> (Karen and David, IV1)

Ethnographic notes from consultations with other families provide further indication of how present fathers are excluded:

> William had taken the afternoon off work to go with his partner and son to see the paediatric consultant. It was a shame that the consultant (incidentally a woman) directed all her attention towards Jennifer, who was clearly viewed as the main carer. William was only addressed towards the end of the consultation in a manner that made it clear that she (the consultant) expected his contribution to consist mainly in carrying baby paraphernalia.
>
> (Ethnographic notes)

The researcher discussed the issue with Jennifer and William after the consultation. Both felt that William's role as a father had been inadvertently devalued.

What is evident in these examples is a clash between attempts by parents to make joint decisions together and institutional requirements for a 'primary' carer to be identified. It is here that we see an important source of rigidity in the care division of labour. Institutional mechanisms are part of the broader social conditions, which generate and legitimise gender ideologies around care practices. As other writers have pointed out, the caring roles men do play are often made invisible and unsupported (Campbell & Carroll, 2007). It is not just bureaucracy that contributes to such invisibility; the day-to-day assumptions people make around who can be a carer also play a significant part. The ways in which the father can be ignored and constructed as outside of the caring relationship became evident in an observation of house-based therapies of Daniel:

> Throughout the session Daniel was either on the floor being encouraged to move with some supporting physio exercises or in a specially adapted padded chair. Most of this time, Daniel was handled by the physiotherapist who tried to help him sit and push himself up independently. Karen then sat between Daniel and the physiotherapist. With the action generally happening on the floor, David seemed somewhat removed from events. Conversation flowed fairly smoothly between the women, though there were times when David made a comment and did manage to interject. I wondered whether David was taking more of a back seat here because of the way these sessions have happened in the past when he has been mostly out at college, hence a protocol/tradition was already established, defining the caring roles with the focus placed on Karen?
>
> (Ethnographic Notes)

As Campbell and Carroll (2007) argue dominant narratives associated with masculinity, in addition to those associated with femininity, contribute to both excluding men from care and denying the roles they play. However, it is important to guard against treating concepts of legitimate care identities, for both men and women, as inherently fixed and instead consider what transformative possibilities there are at the level of identity in playing a part in the day-to-day activities of care.

Transformative potential of care

Earlier we saw how feminists noted the significance of caring roles to formations of identity and subjectivity. Caring can become a constitutive element of identity, encouraged by wider contexts and frameworks, which make it a legitimate one for women in particular social positions and make other forms of identity less available (McLaughlin, 2006). Such processes of identity recognition are particularly marked for mothers of disabled children. In our research we have seen fathers' identities as carers unrecognised by others, while mothers are readily identified and identify themselves as carers: 'This is who I am now'. In Skeggs's (1997) terms, caring identities are available and respectable for mothers. We would add that this is particularly so when the child is disabled and the mother is assumed to make the sacrifice and become the full time, permanent carer. So in one sense this is a problematic identity construction; while one can understand why women adopt it, it also leads to a confirmation of the existing gender division, making it more difficult for men to adopt it (Orme, 2001) and for women to reject it. In addition, even if mothers get a sense of self out of such roles and identities, this can have costs, including a reduced identity as noted by Maria (IV2): 'Some people, a couple of the staff in Waitrose have said to me, "oh you're Luke's mam aren't you?" I've lost my identity, I'm Luke's mam.'

However, if we look at the kind of care identity the women articulate we can also see its expansive possibilities and political potentialities. Mothers talked of a changed life, where accomplishment, as well as exhaustion, was now part of not just what they did, but also who they were. In so doing they challenged the notion that the caring identity should be framed as sacrifice, tragedy and burden. As mothers talked of the positive aspects of being a carer, they were also critical of accounts of raising a disabled child, which concentrated on difficulties and problems:

> I got this book after I had Luke, I was pleased I didn't get this when I was pregnant; it was the story of this girl and this mum and it was all how the mum felt, how she felt sorry for herself and it was about the girl growing up and how the mam found it was difficult and, I found it a very selfish book.
>
> (Maria, IV2)

As part of changed subjectivities mothers talked of seeking out new ways of developing the skills they had acquired. So, for example, Jemma talked of going to college to train as a class room assistant to work with children with learning disabilities after spending time volunteering in her daughter's class room. As mothers' skills and experiences developed they were often likely to develop other extended roles. As discussed in Chapter 5, the experience of parenting a disabled child encouraged mothers to train as educational professionals and inform existing professional practices; something other research has also found (Cole, 2004). For example, we came across more than one mother who had taken on the role of school governor:

> Then there was a position for a Special Education Needs (SEN) governor when somebody resigned and two of us were very interested in doing it, the other lady that's doing it with me does lots of fundraising work and she's a teacher as well, so she's got that side of it and I've got the parental side of it … because as a parent you know what you want out of the school for your child and if you can communicate that to the Board of Governors, they know what they should be working on and what training the staff need or there is anything that can be done that is not being done, so confidence to be able to do things and organise things.
>
> (Cheryl, IV1)

Feelings of accomplishment can emerge out of the work mothers do. It is inappropriate to see such feelings as coping mechanisms to make life bearable when living in a tragedy. What is frustrating is that, as Grant and Whittell (2001) found, professionals do not always recognise the expertise of mothers. This is particularly sad when some of the most marginalised groups of parents – for example, lone parents and older carers – actively embraced caring activities in spite of financial barriers and professional prejudice.

Caring also led to broader changes to patterns of life, which led to fundamental re-writes of previous narratives in ways families found life enhancing. This is an important element of the productive parenting discussed in Chapter 5. Parents, alongside their children, are active in the development of counter narratives of what present and possible futures hold:

> I can sit and say well, yes what's happened to Joe is sad and I wish it hadn't, *but* because of that, we've changed as a family, I've changed as a person, I've changed my job, we've moved house. We're doing things that we would never have done if we hadn't had

Joe, and actually a lot of good has come out of it. So I can be positive about it too, I mean, it has made our lives harder, and it's made it different but in some ways it's made it better as well.

(Kay, IV2, our emphasis)

Kay's narrative shows a way of recognising the transformative nature of not just care, but of the child too; Joe's presence in the family's life changes it. As such he exercises an ability to shape the lives around him and is an active agent in the emerging forms of family living that develop with him.

The approaches of these mothers point to something crucially important for closing the gap between the concerns of disability writers and feminists. If we only highlight ways in which caring for a disabled child brings sorrow and burden, particularly to women, then we fail to do justice to both disabled children and the nature of the care relationship between mother and child. Caring for the disabled child generates a level of change that goes broader than how carers think about their own identity. In addition, it is closely connected to changing views regarding social responsibility and disability. Mothers find new meaning and senses of self in their caring role; in particular fighting injustice against their children and others becomes an important part of what they define as the caring role and is embedded in their identity:

Well, I have changed, I have become more assertive and not letting things lie, and really pushing ... and I think getting out there and finding out the information for yourself, and finding out your rights and your wrongs, and talking to other parents who've been through similar things before you, that's definitely helped.

(Angela, IV1)

In defining their caring role, mothers include their battles with statutory services on behalf of their child. As Corinne (IV1) asserted: 'but like a normal person, her rights need to be respected as well, as the rights of a normal person are respected.' Mothers spoke proudly of their strategies for getting what they can for their child. Therefore their caring identity is not perceived as a private role, it sits in the public realm of the care plan meeting and the statementing process required for resources to be allocated to the child when in school.

Transformative care activities engage with re-evaluation of identity, the future, family templates and biographies and political and ethical values. It is very difficult to separate out ways in which mothers rethink the caring roles they play within the family, from new articulations they produce about their own identities now and into future, and from shifts they notice in their broader world views and actions around disability and other political concerns they have. The difficulty points to the co-production of private caring identities and public political and ethical values, which some families work through in their developing life around their children. As 'private' biographies are purposively changed, so too are broader social biographies; in the process new allegiances and partnerships are created. What this highlights is the interconnections between the categories of the public and private and between the activities we associated with productive parenting in Chapter 5 and the community connections we mapped out in Chapter 6. Mothers, and fathers involved in caring practices, along with their children, move through transitions which ultimately broaden care to encompass political dimensions. Through collective friendships and bonds they actively seek to incorporate political values and activities into the caring role they embed in their lives and identities.

Exploring the boundaries of care

A proper consideration of the social and political significance of care involves examining what activities and practices are defined as part of care and being a carer. We have already seen mothers challenge normative constructions of care by incorporating within it political and public dimensions. Through examining what parents refute to be part of their caring/parental responsibilities, we can think further about the broader social and political significances in how families approach the caring relationships they are part of. In Chapter 5 we discussed the tension between how parents developed skills and expertise as 'professionals' in dealing with the medical and developmental needs of their children, and the governmentality associated with the demands on them. We return to this tension here and explore how their response is related to what they define as within and outside the boundaries of care. As with many aspects of parenting disabled children, mothers and their identities and values, are the centre of much of this.

Caring limits

As has been seen in other research with mothers with disabled children (Traustadóttir, 1991, 1995), mothers talk of the multiple roles they play. The assumption, drawn from gendered norms and discourses, is that mothers play such multiple caring roles because they are mothers.

However, mothers do not necessarily see the ever expanding list of activities added to care as being something they should do and be able to do simply because they are mothers. In her first interview, Jane (IV1) commented: 'you're more of a carer than a parent: carer, psychologist, teacher, you name it you've got every role to play.' The list is significant in the way that it makes a distinction between caring and parenting. Jane went on to emphasise that for her there was a difference; when asked which of the roles came first she again maintained the distinction between parenting and caring: 'a parent, first hand, but definitely carer as well, and I suppose representative as well.' Looking closely at the language and narratives generated by mothers we can track aspects of the mothers' care of their disabled children that they define as something outside of what they perceive parenting should be.

For example, we saw earlier that mothers noted that their caring role would continue into their child's adult life; however, this was not always presented as an extension of the parental role:

> Emma: You called yourself a carer now, is that how you see your parenting role, or is that an add on to your parenting role?
> Jane: An add on. I know he's only seven but I'm quite aware that he might not leave home when he's 16 or 18 and, go off to university and things like that. He could be a lot more based at home. If not all his adult life, for a much longer time that you would expect. I think of myself as a carer. I think it's just, it's another one of these like balls that you're trying to juggle, as well as being a parent, you're not a parent of a child who can even dress himself and things like that, Jack still needs a lot of help getting socks and shoes and can't do buttons, things like that. In the morning when I'm trying to get the two of them ready, really, a seven year old will probably be able to get themselves ready, socks, shoes, coat everything. Jack would put his coat upside-down, back-to-front and god knows what if we didn't stop him.
>
> (Jane, IV3)

Part of the attempts to keep such caring distinct from being a parent is read through the previous expectations they have for what parenting involves, crucially that it has a normal trajectory towards the child developing into an independent adult (Gray, 2001; Rehm & Bradley, 2005; Taylor, 2000). This trajectory is not as clear-cut for those with disabled children, and the added responsibilities they associate with this possibility are not something all mothers defined as parental care. The normal expectations and narratives of what parenting constitutes unravel quickly as the child's development begins to 'deviate' from what normally would be the case:

> But I think it's more the fact that Julie is still a baby when she's with me, she's coming up to three and a half and it's a long time to deal with a baby ... even when you get pregnant you don't expect to have a baby for that long. I can remember, I think Mack was only about eighteen month before he was a real independent little person. I couldn't help him do anything, he had to do everything himself, putting his clothes on back to front and everything, he wanted to do it himself so you just let him get on with it.
>
> (Elizabeth, IV1)

Mothers feel that they are pushed into different roles and a broader set of skills, which they feel an obligation to fulfil:

> I used to spend Monday afternoon every week fighting for services for Joe, or arranging appointments, or administrative stuff. And then instead of just being his mum, I'm kind of his case manager, I'm his physio, I'm his speech therapist, I'm his advocate.
>
> (Kay, IV1)

Lack of public support for their child and their family, is a factor in expanding the role of the carer. Kay (IV1) went on to say, 'the amount of time I must spend in an administrative role, not being his mum, not being a carer, but writing letters of complaint; I wrote to the local MP about 10 o'clock last night about getting adaptations to the house, because we're not entitled to any help with that, so we're still carrying him up and down the stairs. It's all of that kind of stuff; it's very wearing and very stressful.' Likewise Gill (IV1) noted: 'I'm the one who for months didn't feel like a parent, felt like a patient co-ordinator. I just felt all I'm doing is co-ordinating.' What is significant is that mothers rejected the presumption that others make, that such work is an automatic expansion of their caring role (Prussing et al., 2005) and simply evidence of what good and involved mothers they are.

The burden of care, from the parents' perspective, is the time taken up chasing for services nominally they have an entitlement to receive. As conditionality (Dwyer, 2004) increases as an element of welfare provision (see Chapter 4), the implication is that having to pursue services will continue to grow as an element of the caring portfolio of parents of disabled children. In Chapter 5 we saw parents take on the identity of the 'fighter' as part of their caring practices, however it is not necessarily something they wish to see as central to what they do. In the first interview Sarah and Nick had talked of their fighting identity on behalf of their child. In the second interview, partly in response to reading their transcript from the first interview, they had decided to limit the amount of time they spent 'fighting' on behalf of their child. Their aim was to spend more time on the caring activities, which had been drowned out by the focus on fighting with services:

> Sarah: It was like an existence where everything was … we were not enjoying our lives … I never seemed to do anything because I was anticipating, 'Oh, I'm going to talk to the social worker today, it's going to be a fight.' Or, 'I'm going to talk to Katy's school today, and I'm probably going to fight about that too.' It is disheartening to the point where you don't want to go out and deal with anybody, you don't want to get on that phone and talk to anybody, because I anticipated the fight before it began. And if life is a constant fight then you just don't want to. You get tired of fighting eventually. I go out, I do my Tai Chi, and I've got the time to do it. Nick goes to the gym finally, now, and it's all because we looked at our lives and decided from that transcript, that it's not going to be, for me, I decided, I'm not going to be like that any more … It shouldn't have to be a fight.
>
> (Sarah and Nick, IV2)

Medical care

Participation in medical interventions is assumed to be something mothers will incorporate into their caring role. As discussed in Chapter 5 this enables the creation of new skills and knowledge, while also involving mothers in heightened patterns of governance. Many mothers felt they had little choice but to participate in such interventions; however they did not always see it as a logical extension of their caring role. In such instances mothers were more likely to question both the validity of the intervention and their participation in it; a questioning at times that was shared by both parents, providing additional support and legitimacy to their doubts.

Frank was first released from hospital after being born premature, still dependent on oxygen and tube feeding; technological supports Debbie willingly took on in order that he could come home. Later, once Frank had improved and was no longer on regular oxygen, he suffered a serious infection that placed him back in the hospital and back on oxygen. Once the immediate crisis passed, the hospital consultant moved to get the child back in the home as soon as possible. A plan was developed that would see the parents again in charge of monitoring his oxygen, this time Debbie and Bob said no:

> we'd dealt with oxygen, but not at those levels, and there's only so much you can cope with. We knew what was normal, for us 'normal' was the low levels of oxygen, whereas Frank was on high levels of oxygen. It gets to the point where you have got too many things to think about, I couldn't do it, we didn't want to do it ... we'd had a period of nearly a year where he'd had none of that, he wasn't on oxygen. And then when it came to the point where we might have to do some of those things again, you don't want it. You're tired, it's then not normal ... it's then a medical problem and somebody else will have to deal with it. So we actually stayed in hospital a week longer than the other consultant felt we needed to.
>
> (Debbie, IV1)

Debbie was concerned that their involvement in the medical management necessary to keep Frank alive, left little space or time to be his parents: 'If we'd come home and he was monitored continuously, you get to the point where we would be watching the monitor and not Frank' (IV1). Such interventions were someone else's responsibility and did not belong in the home, where they turned an intimate family space into a medical arena. The intensity of medical intervention, in particular the presence of technologies that kept Frank alive, became, from Debbie's point of view, a barrier to parental care and response (Place, 2000):

> You watch the machine, I mean we were watching the machine in the hospital; you can't help because they're wired to so much. We would walk in the unit when Frank was little and poorly, and you'd walk in, you'd see him. And before, you would immediately look up, you would assess what the things were, by then you knew what it meant. You do get quite obsessed by the machine.
>
> (Debbie, IV1)

Debbie and Bob's decision is counter intuitive to the assumption that parents will always want their child home as soon as possible and will willingly take on the role of nurse or therapist in order to do so. In many a case this is what parents would choose to do, but the actions of

Debbie and Bob also highlight the implications of home-based thera-pies. Such therapies necessitate a change in identity for both parents and the intimate space of the family, which is not without cost. In con-trast, any reduction in medical interventions provides a space within which parents feel they can do the things they associate with being car-ing parents, rather than being surrogate medical actors:

> Frank isn't poorly any more, which he was when he first came home. I mean he was a very unwell baby when we first had him home. I mean he was tiny and constantly connected to oxygen and tube fed and it was just this little boy with his tube and everything. We've just got a normal life now ... And I think our approach has changed because this is our life and we want Frank to have a normal life.
>
> (Debbie, IV2)

Over time, some mothers became increasingly likely to question med-ical advice and refuse to participate in some treatments and interven-tions. During the course of the fieldwork Luke, a child who had the label of Down's syndrome, was given the additional label of Attention Deficit Hyperactive Disorder (ADHD). This quickly led to the offer of medication, a route the school was particularly keen to see taken. Maria refused, arguing for Luke to have the space to develop his personality, unclouded by medication. Instead she suggested that other ways could be found to respond to his 'disruptive' behaviour. Other mothers ques-tioned the forms of medical treatment and therapies taking place within their home, particularly those forms unwilling to break free of medical models of development:

> The portage worker is an example of somebody who did nothing constructive to help. One time she brought me a chart to fill in and tick off tasks each day: achieved, not achieved, partially achieved, which is just too controlling and you can't do that. I felt she was policing how much I was doing each day, because she seemed to be disappointed with the level of progress that Joe was making. And, after that my feeling from her, was always this hidden agenda of, well you're not doing enough that's why you're not making progress, that's always what I got from her.
>
> (Kay, IV2)

Kay eventually asked the portage worker to stop coming, her decision came from a view that setting and achieving goals for Joe, made against markers of medically defined physical and mental development, was being privileged over broader criteria of what creates a child's quality of life. In addition the portage worker did not seem to allow Joe any choice or agency over whether he wished to participate in such treatments. Home visits occur in a space that has a set of multiple intimate and complex meanings around family lives and identities (Levine, 2005), yet it is within this space 'that professionals impart their expectations of children's development' (Leiter, 2004: p. 840).

Mothers became choosier about medical interventions and appointments they felt it necessary to attend; in so doing they sought to reclaim their child and provide space for a range of their development to occur more freely and under less regulatory scrutiny. The expertise they developed as 'professional parents' helps them do this; as they become more adept at understanding medical practices, they become more active in decisions about what treatments their child will have. Debbie (IV2) explained that she had reduced the number of appointments Frank went to because 'We've got our own lives to lead now, we don't need to be constantly in hospitals.' The sessions she withdrew him from were those that she felt treated him only as a medical object: 'It's probably the medical side of him they're more interested in, and his weight and things, than how he actually is as a little boy.'

While the societal and medical assumption is that the 'good mother' incorporates medical care into her caring portfolio, mothers themselves do not always agree. Instead for them it can be more important to question medical intervention, rather than participate in it. In this way questioning medical recommendations is incorporated into the scope of the mother's care, while participating in therapies is positioned as outside its boundaries. Rejection of certain medical practices and the refusal to incorporate certain activities into caring is best understood as elements in ongoing processes of redefining family life, what it means to be a carer, and a mother, and what different futures lie ahead (Frank, 1995; Jenks, 2005; Taylor, 2000).

Narratives of care

Parents construct boundaries around their expectations and understandings of what caring for a disabled child involves. By thinking through how the parents, particularly mothers, created boundaries around what was reasonable and unreasonable to see as additional elements of their caring role as parents, we have identified four narratives that influence the production of such boundaries.

First, parents such as Jane and Elizabeth, draw on societal ideals of what *normal* parental care involves, in particular the nurturing of a child into adult independence and responsibility. Maintaining this narrative means that the added intensity and extended commitment involved in caring for a disabled child is not framed as parental care, instead it is an additional burden produced by disability. Such a narrative is problematic in the way in which it continues to present disability as the problem, as the source of burden and tragedy, and fails to question the societal constructions of what normal parental care entails. Second, parents such as Debbie and Bob ('it is someone else's responsibility') draw upon a politically based *rights and entitlements* narrative, which highlights the social and gendered injustice involved in assuming that mothers, and at times fathers, will play roles that the state and society should have a greater responsibility to fulfill. Parents are not demanding that their children be removed from them and placed in residential care; instead they are calling for a reconsideration of the boundaries and content of what care constitutes and how it is shared across a broad range of potential participants. The third, articulated by Kay (a doctor herself), is a *resistant* narrative, resistant of the professionalisation of parental care. Influenced by wider societal suspicion of medical authority, this narrative contains a critical power in its ability to question the authority and presumed superiority of medical knowledge. The fourth narrative, articulated by both Debbie and Kay, seeks to place outside of parenting, practices associated with the instrumentality of medical practices that objectify the child. To challenge the instrumentality of particular medical practices, the mothers articulate a counter narrative of *responsive and connected care*. There are aspects of the caring role they define as part of their parenting practice, which do not fit within the rationality and governmentality of medical practices geared towards narrow models of developmental progress. This challenge and refusal to be co-opted into the regulatory model of child development is politicised. It is politicised in its refusal to accept that alternative caring practices are less significant than medical practices and in its challenge to the public sphere to think about disability and care in different ways.

Conclusion

When a young child is ill or disabled, the caring roles appear to expand exponentially and the assumptions made by both services and society is that parents, in particular mothers, will integrate such roles into their parental care portfolio. However, a number of problems are raised by such assumptions. First, it is based on gendered normative notions about the different parental roles, which direct such increased caring activities towards women. Such assumptions both encourage the continuation of this division and disguise or hinder varied patterns of role across parents and others, which families seek to develop. Caring roles across participants can change over time, influenced by broader social conditions and possibilities; such conditions can either enable or make more difficult such transitions.

Second, it fails to capture the dynamic nature of care and its relationship to subjectivity. As care becomes an element in the ongoing construction of identity, the process is influenced by wider cultural frameworks that both delimit possibilities and also provide alternative versions of caring identities. Third, it abdicates a broader political discussion, which is required, about who is responsible for such caring activities and why the private sphere is assumed to be their location. Without a debate about the responsibilities of the state and society to care, rather than just parents, the privatisation of care goes on unquestioned and the marginalisation of such families continued. Where care provision is presented as individualistic, as focused only on the 'condition' rather than the child, as a form of charity and private responsibility, rather than public right and entitlement, families remain locked in marginalised positions that construct them as 'troubling' to society and enforce the caring role on the mother. Finally, it fails to query the nature of the caring activities parents in this position are asked to play and whether such activities may be incompatible with alternative narratives of parenthood and care, which parents of disabled children may wish to assert in order to challenge societal and state marginalisation of them and their children.

9
Values of Enabling Care and Social Justice

Janice McLaughlin and Dan Goodley

The previous chapters have highlighted disability discourses, across familial, institutional and community settings, that position disabled children and their families in exclusionary and inclusive ways. We have also shown how families respond in creating alternative discourses and practices to those normatively associated with the marginalisation of the disabled family. They remind us of the rights of such families to have access to material and cultural resources that enable them to be full participating members of society (Danermark & Gellerstedt, 2004; Goodland & Riddell, 2005). This chapter brings together some of the key areas of analysis and looks beyond them to consider their implications for how we can think about care, justice and rights in the context of disability. It begins by considering the relationship between enablement and regulation. It then moves on to discuss the social and political categories of recognition around disabled children, before concluding with a proposal that greater recognition of interdependency lies at the core of obtaining greater justice and citizenship for disabled children and their families.

Enabling regulation

The lives of families raising disabled children are complex. They are engaged in heightened relationships with actors and judgments of the public sphere: both in terms of the formal institutions they intersect and also as a consequence of their visibility as 'different' in normal, governed social spheres. There are levels of scrutiny and interventions by the state and professionals distinctive to the disabled family. Such interventions, alongside broader social contexts, have the potential to be either (or indeed both) enabling or regulative. By enabling, we mean values and practices that provide space for children and parents to shape their lives and the support they receive; which respect their visions of a life worth living and worthy of affirmative recognition (Clavering, 2007). Regulation, on the other hand, emerges from the requirement of particular presentations of self in order to receive help and via the ability of institutional actors and processes to define appropriate and inappropriate identities (Foucault, 1982; Rose, 1989). Interventions may seek to enable but generate regulation through the lack of fit between expansive ways of living with disability and instrumental categories of response maintained by institutions. Conversely within familial responses to regulative governance there is also the possibility for the constitution of affirmative and productive forms of subjectivity, relationships, parent-professional partnerships and the constitution of new identities and social movements. In various areas of the families' lives we saw cross-cutting experiences of both enablement and regulation. As a way to briefly pull together some of the key areas of analysis in the book we will highlight some of those experiences.

Knowledge and expertise

As discussed in Chapter 5, part of the productive identities of parents is to be a seeker of knowledge and acquirer of expertise. Knowledge and expertise are important parts of what they do (and who they are as caring and activist parents). They draw on a range of sources of knowledge and expertise, which help them become partners with service providers, where recognition of their expertise is acknowledged, appreciated and used in the support of the child. Such knowledge and expertise is distributed via the role of various alliances with others – other parents, other parent/support groups, other professionals – in acquiring knowledge and expertise. It is productive in the role it plays in providing parents, most often mothers, with an identity that is recognised by others and is supportive of a positive psycho-emotional life. Parent-professional partnership discourses too often are predicated on professionals having knowledge and responding sensitively to the needs and wants of parents. However, across the book, we are reminded of the sophisticated knowledge not only gathered by parents (for example, using the Internet to understand a newly proffered diagnosis), but also created by parents (through, for example, their engagement with other parents and in response to the normalising judgments of other community members).

At the same time participation in knowledge claims about their children can bring with it incorporation, framing the child and the disability, within a particular register, which can contribute to fixing particular expectations about the child and the parents that are regulative. For example, as discussed across the analysis, parents develop medical knowledge and expertise to help with the care of their child and also to encourage professionals to treat them as legitimate partners in decision making. In the process they can also become participants in shaping the child via medical categories and validating normality as a better form of life. Parents are not necessarily unknowing about the forms of regulation that come with particular knowledge claims and expertise. In response they may move away from privileging categories of knowledge and expertise that bring with them disabling ways of thinking about disability. By, for example, turning away a portage worker because their approach to pushing therapy onto the parent (mother) and child does not provide a space for either to adapt the therapy to their own sense of what might work and be beneficial. Parents can become strategic in their use of officially sanctioned knowledge and expertise, while at other times drawing upon intimate forms of knowledge and expertise that encompass enabling values.

Categorising the child

Parents seek social and medical understandings of the child, in part because of what they make possible in terms of understanding, legitimacy, support and services. An accepted diagnosis brings with it medical and support resources that have the potential to help the child. It can also provide a socially recognised identity the child can invest in and, in this sense, is enabling as an entry point to social participation. This is particularly marked, as discussed in Chapter 4, when the disability is invisible and the child is misread as naughty or criminal, and the parent as bad or unfit. In such contexts parents talked of wanting something equivalent to the blue badge on a car (in the UK this allows disabled people to park in allocated spaces) in order for people to categorise their child correctly and for both of them to have unhindered access to the social sphere. While medical categories are prominent in shaping the child, they are not the only categories around the child, in broader participation in different settings other categories can appear that can be either enabling or regulative. For example, as we showed in Chapter 6, within support groups, the child may be just like everyone else and therefore not in the category of the other, while in a mainstream setting, depending on how the school approaches inclusion, they can either be categorised as just another child or as the disabled/disruptive child/other. What label the child falls under depends on context; reminding us of Braidotti's (1994) notion of nomadic subjectivity. Identities belong or are out of place depending on their location and both parents and children can be active in the development of the right identity for the right occasion.

Regulation appears through the encompassing scope such categories can have to define the child in particular ways. Medical categories can enforce the sense of lack and failure – for both child and parent – in the child's perceived inability to be normal. Psychological and medical therapies directed to get the child's development closer to normality help secure the importance of being normal to be able to participate in society. It emphasises that the child should adapt to the social requirements of a society ill-equipped to deal with disability, rather than looking at adapting society to the differences created by impairment. It is understandable, as discussed in chapters 4 and 8, in the context of such a society that parents participate in the regulative adaptation of their child, whether this is behavioural adaptation to be more 'acceptable', or physical therapies aimed at helping the child speak or walk. Parents recognise the social consequences of not being able to do these things. The implication though is the production of subjectivities fixed around a notion of cure and normality, hindering the ability to explore varied forms of subjectivity across different locations and interactions.

However, because parents identify the regulative potential of certain categories, they can resist, as well as adopt them. As discussed in Chapter 4, refusing to explain why a child behaves in a particular way, usually via a medical label, was a refrain from parents, often mothers, when faced with social disapproval of their child. Instead in such contexts, as explored within Chapter 6, parents challenged the scope of the social sphere to demand explanation. Rather than legitimise their child and themselves as good mothers via a medical category – he is not naughty, he is autistic – they at times challenge the social judgments embedded in the requirement for a category. For example, we saw parents in chapters 4, 6 and 8, challenge the right of strangers to caste judgment on them or their child. Such processes involve the child's own developing sense of self. Creating a distance from regulatory categories provides an enabling space within which we have seen children explore their own sense of self, adopting and choosing categories and labels for themselves, encompassing disability and potential. The work they and their parents do, in a context of medical and social categories that seek to fix identity, takes courage and energy.

Parental identities

As suggested above, categorisations of the child often have embedded within them categorisations of the parents. Parental identities are not unchanged by the experience of raising a disabled child; parents seek to develop new identities outside existing scripts of parenthood. As discussed in Chapter 8, gender, alongside other factors such as age, race and ethnicity, disability and class, are vital in the shaping of identities in terms of what appear as the most available (socially recognised) (Finch, 1989; Lawler, 2000; Skeggs, 1997). In Chapter 5 we saw how new positive articulations of identity are made possible via the roles parents take on, the expertise they develop and the relationships they form. Parents talked of incorporating various new aspects of identity in who they are. New aspects included activist, ally to disability politics, expert care worker, institutional negotiator as well as others. Such identities are not just forms of psychological coping, they are products of the possibility of imagining a life that encompasses disability and is still valuable. They are also part of the active, dynamic and sometimes uncertain labours of parenting.

At the same time, framing identity around particular identities brings with it forms of regulation that limit the possibilities for what kind of identity is socially legitimate for a parent of a disabled child to have. For example, certain identities are useful to the services around families, providing either a basis on which to demonise parents (the fighter parent as the problem parent) or celebrate them (the well presented/middle-class parent as the appropriate parent). In addition, due to the significance of categories such as gender or class in the framing of such identities, particular identities are only available to some. For example, gender notions of who is the family carer can make it difficult for men to articulate a caring identity and, when they do, to have this recognised by others. In our study, fathers actively involved in the care of their children, all noted the inability of others to recognise the role they played and the identity they had taken on. Nevertheless, parents become astute at reading what are the appropriate identities for particular contexts and interactions, for example performing as the well-dressed mother, including suit and smart bag, in order that others might listen to them.

Parent groups offer possibilities for both enabling and regulative parental identities. As noted in Chapter 6 these groups are complex in terms of their ideologies, visions and values. In one way they offer a space where parents can have their identities easily recognised by others. However, such groups can contain their own forms of policing identity through the need to echo the dominant identities available within that group. For example, some groups may advocate the notion of the parent as therapist geared towards medical priorities around cure and overcoming disability, which some parents may find confining (Hughes, 2007). Or fathers may find themselves marginalised via the lack of recognition mothers in the group provide to their identity as caring fathers. When faced with such reactions, parents can become active in either developing parents groups within which their identity is recognised or challenging the patterns of identity regulation found in the groups they join.

Community

Identity is socially produced and acknowledged, among the community dynamics and spaces families move within. In Chapter 6 we saw how community dynamics can be regulative for families; everyday trips to the supermarket, the park or the leisure centre can become opportunities for families to experience intolerance and rejection. These patterns of exclusion can be replaced by new forms of community-enabling connection, some made via connections around disability, others not. Such community connections enhance family life by acknowledging the legitimate social space the families have a right to be participants in. Parents and children are active in creating new spaces, sometimes virtual, within which they bring together people around values of both commonality and difference. The alliances parents make are vital to them and their disabled children and provide an important challenge to the everyday realities of supermarkets and schools. It is important to stress that parents are not satisfied with simply receiving the tolerance of others. As well as challenging and attempting to educate community and familial members about disability and diversity, parents also demonstrate subtle and sophisticated ways of refashioning community contexts and relationships in ways that value their children and unsettle the normative.

Care practices

Parents, alongside others involved in the care dynamics from within informal and formal sectors, create care practices that envision enabling possibilities for them and their children. Such forms of support and interaction with the child contain values of respect and responsiveness. Enabling care also blurs the boundaries of the private and the public by containing practices that are about social engagement and activism. Becoming a school governor or appealing service decisions take the caring role into broader contexts and alliances where the marginalisation of disabled people is challenged. Not all parents would define themselves as political actors or join advocacy groups or maintain a static way of 'fighting' on behalf of their children, but few fail to develop different understandings of disability through their experiences of caring and interacting with their child. Such understandings filter into their surrounding social worlds and are part of developing enabling understandings of disability engaged in care and spread through the social body.

As discussed in Chapter 8, the contexts of care limit the possibilities of such caring practices and values, constraining and regulating their potential through a number of routes. First, when care is assumed to be a private act, on the part of individuals in families, there is a refusal to consider broader social responsibilities to be involved in caring relations. Second, the current contexts of support for carers within the welfare system encourages an audit culture around care, which seeks to minimise its meaning, where either the care provided by services or the care that parents or other informal carers provide is assumed to be focused on tasks that can be measured, quantified and costed. Third, the greater emphasis that is now being given to early interventions for young disabled children and the role parents (read mothers) are supposed to provide as surrogate therapists, channels care into the goals of normalisation via medical, therapeutic and psychological models of care. Finally, as implied throughout this discussion, the gendering of care is a major factor in the regulatory aspects of care, both in terms of how it directs care responsibilities towards mothers and also through how it leads to a lack of recognition for the role fathers may play within care.

This discussion shows how disability studies can be enhanced by exploring the experiences of parents who care for disabled children. Capturing the difficulties parents face in the refusal by others to care for them as well as their children identifies the social exclusion of people (parents and children) who experience disability. Highlighting the processes that confine women as the primary carers does not need to occur in a way that excludes those being cared for from the discussion. It is not to the benefit of disabled children to assume that the responsibility for care lies with the mother. Mothers, and at times fathers, are important political actors who challenge, through their care activities, the privatisation and marginalisation of care for disabled children. Exploring the transformations, which occur for them through the intensive caring relationships they have with their children allows for appreciation of the injustices embedded in societal and medical judgments about disability and the political importance of placing care within a rights model of inclusion and recognition for the family as a whole.

Throughout this discussion the phrase 'recognition' has appeared as an important element in both enablement and regulation. What this points to is the political significance of modes of recognition to the social place and rights of disabled children and it is to this we now turn.

Politics of recognition

Honneth (1996), along with others such as Fraser (1997, 2001), suggests that recognition is a central component of social justice. Citing Smith's (1976: pp. 869–70) notion that the individual subject develops by 'being able to appear in public without shame' (2004: p. 355), Honneth argues that questions of equality cannot be separated from the development of self, because that development is a socially embedded process. A good, modern, liberal society is one where growing numbers of its members are provided with both social recognition and the opportunity to develop as autonomous individuals. As the individual develops in this context, through the space afforded to them, they also recognise that 'rights and duties are reciprocally distributed' (2002: p. 501). They sign up to both rights and responsibilities because it provides for their individuality. This level of social accountability holds in check 'anti-social striving for independence' (2002: p. 504). This lies at the heart of Honneth's (1996) notion of struggles over recognition. The struggle is between individuals' efforts at self-realisation of their own unique identity, and the social benefits of those same individuals recognising others and mutual needs. Disputes over recognition emerge from a feeling that as individuals we have not had our uniqueness recognised or respected, that within existing modes of recognition there is a lack of space to 'recognize certain aspects of who one is' (2002: p. 504). Honneth, with a nod to Rawls (1993), argues that the 'just society' can be measured by 'the degree of its ability to secure conditions of mutual recognition in which personal identity formation, and hence individual self-realization, can proceed sufficiently well' (2004: p. 354).

How can this relate to disability? Disabled people have been one of the groups said to be the 'strangers' (Hughes, 2002) of both modernity and postmodernity. Disability politics and critical disability studies have spent much of the last 20 years demanding that disabled people be 'positively incorporated into the social body' (Rapp & Ginsburg, 2001: p. 535). Such work has produced greater appreciation of disabled people's lives and acknowledgement of discrimination; as a result there is now a stronger visible presence of disabled people in the public sphere

(Silvers et al., 1998). We have seen legislative change in the form of the Disability Rights Commission and the Disability Discrimination Act 1995 in Britain – with similar legislation in the US (Americans with Disabilities Act 1990) and other countries – and the filtering through of ideas and values of the disability movement into areas such as social work, health care and education. Disability is now part of citizenship and social justice debates; it is more difficult (although not impossible) to exclude disability from discussion in these areas (Silvers & Francis, 2005). In theory then such greater social recognition provides a context within which social validity helps the development of positive articulations of self and identity. Are disabled children living in a context where they receive social recognition? Such aspirations lie behind the inclusion agenda, particularly within education, and we did see examples of young disabled children being included within educational settings. We also saw the difference that made not just to them but to the lives of those around them in rethinking understandings of disability. We are reminded of Nick's final comments about his young daughter Katy quoted earlier in the book:

> I think Katy belongs to the world too. Because she's her own person, so she does belong out there in the world, and I think the world will be a horrible place without her.
>
> (Sarah and Nick, IV3)

In Katy's first years in primary school her parents found a context where the broader social community also expressed their view that she belonged in the world. Nevertheless at the same time we also saw families continue to struggle over social recognition, as they had to fight to have a space within society where they and their children could be recognised as legitimate subjects.

As political agents, parents continue to be, in alliances with others, key participants in recognition struggles within the public sphere that are far from over. While the public sphere may be developing messages of social recognition around disability, they are also sending out counter messages that continue within understandings of pathology, tragedy and stigma. Rapp and Ginsberg propose that this is because sitting alongside the successes of the disability movement and institutional recognition, sit other processes that continue the messages of discrimination, in particular 'neoeugenic technologies' (2001: p. 538). Prenatal and antenatal screening, whose scope continues to grow, provides a very different social message around disability, refuting assertions that a disabled life is a life worth living (Jennings, 2000). Levine picks up the same inconsistency when she comments that

> there is a conflict between the value of including all people in society's benefits, with whatever accommodations and expenditures are necessary to make that possible, and the disvalue generally placed on disability and dependence. In simplistic terms, it is a conflict between acceptance and avoidance, with a lot of ambiguity in between.
>
> (2005: p. 374)

Recognition thus remains a contested and troubling concept in relation to disability. This is because disability provides particular challenges to the current mechanisms through which recognition is made possible in society. Therefore, those, such as Honneth, who advocate recognition as a component of social justice, need to pay greater attention to the tools of recognition. In particular their ability to create what Brown (1993) suggests are 'wounded attachments'. Recognition implies certain levels of fixedness, where a group has certain needs and identities, which must be acknowledged for rights to be considered and equality obtained. When this happens recognition is an element in defining and securing difference in a way that does not allow for ambiguity, flexibility and reinvention. By acknowledging an identity, recognition defines it and closes off opportunities to articulate it different ways. The language of identity and recognition can become the 'language of unfreedom' (Brown, 1995: p. 66) within the categories used to mark them.

Categories of recognition

Disabled children appear stuck within contradictory social patterns of recognition, regulation, acknowledgement, judgment and categorisation. Acknowledgement of their impairment by parents, family, professionals and societal actors allows for certain rights to be provided. However, the acknowledgement also makes both family and child different. This difference is secured over time and place via the technologies that keep them alive or help them develop; through the identities people, including parents, confer on them; through the regulatory medical practices and treatments they are compelled to participate in; and through the segregated lives they lead, even in mainstream social settings. The apparently only other social option – for their disability not to be labelled – does not necessarily put them in a better position, as it leads to them being labelled in other ways: as naughty children with parents who cannot cope, or as welfare dependents who are claiming resources they have no right to. What is apparently inescapable is categorisation, the regulatory power of assertions of who the normal child is, what is required to produce and maintain that normal child and what rights and responsibilities are conferred on them.

A discussion of recognition needs to broaden out to consider the mechanisms through which it is signified: different forms and practices of recognition bring with them different consequences. Institutional forms of recognition bring with them the power to validate and invalidate different identities, values, ways of living and demands to redistribution. This raises vital questions about which forms of recognition claims are acknowledged, what methods and practices are used to construct categories of recognition, what new boundaries around normalising and normative identities do such responses create and how useful are they are in dealing with disputes over justice and material inequality.

Conditionality and recognition

Current tools of recognition within the state and society are not conducive to recognising disability in ways that offer emancipatory potential. One example, already discussed above, is the current articulations of what makes up the category of the good and productive family. Dreams of human perfection via genetics and reproductive technologies hold up visions of normality that can limit the scope for social recognition of those who do not fit such dreams (Asch, 1999; McLaughlin, 2003). Alongside creative work done by families with disabled children to envision a version of kinship where disability is present, are technologies such as amniocentesis which 'construct the limits of kinship' (Rapp & Ginsburg, 2001: p. 542). Therapeutic practices associated with seeking improved development have the potential to disallow recognition of other forms of development and quality of life. Within contemporary society, with advancing medical technologies and scientific imaginaries promising the ability to create the perfect, selected, designed child; with increasing surveillance of early development through early intervention; and with increasing scrutiny of the skills and expertise of parents, the categorisation and subsequent regulation of children is increasing. The dreams of the perfect family are connected to neoliberal constructions of personhood, which threaten the exclusion of disabled children and their families. As Rapp and Ginsberg argue (in the context of the US, but we would suggest equally valid here) there is work to be done to 'subvert the hegemonic discourse of perfectability disseminated by such sites as obstetric medicine, middle-class parenting literature and, more generally, contemporary U.S. models of personhood that valorize celebrity and individual will' (2001: p. 544). Parents in our study were involved in such subversive activities; one key example is through giving up on the norm – and therefore refusing the perfect child. We saw parents challenging communities to adopt more productive versions of their children which stand in opposition to the perfect family imagery produced via neoeugenics.

We are also seeing the increasing presence of categories of conditional entitlement. There is a conditionality built into screening, which seeks to establish who should and should not inhabit the world (Hubbard, 1997). In Britain, but echoed in other welfare states, welfare entitlements are increasingly framed as conditional (Dwyer, 2004). Conditionality requires practices of recognition in order for claimants to access resources, which previously would have been seen as automatic entitlements. Medical categories dominate in authorising 'entitled bodies' (Kelly, 2005: p. 197), creating yet more focus on and techniques for categorising disabled children and their families in order to qualify for resources and recognition. Children are recognised via categories which identify their failure to live up to certain social ideals of acceptable living and capability. Surveillance of acceptable family lives recognise some as fitting in and others as disruptive, with disability merging with other demonised categories such as criminality.

Such social shifts are problematic for disabled children. They increase the requirement for them and their parents to work to overcome their disability, or they will be judged as different, other and less than those defined as normal. Labels are what, in current society, one must have to access certain rights. In the process Brown's (1993) 'wounded attachments' are being produced, where the categories of recognition provide social stigma and identities that imprison the child (Gillman et al., 2000). Parents of disabled children want recognition of the needs and interests of their child. Their difficulty is that the modes of recognition dominant in contemporary society operate via medical and social categories of objectification, which are incapable of recognising children in complex and responsive ways. The Disability Living Allowance application form, as discussed in Chapter 7, provides no space to do anything other than catalogue inadequacy, fixing the child in the category of the disabled other to normal society. Welfare mechanisms for attributing rights demand a level of categorisation that strip the individual of broader aspects of who they are and what contexts inform their social position. Fault comes with the categories of contemporary identification, either as a welfare dependent (Fraser & Gordon, 1997) or as a disabled child unable to be the normal child. Access to rights and justice are contingent on spoiled categories of failure and lack. The challenge to governing recognition comes from the agency of children themselves, through their creative development of a productive, embodied, disabled self.

Recognition and dependency

Political conflicts over recognition point to different versions of what are acceptable lives, highlighting the role of recognition in the removal as well as the provision of rights. In trying to work through this, we find the limits to models of recognition that stress the needs of the autonomous individual. The liberal fascination with individual autonomy is in itself a factor in the creation of beliefs that the disabled self cannot be recognised as valuable, without shame. While disabled people are not recognised as full citizens, because they fail, or are believed to fail to live up to the vision of the fully autonomous individual, they continue to be seen as 'outside the range of human acceptability' (Landsman, 2003: p. 1950). In all of the liberal talk of autonomy, as various writers have highlighted, there is a discomfort with dependency:

> We admire the powerful wheelchair racer, the accomplished deaf drummer, the renowned paraplegic artist, the popular blind singer. They have disabilities, to be sure, but they have overcome them in ways that society values – by having an unusual talent, by being competitive and successful, and above all by being apparently independent.
>
> (Levine, 2005: p. 378)

Dependency is neglected in considerations of justice, when justice is framed as what is the right of the autonomous individual. In part this is because being dependent is seen as a signal of an inability to be a full citizen (a view held by Rawls (1985) for example), leading to others becoming the voice of those identified as such: whether children (disabled or not), the 'mentally ill' or the 'intellectually impaired'. Such judgments have led to the marginalisation of disabled people and others, as they have been seen as incapable of participating in society. Assumed to lack the abilities of the autonomous individual, they are also denied the rights of the individual. It is in this context that charities, state institutions and relatives have been able to make decisions on their behalf, which have contributed to their marginalisation and discrimination. The problem is that those who act on the behalf of disabled people do not always do so with knowledge of what is in their best interests:

> In their [disabled people's] absence from the conversation, terms inimical to them, or inconvenient or ineffective for them, may have seemed to other people to be compatible with justice.
>
> (Silvers & Francis, 2005: p. 47)

The disability movement has struggled, and in some areas been very successful, in dismissing such assumptions and implications, calling instead for recognition of the potential for disabled people to participate in society and decisions about their own lives. Much of this work, understandably due to the counter it provides, maintains the centrality of independence and autonomy (Morris, 1993b). Alternatively, by acknowledging relations of dependency and mutual obligation that are central to the human condition, it may be beneficial to bring dependency and justice together rather than separating them. Without this the resolution of dependency remains within the family, in particular the woman care provider. An injustice is maintained when care is seen as a value of the private domain, keeping hidden the connections of dependency, which allow the allegedly autonomous individual to function in the public sphere (Nelson, 2002). Levine, quotes Okin's (1989: p. 9) point that theories of justice 'take mature, independent human beings as the subject of their theories without any mention of how they got to be that way' (2005: p. 381). Caring is a social practice (Sevenhuijsen, 1998), which emerges from the 'reciprocal dependencies' (Fine & Glendinning, 2005: p. 616) inherent in the human condition and denied by false models of individuality and autonomy. Recognising dependence, also recognises interdependency. As has been discussed at various points in the book, there is no easy line to draw between those who are dependent and those who provide the solution to that dependency.

Recognising interdependency brings important dimensions to questions of justice. Honneth asserts that recognition is a matter of justice because social validation enables positive realisation of the self. If we adapt his position to argue that the self develops via caring relations of interdependence, then there is an obligation within the social to recognise, and more significantly incorporate, interdependency into our ties of citizenship and responsibility. It points to the broader social responsibility to participate in care practices with all kinds of people. Alongside formal concepts of justice, 'fair treatment for people with disabilities'

(Goering, 2002: p. 375), recognition of interdependency means that independence is not a precursor to being a citizen. There are ways in which disabled people can be independent and autonomous individuals, but like the rest of us and to varying degrees, there are a ways in which they may not. It is not enough to ask that the state ensures that all have a right to participate fully in the public sphere. What is needed instead is an appreciation that being fully independent is not a requirement to participate and take decisions about one's own life. Like a redistributive model of justice, it calls for the state to do more than not hamper the opportunities of the individual to be who they would want to be; it requires the just state provides support and material resources. It also broadens the responsibilities of good citizens to include participation in ties of caring interdependence. Care becomes, as Held proposes, a moral framework within which to realise justice:

> As a practice, empirically described, we can say that without care we cannot live at all. All human beings require a great deal of care in their early years, and most of us need and want caring relationships throughout our lives. As a value, care indicates what many practices ought to involve. When, for instance, necessities are provided without the relational human caring children need, children do not develop well, if at all. And when, in society, individuals treat each other with only the respect that justice requires, the social fabric of trust and concern can be missing or disappearing.
>
> (1995: p. 28)

In practice, this recognition of interdependency leads to a host of enabling and social just practices (Lister, 1997; MacKay, 1998; McKie et al., 2002). As one of us has argued elsewhere, in relation to education (Goodley, 2007b), socially just views of disabled children are drawn to the *interconnection of bodies* where we are no longer singularly embodied nor individually recognised. Instead, disabled children are viewed as emergent interconnected subjects, linked to a host of networks including professionals, family members and community settings. Professional, institutional and community settings can be reviewed to assess the extent to which they provide spaces for development of affirmative and productive relationships with disabled children and their families. This highlights the notion of distributed competence – where we no longer demand recognition of individual impairment, but ask more searching questions about the contributions of all those involved in the making of competent, and by definition, socially just contexts for disabled children.

Concluding thoughts

In this book we aimed to develop a critical disability studies analysis of parents, professionals and disabled babies that maintained an emphasis on the social, cultural and political foundations of disablism and united these with nuanced analyses of other transformative agendas including feminist critique and critical and community psychologies. In concluding our discussion with an emphasis on recognition and interdependence, we reposition the disabled family as a key site for the exposition of a whole host of practices including productive identity work, development of activism and alliance, the constitution of community, the foundations of responsive care practices, the maintenance of reflexive professional ethics and understandings of gendered elements of psychoemotional life. Parents of disabled children are not found to be lacking in the contribution they make to articulating the realities and struggles of these practices. In order to understand disabled children and their families, we must raise serious questions about the kinds of subjects that are valued by contemporary capitalistic, marketised, neoliberal and individualising societies. We must also be mindful of the ways in which our theoretical orientations and emphases might rely upon these values. As an alternative, a turn to the complexities of interdependency might provide us with more productive possibilities of working with parents and their disabled children, as they trouble the certainties of everyday life.

References

Abberley, P. (1987). The Concept of Oppression and the Development of a Social Theory of Disability. *Disability, Handicap and Society*, 2 (1), 5–21.

Abel, E. (1991). *Who Cares for the Elderly? Public Policy and the Experiences of Adult Daughters*. Philadelphia, PA: Temple University Press.

Ackroyd, S., Kirkpatrick, I., & Walker, R. M. (2007). Public Management Reform in the UK and Its Consequences for Professional Organization: A Comparative Analysis. *Public Administration*, 85 (1), 9–26.

Agamben, G. (1998). *Homo Sacer: Sovereign Power and Bare Life*. Stanford, CA: Stanford University Press.

Ainslie, D. C. (2002). Bioethics and the Problem of Pluralism. *Social Philosophy & Policy*, 19 (2), 1–28.

Albrecht, G., Seelman, K. D., & Bury, M. (2001). *Handbook of Disability Studies*. Thousand Oaks, CA: Sage.

Alcoff, L., & Potter, E. (Eds) (1992). *Feminist Epistemologies*. London: Routledge.

Allan, J. (1999). *Actively Seeking Inclusion: Pupils with Special Needs in Mainstream Schools*. London: Falmer Press.

Allen, C. (2004). Bourdieu's Habitus, Social Class and the Spatial Worlds of Visually Impaired Children. *Urban Studies*, 41 (3), 487–506.

Allen, I. (2000). Challenges to the Health Services: The Professions. *British Medical Journal*, 320, 1533–5.

Angrosino, M. V. (1994). On the Bus with Vonnie Lee: Explorations in Life History and Metaphor. *Journal of Contemporary Ethnography*, 23 (April), 14–28.

Armstrong, D. (2005). Reinventing 'Inclusion': New Labour and the Cultural Politics of Special Education. *Oxford Review of Education*, 31 (1), 135–51.

Armstrong, F. (2002). The Historical Development of Special Education: Humanitarian Rationality or 'Wild Profusion of Entangled Events'? *History of Education*, 31 (5), 437–56.

Artaraz, K. (2006). The Wrong Person for the Job? Professional Habitus and Working Cultures in Connexions. *Critical Social Policy*, 26 (4), 910–31.

Asch, A. (1999). Prenatal Diagnosis and Selective Abortion: A Challenge to Practice and Policy. *American Journal of Public Health*, 89 (11), 1649–57.

Atkinson, P., Coffey, A., Delamont, S., et al. (2001). *Handbook of Ethnography*. Thousand Oaks, CA: Sage.

Audit Commission. (2002). *Special Educational Needs: A Mainstream Issue*. London: Audit Commission.

Avery, D. (1999). Talking Tragedy-Identity Issues in the Parental Story of Disability. In Corker, M. & French, S. (Eds), *Disability Discourse*. Buckingham: Open University Press / Macmillan.

Avis, J., Bathmaker, A-M., & Parsons, J. (2002). Communities of Practice and the Construction of Learners in Post-Compulsory Education and Training. *Journal of Vocational Education & Training*, 54 (1), 27–50.

Azzopardi, A. (2005). Narratives of Inclusion. Unpublished Phd Thesis. Sheffield: University of Sheffield.

Baines, D. (2004). Caring for Nothing: Work Organization and Unwaged Labour in Social Services. *Work Employment and Society*, 18 (2), 267–95.

Baldwin, S., & Twigg, J. (1991). Women and Community Care: Reflections on a Debate. In Groves, D., & Maclean, M. (Eds), *Women's Issues in Social Policy*. London: Routledge.

Banks, A., & Banks, S. (Eds) (1998). *Fiction and Social Research: By Ice or Fire*. London: AltaMira Press.

Bannerji, H. (1995). *Thinking Through: Essays on Feminism, Marxism and Anti-Racism*. Toronto: Women's Press.

Barnes, C. (1990). *The Cabbage Syndrome: The Social Construction of Dependence*. London: Falmer Press.

Barnes, C. (1992). Institutional Discrimination and Disabled People and the Campaign for Anti-Discrimination Legislation. *Critical Social Policy*, 12 (Summer), 5–22.

Barnes, C. (1993). *Disabling Imagery & the Media: An Exploration of the Principles for Media Representations of Disabled People*. Halifax: Ryburn and The British Council of Organisations of Disabled People.

Barnes, C., & Mercer, G. (2003). *Disability*. Cambridge: Polity Press.

Barnes, C., & Mercer, G. (2005). Disability, Work, and Welfare: Challenging the Social Exclusion of Disabled People. *Work Employment and Society*, 19 (3), 527–45.

Barnes, C., & Mercer, G. (Eds) (1996). *Exploring the Divide: Illness and Disability*. Leeds: The Disability Press.

Barnes, C., & Mercer, G. (Eds) (1997). *Doing Disability Research*. Leeds: The Disability Press.

Barnes, C., Oliver, M., & Barton, L. (Eds) (2002). *Disability Studies Today*. Cambridge: Polity Press in association with Blackwell Publishers.

Barnes, M. (1999). Users as Citizens: Collective Action and the Local Governance of Welfare. *Social Policy & Administration*, 33 (1), 73–90.

Barrett, M. (1992). Words and Things: Materialism and Method in Contemporary Feminist Analysis. In Barrett, M. & Phillips, A. (Eds), *Destabilizing Theory: Contemporary Feminist Debates*. Cambridge: Polity Press.

Barron, J. D. (1999). *She's Had a Baby: And I'm Having a Meltdown*. Whitby: Quill Publishing.

Bartolo, P. A. (2002). Communicating a Diagnosis of Developmental Disability to Parents: Multiprofessional Negotiation Frameworks. *Child: Care, Health and Development*, 28 (1), 65–71.

Barton, L. (Ed.) (2001). *Disability Politics and the Struggle for Change*. London: David Fulton.

Baxter, J. (1992). Power, Attitudes and Time: The Domestic Division of Labour. *Journal of Comparative Family Studies*, 32 (2), 165–82.

Bayliss, P. (2006). Breaking Out: Intellectual Disability and Inclusion. Paper presented at The British Disability Studies Association 3rd Annual Conference. Lancaster University, Lancaster.

Begum, N. (1990). *The Burden of Gratitude*. Warwick: University of Warwick and SCA.

Begum, N. (1992). Disabled Women and the Feminist Agenda. *Feminist Review*, 40 (Spring), 70–84.

Bell, V. (1999). Performativity and Belonging: An Introduction. *Theory, Culture and Society*, 16 (2), 1–10.

Bell, V. (Ed.) (1999). *Performativity and Belonging*. London: Sage.

Beresford, B. (1994). Positively Parents: Caring for a Severely Disabled Child. London: HMSO.

Beresford, B. (1997). *Personal Accounts: Involving Disabled Children in Research*. London: HMSO.

Beresford, B., Clark, S., & Sloper, P. (2005). *Integrating Services for Disabled Children, Young People and Their Families: Consultation Project*. York: Social Policy Research Unit, University of York.

Beresford, B., Sloper, P., Baldwin, S., et al. (1996). *What Works in Services for Families with a Disabled Child*. Ilford: Barnardo's.

Berg, M. (1997). *Rationalizing Medical Work: Decision-Support Techniques and Medical Practices* Cambridge, MA: MIT Press.

Bertaux, D. (1981). *Biography and Society: The Life History Approach in the Social Sciences*. Beverley Hills, CA: Sage.

Birch, M., & Miller, T. (2000). Inviting Intimacy: The Interview as Therapeutic Opportunity. *International Journal of Social Research Methodology*, 3 (3), 189–202.

Birkett, D. (2000). There Was Nothing on My List About This.... In Murray, P. & Penman, J. (Eds), *Telling Our Stories: Reflections on Family Life in a Disabling World*. Sheffield: Parents with Attitude.

Blackburn, C., & Read, J. (2005). Using the Internet? The Experiences of Parents of Disabled Children. *Child: Care, Health and Development*, 31 (5), 507–15.

Bogdan, R., & Taylor, S. J. (1976). The Judged Not the Judges: An Insider's View of Mental Retardation. *American Psychologist*, 31, 47–52.

Bogdan, R., & Taylor, S. J. (1982). *Inside Out: The Social Meaning of Mental Retardation*. Toronto: University of Toronto Press.

Bookman, A., & Harrington, M. (2005). A Shadow Workforce in the Health Care Industry? Rethinking the Job of the Family Caregiver. Paper presented at The Community, work and Family: Change and Transition Conference. Manchester Metropolitan University, Manchester.

Booth, T., & Booth, W. (1994). *Parenting under Pressure: Mothers and Fathers with Learning Difficulties*. Buckingham: Open University Press.

Booth, T., & Booth, W. (1998). *Growing up with Parents Who Have Learning Difficulties*. London: Routledge.

Bourdieu, P. (1977). *Outline of a Theory of Practice*. Cambridge: Cambridge University Press.

Bourdieu, P. (1996). On the Family as a Realized Category. *Theory, Culture & Society*, 13 (3), 19–26.

Bowker, G. (1993). The Age of Biography is Upon Us. *Times Higher Education Supplement*, 8 January, 9.

Bowker, G., & Star, S. L. (1999). *Sorting Things Out: Classifications and Their Consequences (inside Technology)*. Cambridge, MA: MIT Press.

Boyte, H. C. (2005). Reframing Democracy: Governance, Civic Agency, and Politics. *Public Administration Review*, 65 (5), 536–46.

Braidotti, R. (1994). *Nomadic Subjects*. New York, N.Y.: Columbia University Press.

Braidotti, R. (2006). *Transpositions: On Nomadic Ethics*. Cambridge: Polity Press.

Brazier, M., Archard, D., Franck, L., et al. (2006). *Critical Care Decisions in Fetal and Neonatal Medicine: Ethical Issues. Nuffield Council on Bioethics Report*. London: Nuffield Council on Bioethics.

Brett, J. (2002). The Experience of Disability from the Perspective of Parents of Children with Profound Impairment: Is it Time for an Alternative Model of Disability. *Disability & Society*, 17 (7), 825–43.

Brinchmann, B. S. (1999). When the Home Becomes a Prison: Living with a Severely Disabled Child. *Nursing Ethics*, 6 (2), 137–43.

Bronfenbrenner, U. (1977). Toward an Experimental Ecology of Human Development. *American Psychology*, 32, 513–31.

Brown, A. P. (2004). Anti-Social Behaviour, Crime Control and Social Control. *The Howard Journal of Criminal Justice*, 43 (2), 203–11.

Brown, S. (1997). *The Life of Stress: Seeing and Saying Dysphoria*. University of Reading: Unpublished Phd Thesis.

Brown, W. (1993). Wounded Attachments. *Political Theory*, 21 (3), 390–410.

Brown, W. (1995). *States of Injury: Power and Freedom in Late Modernity*. Princeton, N.J: Princeton University Press.

Brownlie, J. (2001). The 'Being-Risky' Child: Governing Childhood and Sexual Risk. *Sociology*, 35 (2), 519–37.

Brownlow, C., & O'Dell, L. (2002). Ethical Issues for Qualitative Research in On-Line Communities. *Disability & Society*, 17 (6), 685–94.

Brownlow, C., & O'Dell, L. (2006). Constructing an Autistic Identity: As Voices Online. *Mental Retardation and Developmental Disabilities*, 44 (5), 315–21.

Bruner, J. S. (1986). *Actual Minds, Possible Worlds*. Cambridge, MA: Harvard University Press.

Bruner, J. S. (1990). *Acts of Meaning*. Cambridge, MA: Harvard University Press.

Bull, C., & Whelen, T. (2006). Parental Schemata in the Management of Children with Attention Deficit-Hyperactivity Disorder. *Qualitative Health Research*, 16 (5), 664–78.

Burchell, B., Fagen, C., O'Brien, C., et al. (2007). *Working Conditions in the EU: The Gender Perspective*. Dublin: European Foundation for the Improvement of Living and Working Conditions.

Burman, E. (2008). *Developments: Child, Image, Nation*. London: Routledge.

Burr, V. (2003). *Social Constructionism*. London: Psychology Press.

CAF (2003). *Relationships – No Time for Us*. Contact a Family: http://www.cafamily. org.uk/relationshipsurvey.html.

Campbell, J., & Oliver, M. (1996). *Disability Politics: Understanding Our Past, Changing Our Future*. London: Routledge.

Campbell, L. D., & Carroll, M. P. (2007). The Incomplete Revolution – Theorizing Gender when Studying Men Who Provide Care to Aging Parents. *Men and Masculinities*, 9 (4), 491–508.

Canam, C. (1993). Common Adaptive Tasks Facing Parents of Children with Chronic Conditions. *Journal of Advanced Nursing*, 18 (1), 46–53.

Carby, H. (1997). White Women Listen! Black Feminism and the Boundaries of Sisterhood. In Mirza, H. S. (Ed.), *Black British Feminism*. London: Routledge.

Carey, M. A. (1994). The Group Effect in Focus Groups: Planning, Implementing, and Interpreting Focus Group Research. In Morse, J. M. (Ed.), *Critical Issues in Qualitative Research Methods*. Thousand Oaks, CA: Sage.

Carpenter, B. (2002). Inside the portrait of a family: The importance of fathers. *Early Child Development and Care*, 172 (2), 195–202.

Case, S. (2000). Refocusing on the Parent: What are the Social Issues of Concern for Parents of Disabled Children? *Disability & Society*, 15 (2), 271–92.

Chamba, R., Ahmad, W., Hirst, M., et al. (1999). *On the Edge: Minority Ethnic Families Caring for a Severely Disabled Child*. Bristol: The Policy Press and Joseph Rowntree Foundation.

Chancer, L. S. (1998). *Reconcilable Differences*. Berkeley, CA: University of California Press.

Chappell, A. (1998). Still out in the Cold: People with Learning Difficulties and the Social Model of Disability. In Shakespeare, T. (Ed.), *The Disability Reader: Social Science Perspectives*. London: Cassell.

Charles-Jones, H., Latimer, J., & May, C. (2003). Transforming General Practice: The Redistribution of Medical Work in Primary Care. *Sociology of Health & Illness*, 25 (1), 71–92.

Charles, N. (2000). *Feminism, the State and Social Policy*. Basingstoke: Macmillan.

Chataika, T. (2007). Inclusion of Disabled Students in Higher Education in Zimbabwe: From Idealism to Reality – a Social Ecosystem Perspective. Unpublished Phd Thesis. Sheffield: The University of Sheffield.

Chevannes, M. (2002). Social Construction of the Managerialism of Needs Assessment by Health and Social Care Professionals. *Health and Social Care in the Community*, 10 (3), 168–78.

Clandinin, D. J., & Connelly, F. M. (1994). Personal Experience Methods. In Denzin, N. & Lincoln, Y. (Eds), *Handbook of Qualitative Research*. Thousand Oaks, CA: Sage.

Clavering, E. K. (2007). Enabling Carers to Care: Processes of Exclusion and Support for Parents of Young Disabled Children. *Benefits: Journal of Poverty and Social Justice*, 15 (1), 33–44.

Clavering, E. K., & McLaughlin, J. (2007a). Community Practices: Community Support for and Withdrawal from Families with Disabled Children. Paper presented at the ESA Conference. Glasgow University, Glasgow.

Clavering, E. K., & McLaughlin, J. (2007b). Crossing Multidisciplinary Divides: Exploring Professional Hierarchies and Boundaries in Focus Groups. *Qualitative Health Research*, 17 (3), 400–10.

Clough, P. (2002). *Narratives and Fictions in Educational Research*. Buckingham: Open University Press.

Coffey, A. (1999). *The Ethnographic Self: Fieldwork and the Representation of Identity*. London: Sage.

Cole, B. A. (2004). *Mother-Teachers: Insights into Inclusion*. London: David Fulton.

Cole, B. A. (2005). 'Good Faith and Effort?' Perspectives on Educational Inclusion. *Disability & Society*, 20 (3), 331–44.

Colebrook, C. S. (2006). *Deleuze: A Guide for the Perplexed*. London: Continuum.

Connell, R. W. (1987). *Gender and Power*. Cambridge: Polity Press.

Connors, C., & Stalker, K. (2003). Children's Experiences of Disability: A Positive Outlook. Paper presented at The Disabilities Studies: Theory, Policy and Practice Conference. Lancaster University, Lancaster.

Conrad, P., & Potter, D. (2000). From Hyperactive Children to ADHD Adults: Observations on the Expansion of Medical Categories. *Social Problems*, 47 (4), 559–82.

Crompton, R. (1990). Professions in the Current Context. *Work, Employment and Society*, 3/2, 147–66.

Crow, L. (1996). Including All of Our Lives: Renewing the Social Model of Disability. In Barnes, C. & Mercer, G. (Eds), *Exploring the Divide*. Leeds: The Disability Press.

Cunningham, A. (2000). Where Have All the Activists Gone? *Greater Manchester Coalition of Disabled People*, Coalition, 8–12.

Cunningham, C. C. (1994). Telling Parents Their Child Has a Disability. In Mittler, P. & Mittler, H. (Eds), *Innovations in Family Support for People with Learning Disabilities*. Whittle-le-Woods: Lisieux Hall.

Cunningham, C. C., Morgan, P. A., & McGucken, R. B. (1984). Down's Syndrome: Is Dissatisfaction with Disclosure of Diagnosis Inevitable? *Developmental Medicine and Child Neurology*, 26, 33–9.

Dale, N. (1996). *Working with Families of Children with Special Needs: Partnership and Practice*. London: Routledge.

Danermark, B., & Gellerstedt, L. C. (2004). Social Justice: Redistribution and Recognition - a Non-Reductionist Perspective on Disability. *Disability & Society*, 19 (4), 339–53.

Davies, S., & Hall, D. (2005). 'Contact a Family': Professionals and Parents in Partnership. *Archives of Disease in Childhood*, 90 (10), 1053–7.

Davis, A., Ellis, K., & Rummery, K. (1997). *Access to Assessment: Perspectives of Practitioners, Disabled People and Carers*. Bristol: The Policy Press.

Davis, J. M., & Watson, N. (2001). Where are the Children's Experiences? Analysing Social and Cultural Exclusion in 'Special' and 'Mainstream' Schools. *Disability & Society*, 16 (5), 671–87.

Dean, M. (1999). Hospitals and New Ways of Organisation of Medical Work in Europe: Standardisation of Medicine in the Public Sector and the Future of Medical Autonomy. In Thompson, P. & Warhurst, C. (Eds), *Workplaces of the Future*. Basingstoke: Macmillan.

Deeley, S. (2002). Professional Ideology and Learning Disability: An Analysis of Internal Conflict. *Disability & Society*, 17 (1), 19–33.

Deleuze, G., & Guattari, F. (1987/2004). *A Thousand Plateaus. Capitalism and Schizophrenia*. London: Continuum.

Department for Education and Skills (2003). *Every Child Matters*. London: The Stationery Office.

Department for Education and Skills (2004a). *Every Child Matters: Change for Children*. London: Stationery Office.

Department for Education and Skills (2004b). *Every Child Matters: Next Steps*. London: Stationery Office.

Dickinson, H. O., Parkinson, K. N., Ravens-Sieberer, U. et al. (2007). Self-Reported Quality of Life of 8–12-Year-Old Children with Cerebral Palsy: A Cross-Sectional European Study. *Lancet*, 369, 2171–8.

Dingwell, R., & Lewis, P. (Eds) (1983). *The Sociology of the Professions: Lawyers, Doctors and Others*. London: Macmillan.

Dixon-Woods, M. (2001). Writing Wrongs? An Analysis of Published Discourses About the Use of Patient Information Leaflets. *Social Science and Medicine*, 52, 1417–32.

Dobson, B., Middleton, S., & Beardsworth, A. (2001). The Impact of Childhood Disability on Family Life. York: YPS.

DOH (Department of Health) (1991). *The Patient's Charter*. London: HMSO.

DOH (1997). *New NHS: Modern, Dependable*. London: HMSO.

DOH (2000). *The NHS Plan: A Plan for Investment, a Plan for Reform*. London: Stationary Office.

DOH. (2004). *National Service Framework for Children, Young People and Maternity Services.* London: Stationery Office.

Douglas, S., & Michaels, M. C. (2004). *The Mommy Myth: The Idealization of Motherhood and How It Has Undermined Women.* New York: Free Press.

Dowling, M., & Dolan, L. (2001). Families with Children with Disabilities – Inequalities and the Social Model. *Disability & Society*, 16 (1), 21–35.

Dreidger, D. (1989). *The Last Civil Rights Movement.* London: Hurst.

Drewett, A. (1999). Social Rights and Disability: The Language of 'Rights' in Community Care Policies. *Disability & Society*, 14 (1), 115–28.

Duffy, K. G., & Wong, F. Y. (1997). *Community Psychology.* Boston, MA: Allyn Bacon.

Duncan, N. (2003). Awkward Customers? Parents and Provision for Special Educational Needs. *Disability & Society*, 18 (3), 341–56.

Dwyer, P. (2000). *Welfare Rights and Responsibilities: Contesting Social Citizenship.* Bristol: The Policy Press.

Dwyer, P. (2004). Creeping Conditionality in the UK: From Welfare Rights to Conditional Entitlements? *Canadian Journal of Sociology*, 29 (2), 265–87.

Dyer, B. (1996). *Seeming Parted.* Middlesex: New Millenium.

Edgerton, R. B. (1967). *The Cloak of Competence: Stigma in the Lives of the Mentally Retarded.* Berkeley, CA: University of California Press.

Edgerton, R. B. (1984). *Lives in Process: Mentally Retarded Adults in a Large City.* Washington, DC: Monograph #6 American Association on Mental Deficiency.

Education and Skills Select Committee (2005). *Every Child Matters: Ninth Report of Session 2004–05.* London: The Stationery Office.

Eiser, C., Mohay, H., & Morse, R. (2000). The Development of a Theoretically Driven Generic Measure of Quality of Life for Children Aged 6–12 Years: A Preliminary Report. *Child: Care, Health & Development*, 26 (6), 445–56.

Elllis, J. B., & Hirsch, J. K. (2000). Reasons for Living in Parents of Developmentally Delayed Children. *Research in Developmental Disabilities*, 21 (4), 323–7.

Evans, R. (2002). Ethnography of Teacher Training: Mantras for Those Constructed as 'Other'. *Disability & Society*, 17 (1), 35–48.

Every Disabled Child Matters. (2006). Off the Radar: How Local Authority Plans Fail Disabled Children. London: ECDM.

Farrell, C., & Morris, J. (2003). The 'Neo-Bureaucratic' State: Professionals, Managers and Professional Managers in Schools, General Practices and Social Work. *Organization*, 10 (1), 129–56.

Ferguson, P. M. (2001). Mapping the Family: Disability Studies and the Exploration of Parental Response to Disability. In Albrecht, G. L., et al. (Eds), *Handbook of Disability Studies.* Thousands Oaks, CA: Sage.

Ferguson, P. M., Ferguson, D. L., & Taylor, S. J. (Eds) (1992). *Interpreting Disability: A Qualitative Reader.* New York: Teachers College Press.

Ferlie, E., Ashburner, L., Fitzgerald, L., et al. (Eds) (1996). *The New Public Management in Action.* Oxford: Oxford University Press.

Finch, J. (1989). *Family Obligations and Social Change.* Cambridge: Polity Press.

Finch, J., & Groves, D. (Eds) (1983). *A Labor of Love: Women, Work and Caring.* London: Routledge & Kegan Paul.

Finch, J., & Mason, J. (1993). *Negotiating Family Responsibilities.* London: Routledge.

Fine, M., & Glendinning, C. (2005). Dependence, Independence or Inter-Dependence? Revisiting the Concepts of 'Care' and 'Dependency'. *Ageing & Society*, 25, 601–21.

Fisher, P., & Goodley, D. (2007). The Linear Medical Model of Disability: Mothers of Disabled Babies Resist with Counter-Narratives. *Sociology of Health & Illness*, 29 (1), 66–81.

Fitzgerald, L., Ferlie, E., & Hawkins, C. (2003). Innovation in Healthcare: How Does Credible Evidence Influence Professionals? *Health & Social Care in the Community*, 11 (3), 219–228.

Flanagan, A. (8 May 2006). Tarred with the Same Brush. *Guardian Unlimited*, http://www.guardian.co.uk/crime/article/0,1768759,00.html (accessed 29 December 2007).

Foster, P., & Wilding, P. (2000). Whither Welfare Professionalism? *Social Policy & Public Administration*, 34 (2), 143–59.

Foucault, M. (1982). The Subject and Power. In Dreyfus, H. & Rabinow, P. (Eds), *Michel Foucault: Beyond Structuralism and Hermeneutics*. Chicago, IL: University of Chicago Press.

Foucault, M. (1991). *Discipline and Punish*. New York, N.Y.: Vintage Books.

Fournier, V. (2000). Boundary Work and the (Un)Making of the Professions. In Malin, N. (Ed.), *Professionalism, Boundaries and the Workplace*. London: Routledge.

Frank, A. W. (1995). *The Wounded Storyteller: Body, Illness and Ethics*. Chicago, IL: University of Chicago Press.

Fraser, N. (1989). *Unruly Practices: Power, Discourse, and Gender in Contemporary Social Theory*. Minneapolis, MN: University of Minnesota.

Fraser, N. (1997). *Justice Interruptus: Critical Reflections on the 'Postsocialist' Condition*. London: Routledge.

Fraser, N. (2001). Recognition without Ethics? *Theory Culture & Society*, 18 (2–3), 21–42.

Fraser, N., & Gordon, L. (1997). A Genealogy of 'Dependency': Tracing a Keyword of the U.S. Welfare State. In Fraser, N. (Ed.), *Justice Interruptus*. London: Routledge.

Freidson, E. (1994). *Professionalism Reborn*. Cambridge: Polity Press.

Freidson, E. (2001). *Professionalism: The Third Logic*. Chicago, IL: University of Chicago Press.

Freire, P. (1972). *Pedagogy of the Oppressed*. Harmondsworth: Penguin.

Freire, P. (1998). *Pedagogy of the Heart*. New York, N.Y.: Continuum.

French, S. (1993). 'Can You See the Rainbow?' The Roots of Denial. In Swain, J., Finkelstein, V., French, S., et al. (Eds), *Disabling Barriers – Enabling Environments*. London: Sage.

Freund, P. (2001). Bodies, Disability and Spaces: The Social Model and Disabling Spatial Organisations. *Disability & Society*, 16 (5), 689–706.

Gabb, J. (2004). 'I Could Eat My Baby to Bits': Passion and Desire in Lesbian Mother-Children Love. *Gender, Place and Culture*, 11 (3), 399–415.

Gabb, J. (2005a). Lesbian M/Otherhood: Strategies of Familial-Linguistic Management in Lesbian Parent Families. *Sociology of Health & Illness*, 39 (4), 585–603.

Gabb, J. (2005b). Locating Lesbian Parent Families: Everyday Negotiations of Lesbian Motherhood in Britain. *Gender, Place and Culture*, 12 (4), 419–32.

Garland-Thomson, R. (2005). Feminist Disability Studies. *Signs*, 30 (2), 1557–87.

Germov, J. (2005). Managerialism in the Australian Public Health Sector: Towards the Hyper-Rationalisation of Professional Bureaucracies. *Sociology of Health & Illness*, 27 (6), 738–58.

Gilbert, T. P. (2005). Trust and Managerialism: Exploring Discourses of Care. *Journal of Advanced Nursing*, 52 (4), 454–63.

Giles, S. (2006). *You're the Daddy: From Nappy Mess to Happiness in One Year the Art of Being a Great Dad*. Great Ambrook: White Ladder Press Ltd.

Gillies, V. (2005). Raising the 'Meritocracy': Parenting and the Individualization of Social Class. *Sociology of Health & Illness*, 39 (5), 835–53.

Gilligan, C. (1987). Moral Orientation and Moral Development. In Kittay, E. F. & Meyers, D. T. (Eds), *Women and Moral Theory*. Savage, MD: Rowman and Littlefield Publishers, INC.

Gilligan, C. (1993). *In a Different Voice*. London: Harvard University Press.

Gillman, M., Heyman, B., & Swain, J. (2000). What's in a Name? The Implications of Diagnosis for People with Learning Difficulties and Their Family Carers. *Disability & Society*, 15 (3), 389–409.

Glendinning, C. (1992). *The Costs of Informal Care*. London: HMSO.

Glenn, E. N. (1992). From Servitude to Service Work: Historical Continuities in the Racial Division of Paid Reproductive Labour. *Signs*, 18 (1), 1–43.

Goering, S. (2002). Beyond the Medical Model? Disability, Formal Justice, and the Exception for the 'Profoundly Impaired'. *Kennedy Institute of Ethics Journal*, 12 (4), 373–88.

Goodland, R., & Riddell, S. (2005). Social Justice and Disabled People: Principles and Challenges. *Social Policy & Society*, 4 (1), 45–54.

Goodley, D. (1996). Tales of Hidden Lives: A Critical Examination of Life History Research with People Who Have Learning Difficulties. *Disability & Society*, 11 (3), 333–48.

Goodley, D. (1999). Disability Research and the 'Researcher Template': Reflections on Grounded Subjectivity in Ethnographic Research. *Qualitative Inquiry*, 5 (1), 24–46.

Goodley, D. (2000). *Self-Advocacy in the Lives of People with Learning Difficulties. The Politics of Resilience*. Buckingham: Open University Press.

Goodley, D. (2001). 'Learning Difficulties', the Social Model of Disability and Impairment: Challenging Epistemologies. *Disability & Society*, 16 (2), 207–31.

Goodley, D. (2007a). Becoming Rhizomatic Parents: Deleuze, Guattari and Disabled Babies. *Disability & Society*, 22 (2), 145–60.

Goodley, D. (2007b). Towards Socially Just Pedagogies: Deleuzoguattarian Critical Disability Studies. *International Journal of Inclusive Education*, 11 (3), 317–34.

Goodley, D. (forthcoming). *Critical Disability Studies: Expanding Debates and Interdisciplinary Engagements*. London: Sage.

Goodley, D., & Clough, P. (2004). Community Projects and Excluded Young People: Reflections on a Participatory Narrative Research Approach. *International Journal of Inclusive Education*, 8 (4), 331–51.

Goodley, D., & Lawthom, R. (2005a). Journeys in Emancipatory Disability Research: Alliances between Community Psychology and Disability Studies. *Disability & Society*, 20 (2), 135–51.

Goodley, D., & Lawthom, R. (2008). Disability Studies and Psychology: Emancipatory Opportunities. In Gabel, S. & Danforth, S. (Eds), *Disability Studies in Education: A Reader*. New York, N.Y.: Peter Lang.

Goodley, D., & Lawthom, R. (Eds) (2005b). *Disability and Psychology: Critical Introductions and Reflections*. Basingstoke: Palgrave Macmillan.

Goodley, D., Lawthom, R., Clough, P., et al. (2004). *Researching Life Stories. Method, Theory and Analyses in a Biographical Age*. London: Routledge Farmer.

Goodley, D., & Roets, G. (2008). The (Be)Comings and Goings of 'Developmental Disabilities': The Cultural Politics of 'Impairment'. *Discourse*, 29 (2), 239–55.

Goodley, D., & Tregaskis, C. (2006a). Parents of Disabled Babies: Retrospective Accounts of Disabled Family Life and Social Theories of Disability. *Qualitative Health Research*, 16 (4), 630–46.

Goodley, D., & Tregaskis, C. (2006b). Storying Disability and Impairment: Retrospective Accounts of Disabled Family Life. *Qualitative Health Research*, 16 (5), 630–46.

Gordon, T., Holland, J., & Lahelma, E. (2001). Ethnographic Research in Educational Settings. In Atkinson, P., Coffey, A., Delamont, S., et al. (Eds), *Handbook of Ethnography*. London: Sage.

Götlind, K. (2003). Dilemmas in Practice: Handling of Ambivalence in a Neonatal Intensive Care. Paper Presented at The 7th Annual Research Conference for the Nordic Network on Disability Research. Jyväskylä, Finland.

Gottlieb, R. S. (2002). The Tasks of Embodied Love: Moral Problems in Caring for Children with Disabilities. *Hypatia*, 17 (3), 225–36.

Graham, H. (1983). Caring: A Labor of Love. In Finch, J. & Groves, D. (Eds), *A Labor of Love: Women, Work and Caring*. London: Routledge & Kegan Paul.

Graham, H. (1993). Social Divisions in Caring. *Women's Studies International Forum*, 16 (5), 461–70.

Granic, I., & Lamey, A. V. (2000). The Self-Organization of the Internet and Changing Modes of Thought. *New Ideas in Psychology*, 18, 93–107.

Grant, G. (2005). Experience of Family Care. In Grant, G., et al. (Eds), *Learning Disability: A Life Cycle Approach to Valuing People*. Maidenhead: Open University Press.

Grant, G., & Whittell, B. (2001). Do Families and Care Managers Have a Similar View of Family Coping? *Journal of Learning Disabilities*, 5 (2), 111–20.

Gray, D. E. (2001). Accommodation, Resistance and Transcendence: Three Narratives of Autism. *Social Science & Medicine*, 53 (9), 1247–57.

Green, S. E. (2004). The Impact of Stigma on Maternal Attitudes toward Placement of Children with Disabilities in Residential Care Facilities. *Social Science & Medicine*, 59 (4), 799–812.

Gregory, M., & Holloway, M. (2005). Language and the Shaping of Social Work. *British Journal of Social Work*, 35 (1), 37–53.

Groenewegen, P. P. (2006). Trust and the Sociology of the Professions. *European Journal of Public Health*, 16 (1), 3–4.

Guter, B., & Killarky, J. R. (2004). *Queer Crips: Disabled Gay Men and Their Stories*. New York, N.Y.: Harrington Park Press.

Haimes, E. (2003). Embodied Spaces, Social Places and Bourdieu: Locating and Dislocating the Child in Family Relationships. *Body and Society*, 9 (1), 11–33.

Haimes, E. (2006). Social and Ethical Issues in the Use of Familial Searching in Forensic Investigations: Insights from Family and Kinship Studies. *Journal of Law Medicine & Ethics*, 34 (2), 263–76.

Hames, D. (1998). Do Younger Siblings of Learning Disabled Children See Them as Similar or Different? *Child: Care, Health and Development*, 24 (2), 157–62.

Hanlon, G. (1998). Professionalism as Enterprise: Service Class Politics and the Redefinition of Professionalism. *Sociology*, 32 (1), 43–63.

Hannam, C. (1988). *Parents and Mentally Handicapped Children*. Bristol: Bristol Classical Press.

Hansen, D. L., & Hansen, E. H. (2006). Caught in a Balancing Act: Parents' Dilemmas Regarding Their ADHD Child's Treatment with Stimulant Medication. *Qualitative Health Research*, 16 (9), 1267–85.

Hanson, S., & Pratt, G. (1995). *Gender, Work and Space*. London: Routledge.

Haraway, D. J. (1991). *Simians, Cyborgs and Women: The Reinvention of Nature*. New York, N.Y.: Routledge.

Harding, S. (1991). *Whose Science? Whose Knowledge*. Ithaca, N.Y.: Cornell University Press.

Harris, J. (1999). State Social Work and Social Citizenship in Britain: From Clientelism to Consumerism. *British Journal of Social Work*, 29 (6), 915–37.

Harris, S. (2007). *The Governance of Education: How Neo-Liberalism is Transforming Policy and Practice*. London: Continuum Press.

Hartsock, N. (1998). *'The Feminist Standpoint Revisited' And Other Essays*. Boulder, CO: Westview.

Hasler, F. (1993). Developments in the Disabled People's Movement. In Swain, J., et al. (Eds), *Disabling Barriers – Enabling Environments*. London: Sage.

Hays, S. (1996). *The Cultural Contradictions of Motherhood*. New Haven and London: Yale University Press.

Hebson, G., Grimshaw, D., & Marchington, M. (2003). PPPs and the Changing Public Sector Ethos: Case-Study Evidence from the Health and Local Authority Sectors. *Work Employment and Society*, 17 (3), 481–501.

Held, V. (1995). The Meshing of Care and Justice. *Hypatia*, 10 (2), 128–34.

Heller, K., Price, R., Reinharz, S., et al. (1984). *Psychology and Community Change*. Homewood, IL: Dorsey Press.

Hemmings, C. (1999). Out of Sight, out of Mind? Theorizing Femme Narrative. *Sexualities*, 2 (4), 451–64.

Hennessy, R. (2006). The Value of a Second Skin. In Richardson, D., et al. (Eds), *Intersections between Feminist and Queer Theory*. Basingstoke: Palgrave Macmillan.

Hevey, D. (1992). *The Creatures Time Forgot: Photography and Disability Imagery*. London: Routledge.

Heywood, C. (2001). *A History of Childhood: Children and Childhood in the West from Medieval to Modern Times*. Cambridge: Polity Press.

Hoggett, P., Mayo, M., & Miller, C. (2006). Private Passions, the Public Good and Public Service Reform. *Social Policy & Administration*, 40 (7), 758–73.

Honneth, A. (1996). *The Struggle for Recognition: The Moral Grammer of Social Conflict*. Cambridge: Polity Press.

Honneth, A. (2002). Grounding Recognition: A Rejoinder to Critical Questions. *Inquiry-an Interdisciplinary Journal of Philosophy*, 45 (4), 499–519.

Honneth, A. (2004). Recognition and Justice - Outline of a Plural Theory of Justice. *Acta Sociologica*, 47 (4), 351–64.

Hubbard, R. (1997). Abortion and Disability: Who Should and Who Should Not Inhabit the World? In Davis, L. J. (Ed.), *The Disability Studies Reader*. London: Routledge.

Hughes, B. (1999). The Constitution of Impairment: Modernity and the Aesthetic of Oppression. *Disability & Society*, 14 (2), 155–72.

Hughes, B. (2002). Bauman's Strangers: Impairment and the Invalidation of Disabled People in Modern and Post-Modern Cultures. *Disability & Society*, 17 (5), 571–84.

Hughes, B. (2007). Disability Activisms: Social Model Stalwarts and Biological Citizens. Paper Presented at The ESA Conference. Glasgow University, Glasgow.

Hughes, B., & Paterson, K. (1997). The Social Model of Disability and the Disappearing Body: Towards a Sociology of Impairment. *Disability & Society*, 12 (3), 325–40.

Hustedde, R., & King, B. (2002). Rituals: Emotions, Community Faith in Soul and the Messiness of Life. *Community Development Journal*, 37, 338–48.

Illich, I. (1977). *Disabling Professions*. London: Marion Boyars Publishers.

Imrie, R. (2000). Disabling Environments and the Geography of Access Policies and Practices. *Disability & Society*, 15 (1), 5–24.

Imrie, R. (2001). Barriered and Bounded Places and the Spatialities of Disability. *Urban Studies*, 38 (2), 231–7.

Jackson, S. (1999). Feminist Sociology and Sociological Feminism: Recovering the Social in Feminist Thought. *Sociological Research Online*, 4 (3), U337–U356.

Jackson, S. (2001). Why a Materialist Feminism Is (Still) Possible–and Necessary. *Women's Studies International Forum*, 24 (3–4), 283–93.

James, A. (1993). *Childhood Identities, Self and Social Relationships in the Experience of the Child*. Edinburgh: Edinburgh: University Press.

James, A., Jenks, C., & Prout, A. (1998). *Theorising Childhood*. Cambridge: Polity Press.

James, O. (2005). The Rise of Regulation of the Public Sector in the United Kingdom. *Sociologie Du Travail*, 47 (3), 323–39.

Jenks, C. (1996). *Childhood*. London: Routledge.

Jenks, E. B. (2005). Explaining Disability – Parents' Stories of Raising Children with Visual Impairments in a Sighted World. *Journal of Contemporary Ethnography*, 34 (2), 143–69.

Jennings, B. (2000). Technology and the Genetic Imaginary. In Parens, E. & Asch, A. (Eds), *Prenatal Testing and Disability Rights*. Washington, D.C.: Georgetown University Press.

Johnston, D. D., & Swanson, D. H. (2006). Constructing the 'Good Mother': The Experience of Mothering Ideologies by Work Status. *Sex Roles*, 54 (7–8), 509–19.

Jones, C. (1999). Social Work: Regulation and Managerialism. In Exworthy, M. & Halford, S. (Eds), *Professionals and the New Managerialism in the Public Sector*. Buckingham: Open University Press.

Jordan, B. (2001). Tough Love: Social Work, Social Exclusion and the Third Way. *British Journal of Social Work*, 31, 527–46.

Kagan, C. (2002). Making the Road by Walking it. Inaugural Professional Lecture. Manchester Metropolitan University.

Kagan, C., Lewis, S., & Heaton, P. (1998). *Caring to Work: Accounts of Working Parents of Disabled Children*. London: Family Policy Studies Centre in collaboration with the Joseph Rowntree Foundation.

Kagan, S. L. (1997). Support Systems for Children, Youths, Families, and Schools in Inner-City Situations. *Education and Urban Society*, 29 (3), 277–95.

Kälvemark, S., Hoglund, A. T., Hansson, M. G., et al. (2004). Living with Conflicts-Ethical Dilemmas and Moral Distress in the Health Care System. *Social Science & Medicine*, 58 (6), 1075–84.

Kearney, P. M., & Griffin, T. (2001). Between Joy and Sorrow: Being a Parent of a Child with Developmental Disability. *Journal of Advanced Nursing*, 34 (5), 582–92.

Keith, L., & Morris, J. (1995). Easy Targets: A Disability Rights Perspective on the 'Children as Carers' Debate. *Critical Social Policy*, 15 (2/3), 36–57.

Kelly, B. (2005). 'Chocolate ... Makes You Autism': Impairment, Disability and Childhood Identities. *Disability & Society*, 20 (3), 261–75.

Kelly, J. (2004). *The Pocket Idiot's Guide to Being a New Dad*. Indianapolis, IN: Alpha Books.

Kelly, S. E. (2005). 'A Different Light' – Examining Impairment through Parent Narratives of Childhood Disability. *Journal of Contemporary Ethnography*, 34 (2), 180–205.

Kenney, S. J. (1997). Politics and Feminist – Standpoint Theories–Introduction. *Women and Politics*, 3, 1–5.

Kitchin, R. (1998). 'Out of Place', Knowing One's Place: Space, Disabled People. *Disability & Society*, 13 (3), 343–56.

Kittay, E. F. (1999a). *Love's Labour: Essays on Women, Equality and Dependency*. New York, N.Y.: Routledge.

Kittay, E. F. (1999b). Not My Way, Sesha, Your Way Slowly: 'Maternal Thinking' in the Raising of a Child with Profound Intellectual Disabilities. In Hanisberg, J. & Ruddick, S. (Eds), *Mother Troubles: Rethinking Contemporary Maternal Dilemmas*. Boston, MA: Beacon Press.

Kittay, E. F. (2002). When Caring is Just and Justice is Caring: Justice and Mental Retardation. In Kittay, E. F. & Feder, E. K. (Eds), *The Subject of Care: Feminist Perspectives on Dependency*. Oxford: Rowan and Littlefield Publishers.

Kittay, E.F. (2006). Thoughts on the Desire for Normality. In Parens, E. (Ed.) *Surgically Shaping Children: Technology, Ethics and the Pursuit of Normality*. Baltimore: The John Hopkins University Press.

Kitzinger, J. (1994). The Methodology of Focus Groups: The Importance of Interaction between Research Participants. *Sociology of Health & Illness*, 16, 103–21.

Klasen, H., & Goodman, R. (2000). Parents and GPs at Cross-Purposes over Hyperactivity: A Qualitative Study of Possible Barriers to Treatment. *British Journal of General Practice*, 50, 199–202.

Koch, T. (2000). Life Quality vs the 'Quality of Life': Assumptions Underlying Prospective Quality of Life Instruments in Health Care Planning. *Social Science & Medicine*, 51 (3), 419–27.

Koffman, L. (2008). Holding Parents to Account: Tough on Children, Tough on the Causes of Children? *Journal of Law and Society*, 35 (1), 113–30.

Kondo, D. K. (1990). *Crafting Selves: Power, Gender, and Discourses of Identity in a Japanese Workplace*. London: University of Chicago Press.

Kremer, M. (2006). Consumers in Charge of Care: The Dutch Personal Budget and Its Impact on the Market, Professionals and the Family. *European Societies*, 8 (3), 385–401.

Kristiansen, K., & Traustadóttir, R. (Eds) (2004). *Gender and Disability Research in the Nordic Countries*. Lund: Studentlitteratur.

Laming, W. H. (2003). *The Victoria Climbié Inquiry: Report by Lord Laming*. London: Stationery Office.

Land, H. (1978). Who Cares for the Family? *Journal of Social Policy*, 3 (7), 357–84.

Landsdown, G. (2001). It's Our World Too! A Report on the Lives of Disabled Children. Disability Awareness in Action.

Landsman, G. (1999). Does God Give Special Kids to Special Parents: Personhood and the Child with Disabilities as Gift and as Giver. In Layne, L. L. (Ed.), *Transformative Motherhood: On Giving and Getting in a Consumer Culture*. New York and London: New York University Press.

Landsman, G. (2003). Emplotting Children's Lives: Developmental Delay vs. Disability. *Social Science & Medicine*, 56 (9), 1947–60.

Landsman, G. (2006). What Evidence, Whose Evidence?: Physical Therapy in New York State's Clinical Practice Guideline and in the Lives of Mothers of Disabled Children. *Social Science & Medicine*, 62 (11), 2670–80.

Larrabee, M. J. (Ed.) (1993). *An Ethic of Care: Feminist and Interdisciplinary Perspectives*. London: Routledge.

Larson, E. (1998). Reframing the Meaning of Disability to Families: The Embrace of Paradox. *Social Science & Medicine*, 47 (7), 865–75.

Latimer, J. (2007). Diagnosis, Dysmorphology, and the Family: Knowledge, Motility, Choice. *Medical Anthropology*, 26 (2), 97–138.

Latimer, J., Featherstone, K., Atkinson, P., et al. (2006). Rebirthing the Clinic – the Interaction of Clinical Judgment and Genetic Technology in the Production of Medical Science. *Science Technology & Human Values*, 31 (5), 599–630.

Lauritzen, P. (1989). A Feminist Ethic and the New Romanticism: Mothering as a Model of Moral Relations. *Hypatia*, 4 (2), 29–44.

Lave, J., & Wenger, E. (1991). *Situated Learning: Legitimate Peripheral Participation*. Cambridge: Cambridge University Press.

Law, I. (2007). *Self Research: The Intersections of Therapy and Research*. Manchester: Manchester Metropolitan Universiy, Unpublished Phd thesis.

Lawler, S. (2000). *Mothering the Self*. London: Routledge.

Lawthom, R., & Goodley, D. (2005). Community Psychology: Towards an Empowering Vision of Disability. *The Psychologist*, 18 (7), 423–5.

Lazarus, R. S., & Folkman, S. (1984). *Stress, Appraisal and Coping*. New York, N.Y.: Springer.

Ledwith, M. (2006). *Community Development: A Critical Approach*. Bristol: The Policy Press.

Le Grand, J. (2003). *Motivation, Agency and Public Policy*. Oxford: Oxford University Press.

Leiter, V. (2004). Dilemmas in sharing care: Maternal provision of professionally driven therapy for children with disabilities. *Social Science & Medicine*, 58, 837–49.

Levine, C. (2005). Acceptance, Avoidance, and Ambiguity: Conflicting Social Values About Childhood Disability. *Kennedy Institute of Ethics Journal*, 15 (4), 371–83.

Levine, M., & Perkins, D. V. (1997). *Principles of Community Psychology: Perspectives and Applications*. Oxford: Oxford University Press.

Lewis, J. (2002). Gender and Welfare State Change. *European Societies*, 4 (4), 331–57.

Lewis, J. (2007). Gender, Ageing and the 'New Social Settlement' – the Importance of Developing a Holistic Approach to Care Policies. *Current Sociology*, 55 (2), 271–86.

Lewis, S., Kagan, C., & Heaton, P. (2000a). Dual-Earner Parents with Disabled Children – Family Patterns for Working and Caring. *Journal of Family Issues*, 21 (8), 1031–60.

Lewis, S., Kagan, C., & Heaton, P. (2000b). Managing Work – Family Diversity for Parents of Disabled Children–Beyond Policy to Practice and Partnership. *Personnel Review*, 29 (3), 417–30.

Lindblad, B. M., Holritz-Rasmussen, B., & Sandman, P. O. (2007). A Life Enriching Togetherness – Meanings of Informal Support when being a Parent of a Child with Disability. *Scandinavian Journal Of Caring science*, 21 (2), 238–46.

Lindemann, K. (2003). The Ethics of Receiving. *Theoretical Medicine*, 24, 501–9.

Lingard, B., Hayes, D., & Mills, M. (2003). Teachers and Productive Pedagogies: Conceptualising, Utilising. Pedagogy. *Culture and Society*, 11 (3), 399–424.

Linton, S. (1998). *Claiming Disability: Knowledge and Identity*. New York, N.Y.: New York University Press.

Lister, R. (1997). *Citizenship: Feminist Perspectives*. Basingstoke: Macmillan.

Lister, R. (1999). Citizenship and the Ethics of Care. *Policy and Politics*, 27 (2), 233–46.

Llewellyn, G. (1997). Parents with Intellectual Disability Learning to Parent: The Role of Informal Learning and Experience. *International Journal of Disability, Development and Education*, 44 (3), 243–61.

Lloyd, L. (2000). Caring About Carers: Only Half the Picture? *Critical Social Policy*, 20 (1), 136–50.

Lloyd, L. (2003). Caring Relationships: Beyond 'Carers' and 'Service Users'. In Stalker, K. (Ed.), *Reconceptualising Work and Carers: New Directions for Policy and Practice. Research Highlights in Social Work 43*. London: Jessica Kingsley.

Long, A. F., Grayson, L., & Boaz, A. (2006). Assessing the Quality of Knowledge in Social Care: Exploring the Potential of a Set of Generic Standards. *British Journal of Social Work*, 36 (2), 207–26.

Longman, P., & Umansky, L. (Eds) (2001). *The New Disability History: American Perspectives (History of Disability)*. New York, N.Y.: New York University Press.

Lundeby, H., & Tøssebro, J. (2003). Struggle and Satisfaction: Parents' Experiences with Services for Families with Disabled Children. Paper presented at the 7th annual research conference for the Nordic network on Disability Research. Jyväskylä, Finland.

Lupton, D., & Barclay, L. (1997). *Constructing Fatherhood: Discourses and Experiences*. London: Sage.

Lynn, M. (2006). Race, Culture and the Education of African Americans. *Educational Theory*, 56 (1), 107–19.

MacDonald, K. (1995). *The Sociology of the Professions*. London: Routledge.

MacDonald, K., & Ritzer, G. (1988). The Sociology of the Professions: Dead or Alive? *Work and Occupations*, 15 (3), 251–72.

MacKay, F. (1998). *Women Politicians and the Ethic of Care in Gender and Scottish Society: Politics, Policies and Participation*. Edinburgh: Unit for the Study of Government in Scotland, University of Edinburgh.

Mallett, R. (2006). A Review of Contemporary Legislation and Policy Related to Disabled Babies, Children, Their Families and Associated Professionals, Practitioners and Supporters. Sheffield: University of Sheffield.

Mann, S. A. (2000). The Scholarship of Difference: A Scholarship of Liberation? *Sociological Inquiry*, 70 (4), 475–98.

Marks, D. (1999). Dimensions of Oppression: Theorising the Embodied Subject. *Disability & Society*, 14 (5), 611–26.

Martin-Baró, I., Aron, A., & Corne, S. (1994). *Writings for a Liberation Psychology.* Cambridge, MA: Harvard University Press.

Mason, M. (1992). Internalised Oppression. In Rieser, R. & Mason, M. (Eds), *Disability Equality in the Classroom: A Human Rights Issue.* London: Disability Equality in Education.

Matarasso, F. (1977). *Use or Ornament. The Social Impact of Participation in the Arts.* Stroud: Comedia.

Mauldon, J. (1992). Children's Risks of Experiencing Divorce and Remarriage: Do Disabled Children Destabilise Marriages? *Population Studies,* 46 (2), 349–62.

Mauthner, N. S. (1998). 'It's a Woman's Cry for Help': A Relational Perspective on Postnatal Depression. *Feminism & Psychology,* 8 (3), 325–55.

McCarthy, J. R., Edwards, R., & Gillies, V. (2000). Moral Tales of the Child and the Adult: Narratives of Contemporary Family Lives under Changing Circumstances. *Sociology,* 34 (4), 785–803.

McConachie, H. R. (1995). Critique of Current Practices in Assessment of Children. In Zinkin, P. & McConachie, H. R. (Eds), *Disabled Children and Developing Countries.* London: MacKeith Press.

McConachie, H. R. (1999). Conceptual Frameworks of Evaluation of Multidisciplinary Services for Children with Disabilities. *Child: Care, Health and Development,* 25 (2), 101–13.

McConachie, H. R., Colver, A. F., Forsyth, R. J., et al. (2006). Participation of Disabled Children: How Should It Be Characterised and Measured? *Disability and Rehabilitation,* 28 (18), 1157–64.

McConnell, D., & Llewellyn, G. (1998). Parental Disability and the Threat of Child Removal. *Family Matters,* 51, 33–6.

McGrath, P. (2001). Findings on the Impact of Treatment for Childhood Acute Lymphoblastic Leukemia on Family Relationships. *Child and Family Social Work,* 6, 229–37.

McKeever, P., & Miller, K. L. (2004). Mothering Children Who have Disabilities: A Bourdieusian Interpretation of Maternal Practices. *Social Science & Medicine,* 59 (6), 1177–91.

McKie, L., Gregory, S., & Bowlby, S. (2002). Shadow Times: The Temporal and Spatial Frameworks and Experiences of Caring and Working. *Sociology,* 36 (4), 897–924.

McLaughlin, J. (2003). Screening Networks: Shared Agendas in Feminist and Disability Movement Challenges to Antenatal Screening and Abortion. *Disability & Society,* 18 (3), 297–310.

McLaughlin, J. (2004). Professional Translations of Evidence Based Medicine. In Harding, N. & Learmonth, M. (Eds), *Unmasking Health Management: A Critical Text.* New York, N.Y.: Nova Science Publishers Ltd.

McLaughlin, J. (2005). Exploring Diagnostic Processes: Social Science Perspectives. *Archives of Diseases in Childhood,* March (90), 284–7.

McLaughlin, J. (2006). Conceptualising Intensive Caring Activities: The Changing Lives of Families with Young Disabled Children. *Sociological Research Online,* 11 (1).

McLaughlin, J., & Goodley, D. (2008). Seeking and Rejecting Certainty: Exposing the Sophisticated Lifeworlds of Parents of Disabled Babies. *Sociology,* 42 (2), 317–35.

McLaughlin, J., & Webster, A. (1998). Rationalising Knowledge: IT Systems, Professional Identities and Power. *Sociological Review,* 46 (4), 781–802.

McLaughlin, K., Osborne, S. P., & Ferlie, E. (Eds) (2002). *New Public Management: Current Trends and Future Prospects*. London: Routledge.

McRuer, R. (2002). Critical Investments: Aids, Christopher Reeve and Queer/ Disability Studies. *Journal of Medical Humanities*, 23 (3/4), 221–37.

Merleau-Ponty, M. (1962). *Phenomenology of Perception*. New York, N.Y.: Humanities Press.

Middleton, L. (1992). *Children First: Working with Children and Disability*. Birmingham: Venture Press.

Middleton, L. (1998). Services for Disabled Children: Integrating the Perspective of Social. *Child and Family Social Work*, 3, 239–46.

Middleton, L. (1999a). *Disabled Children: Challenging Social Exclusion*. Oxford: Blackwell.

Middleton, L. (1999b). The Social Exclusion of Disabled Children: The Role of the Voluntary Sector in the Contract Culture. *Disability & Society*, 14 (1), 129–39.

Molloy, H., & Vasil, L. (2002). The Social Construction of Asperger Syndrome: The Pathologising of Difference? *Disability & Society*, 17 (6), 659–69.

Mooney, A., Statham, J., & Simon, A. (2002). *The Pivot Generation: Informal Care and Work after 50*. London: The Policy Press.

Moons, P., Budts, W., & De Geest, S. (2006). Critique on the Conceptualisation of Quality of Life: A Review and Evaluation of Different Conceptual Approaches. *International Journal of Nursing Studies*, 43 (7), 891–901.

Morris, J. (1993a). Feminism and Disability. *Feminist Review*, 43 (Spring), 57–70.

Morris, J. (1993b). *Independent Lives*. Basingstoke: Macmillan.

Morris, J. (Ed.) (1996). *Encounters with Strangers: Feminism and Disability*. London: The Women's Press.

Murray, P. (2000). Disabled Children, Parents and Professionals: Partnership on Whose Terms? *Disability & Society*, 15 (4), 683–98.

Murray, P. (2003). Reflections on Living with Illness, Impairment and Death. *Disability & Society*, 18 (4), 523–6.

Murray, P., & Penman, J. S. (Eds) (1996). *Let Our Children Be: A Collection of Stories*. Sheffield: Parents with Attitude.

Murray, P., & Penman, J. S. (Eds) (2000). *Telling Our Own Stories: Reflections on Family Life in a Disabling World*. Sheffield: Parents with Attitude.

Nelson, G., & Prilleltensky, I. (Eds) (2004). *Community Psychology: In Pursuit of Liberation and Well-Being*. New York, N.Y.: Palgrave Macmillan.

Nelson, J. L. (2002). Just Expectations: Family Caregivers, Practical Identities and Social Justice in the Provision of Healthcare. In Rhodes, R., Battin, M. P., & Silvers, A. (Eds), *Medicine and Justice: Essays on the Distribution of Health Care*. New York: Oxford University Press.

Newman, J., & Nutley, S. (2003). Transforming the Probation Service: 'What Works', Organisational Change and Professional Identity. *Policy and Politics*, 31 (4), 547–63.

Newman, J., & Vidler, E. (2006). Discriminating Customers, Responsible Patients, Empowered Users: Consumerism and the Modernisation of Health Care. *Journal of Social Policy*, 35 (2), 193–209.

Nightingale, D. J., & Cromby, J. (Eds) (1999). *Social Constructionist Psychology: A Critical Analysis of Theory and Practice*. Buckingham: Open University Press.

Nikander, P. (1995). The Turn to the Text: The Critical Potential of Discursive Social Psychology. *Nordiske Upkast*, 2, 3–15.

Noddings, N. (1984). *Caring: A Feminine Approach to Ethics and Moral Education*. Berkley, CA: University of California Press.

Nussbaum, M. (1986). *The Fragility of Goodness: Luck and Ethics in Greek Tragedy and Philosophy*. Cambridge: Cambridge University Press.

O'Brien, M. (2007). Mothers' Emotional Care Work in Education and its Moral Imperative. *Gender and Education*, 19 (2), 159–77.

O'Connor, S. (1995a). More than what they Bargained For: The Meaning of Support to Families. In Taylor, S. J., et al. (Eds), *The Variety of Community Experience: Qualitative Studies of Family and Community Life*. Baltimore, MD: Paul H. Brookes Publishing Co.

O'Connor, S. (1995b). 'We're All One Family': The Positive Construction of People with Disabilities by Family Members. In Taylor, S. J., et al. (Eds), *The Variety of Community Experience: Qualitative Studies of Family and Community Life* Baltimore, MD: Paul H. Brookes Publishing Co.

Okin, S. M. (1989). *Justice, Gender and the Family*. New York, N.Y.: Basic Books.

Oldenburg, R. (1999). *The Great Good Place*. New York, N.Y.: Paragon House.

Oliver, M. (1990). *The Politics of Disablement*. Basingstoke: Macmillan.

Oliver, M. (1996). *Understanding Disability*. Basingstoke: Macmillan.

Oliver, M., & Barnes, C. (1998). *Disabled People and Social Policy: From Exclusion to Inclusion*. London: Longman.

Oliver, M., & Barnes, C. (2006). Disability Politics and the Disability Movement in Britain: Where did it All Go Wrong? *Coalition*, August, 8–13.

Oliver, M., & Sapey, B. (2006). *Social Work with Disabled People*. Basingstoke: Macmillan.

Ong-Dean, C. (2005). Reconsidering the Social Location of the Medical Model: An Examination of Disability in Parenting Literature. *Journal of Medical Humanities*, 26 (2–3), 141–58.

ONS (Office of National Statistics) (2007). *Unpaid Care: Cohabiting Couples Provide Less Unpaid Care*. London: Stationery Office.

Orford, J. (1992). *Community Psychology: Theory and Practice*. Chichester: John Wiley & Sons.

Orme, J. (2001). *Gender and Community Care*. Basingstoke: Palgrave Macmillan.

Orr, D. (2008). We Must Protect Disabled People against this Wave of Barbaric and Hateful Crimes. *The Independent*. http://www.independent.co.uk/opinion/commentators/deborah-orr/deborah-orr-we-must-protect-disabled-people-against-this-wave-of-barbaric-and-hateful-crimes-775617.html.

Overboe, J. (2007). Disability and Genetics: Affirming the Bare Life (the State of Exception). *Canadian Review of Sociological Anthropology*, 44 (2), 219–35.

Parker, I. (2002). *Critical Discursive Psychology*. London: Sage.

Parker, I., Georgaca, E., Harper, D., et al. (1995). *Deconstructing Psychopathology*. London: Sage.

Parker, T. (1963). *The Unknown Citizen*. London, Hutchinson.

Parker, T. (1990). *Life after Life: Interviews with Twelve Murderers*. London: Secker & Warburg.

Parker, T. (1994). Tony Parker – Writer and Oral Historian: Interviewed by Paul Thompson. *Oral History*, Autumn, 64–73.

Parliamentary Hearings on Services for Disabled Children (2006). *Parliamentary Hearings on Services for Disabled Children. Full Report*. London: Stationery Office.

Partington, K. (2002). Maternal Responses to the Diagnosis of Learning Disabilities in Children: A Qualitative Study Using a Focus Group Approach. *Journal of Learning Disabilities*, 6 (2), 163–73.

Pearson, C. (2000). Money Talks? Competing Discourses in the Implementation of Direct Payments. *Critical Social Policy*, 20 (4), 459–77.

Peim, N. (2001). The History of the Present: Towards a Contemporary Phenomenology of the School. *History of Education*, 30 (2), 177–90.

People First of Washington State and University of Oregon. (1984). Speaking Up and Speaking Out. A Report on the First International Self-Advocacy Leadership Conference. First International Self-advocacy Leadership Conference. Tacoma, Washington.

Perkins, H. J. (1989). *The Rise of the Professional Society: England since 1880*. London: Routledge.

Petratos, P. (2005). Does the Private Finance Initiative Promote Innovation in Health Care? The Case of the British National Health Service. *Journal of Medicine and Philosophy*, 30 (6), 627–42.

Phoenix, A. (1991). *Young Mothers?* Cambridge: Polity Press.

Phoenix, A., Woollet, A., & Llyod, E. (Eds) (1991). *Motherhood: Meanings, Practices and Ideologies*. London: Sage.

Pinder, R., Petchey, P., Shaw, S., et al. (2005). What's in a Care Pathway? Towards a Cultural Cartography of the New NHS. *Sociology of Health & Illness*, 27 (6), 759–79.

Place, B. (2000). Constructing the Bodies of Critically Ill Children: An Ethnography of Intensive Care. In Prout, A. (Ed.), *The Body, Childhood and Society*. Basingstoke: Palgrave Macmillan.

Plummer, K. (1983). *Documents of Life: An Introduction to the Problems and Literature of a Humanistic Method*. London: George Allen & Unwin.

Plummer, K. (1995). *Telling Sexual Stories: Power, Change and Social Worlds*. London: Routledge.

Pols, J. (2006). Accounting and Washing – Good Care in Long-term Psychiatry. *Science, Technology & Human Values*, 31 (4), 409–30.

Poltorak, M., Leach, M., Fairhead, J., et al. (2005). 'MMR Talk' and Vaccination Choices: An Ethnographic Study in Brighton. *Social Science & Medicine*, 61 (3), 709–19.

Preston, G. (2006). Families with Disabled Children, Benefits and Poverty. *Benefits: Journal of Poverty and Social Justice*, 14 (1), 39–43.

Pretty, G., Rapley, M., & Bramston, P. (2002). Neighbourhood and Community Experience, and the Quality of Life of Rural Adolescents with and without an Intellectual Disability. *Journal of Intellectual & Developmental Disability*, 27 (2), 106–16.

Priestley, M. (1999). *Disability Politics and Community Care*. London: Jessica Kingsley Publishers.

Priestley, M. (2000). Adults Only: Disability, Social Policy and the Life Course. *Journal of Social Policy*, 29, 421–39.

Priestley, M. (2003). *Disability: A Life Course Approach*. Cambridge: Polity Press.

Priestley, M. (Ed.) (2001). *Disability and the Life Course: Global Perspectives*. Cambridge: Cambridge University Press.

Prilleltensky, I., & Nelson, G. (2002). *Doing Psychology Critically: Making a Difference in Diverse Settings*. Basingstoke: Palgrave Macmillan.

Prussing, E., Sobo, E. J., Walker, E., et al. (2005). Between 'Desperation' and Disability Rights: A Narrative Analysis of Complementary/Alternative Medicine Use by Parents for Children with Down's Syndrome. *Social Science & Medicine*, 60 (3), 587–98.

Rahi, J. S., Manaras, I., Tuomainen, H., et al. (2004). Meeting the Needs of Parents around the Time of Diagnosis of Disability among Their Children: Evaluation of a Novel Program for Information, Support, and Liaison by Key Workers. *Pediatrics*, 114 (4), E477–E482.

Raines, M. L. (2000). Ethical Decision Making in Nurses Relationships among Moral Reasoning Coping Styles and Ethics Stress. *JONA's Healthcare Law, Ethics and Regulation*, 2 (1), 29–41.

Rapp, R., & Ginsburg, F. (2001). Enabling Disability: Rewriting Kinship, Reimagining Citizenship. *Public Culture*, 13 (3), 533–56.

Rappaport, J. (1977). *Community Psychology: Values, Research, and Action*. London: Holt, Rinehart and Winston.

Rawls, J. (1985). Justice as Fairness: Political Not Metaphysical. *Philosophy and Public Affairs*, 14, 233.

Rawls, J. (1993). *Political Liberalism*. New York, N.Y.: Columbia University Press.

Read, J. (1991). There Was Never Really Any Choice – the Experience of Mothers of Disabled Children in the United Kingdom. *Women's Studies International Forum*, 14 (6), 561–71.

Read, J. (2000). *Disability, the Family and Society: Listening to Mothers*. Buckingham: Open University Press.

Read, J. (2002). Will the Carers and Disabled Children Act 2000 Make a Difference to the Lives of Disabled Children and Their Carers? *Child: Care, Health and Development*, 28 (4), 273–5.

Read, J., & Clements, L. (2004a). Demonstrably Awful: The Right to Life and the Selective Non-Treatment of Disabled Babies and Young Children. *Journal of Law and Society*, 31 (4), 482–509.

Read, J., & Clements, L. (2004b). *Disabled Children and the Law*. London: Jessica Kingsley Publishers.

Reason, P., & Heron, J. (1995). Co-Operative Inquiry. In Harré, R., et al. (Eds), *Rethinking Methods in Psychology*. London: Sage.

Reed, M. I. (1996). Expert Power and Control in Late Modernity: An Empirical Review and Theoretical Synthesis. *Organization Studies*, 17 (4), 573–97.

Reeve, D. (2002). Negotiating Psycho-Emotional Dimensions of Disability and Their Influence on Identity Constructions. *Disability & Society*, 17 (5), 493–508.

Reeve, D. (2005). Towards a Psychology of Disability: The Emotional Effects of Living in a Disabling Society. In Goodley, D. & Lawthom, R. (Eds), *Disability and Psychology: Critical Introductions and Reflections*. Basingstoke: Palgrave Macmillan.

Reeve, D. (2007). Homo Sacer and Zones of Exception: Metaphors for the Contemporary Experience of Disablism? Paper presented at The Nordic Network of Disability Research. Stockholm.

Rehm, R. S., & Bradley, J. F. (2005). Normalization in Families Raising a Child Who Is Medically Fragile/Technology Dependent and Developmentally Delayed. *Qualitative Health Research*, 15 (6), 807–20.

Reindal, S. M. (1999). Independence, Dependence, Interdependence: Some Reflections on the Subject and Personal Autonomy. *Disability & Society*, 14 (3), 353–67.

Riddell, S., & Watson, N. (2003). *Disability, Culture and Identity*. London: Pearson Education.

Rigazio-DiGilio, S. A. (2000). Relational Diagnosis: A Coconstructive-Developmental Perspective on Assessment and Treatment. *Journal of Clinical Psychology*, 56 (8), 1017–36.

Riley, D. (1988). *'Am I That Name?': Feminism and the Category of 'Women' in History*. Basingstoke: Macmillan.

Robins, C. S. (2001). Generating Revenues: Fiscal Changes in Public Mental Health Care and the Emergence of Moral Conflicts among Care-Givers. *Culture, Medicine and Psychiatry*, 25 (4), 457–66.

Roets, G. (2008). Connecting Activism with Academia: A Postmodernist Feminist Perspective in Disability Studies. *Orthopedagogische Reeks Gent*, 30.

Rose, N. (1979). The Psychological Complex: Mental Measurement and Social Administration. *Ideology & Consciousness*, 5, 5–68.

Rose, N. (1985). *The Psychological Complex: Psychology, Politics and Society in England 1869–1939*. London: Routledge and Kegan Paul.

Rose, N. (1989). *Governing the Soul: The Shaping of the Private Self*. London: Routledge.

Rose, N. (1999). *Powers of Freedom: Reframing Political Thought*. Cambridge: Cambridge University Press.

Rowbotham, S. (1973). *Hidden from History. 300 Years of Women's Oppression and the Fight against It*. London: Pluto Press.

Ruddick, S. (1984). *Of Woman Born*. New York, N.Y.: Norton.

Rummery, K., & Glendinning, C. (1999). Negotiating Needs, Access and Gate Keeping Developments in Health and Community Care Policies in the UK and the Right of Disabled and Older Citizens. *Critical Social Policy*, 19 (3), 335–51.

Runswick Cole, K. (2007). 'The Tribunal Was the Most Stressful Thing: More Stressful Than My Son's Diagnosis or Behaviour': The Experiences of Families Who Go to the Special Educational Needs and Disability Tribunal (Sendist). *Disability & Society*, 22 (3), 315–28.

Russell, P. (2003). Access and Achievement or Social Exclusion?: Are the Government's Policies Working for Disabled Children and Their Families? *Children and Society*, 17, 215–25.

Ryan, S. & Runswick Cole, K. (2008). Repositioning Mothers: Mothers, Disabled Children and Disability Studies. *Disability & Society*. 23 (3): 199–210.

Ryan, S. (2005a). Busy Behaviour in the Land of the Golden M: Going out with Learning Disabled Children in Public Places. *Journal of Applied Research in Intellectual Disabilities*, 18 (1), 65–74.

Ryan, S. (2005b). People Don't Do Odd, Do They? Mothers Making Sense of the Reactions of Others to Their Learning Disabled Children in Public Places. *Children's Geographies*, 3 (3), 291–305.

Sapey, B., & Pearson, J. (2005). Do Disabled People Need Social Workers? *Social Work and Social Sciences Review*, 11(3), 52–70.

Sarason, S. B. (1974). *The Psychological Sense of Community: Prospects for a Community Psychology*. San Francisco, CA: Jossey-Bass.

Savage, M., Barlow, J., Dickens, P., et al. (1992). *Property, Bureaucracy, and Culture: Middle-Class Formation in Contemporary Britain*. London: Routledge.

Scandinavian Journal of Disability Research (2004). Special Issue. *Scandinavian Journal of Disability Research*, 16 (6).

Schutzman, M., & Cohen-Cruz, M. (Eds) (1997). *Playing Boal: Theatre, Therapy and Activism*. London: Routledge.

Sevenhuijsen, S. (1998). *Citizenship and the Ethics of Care*. London: Routledge.

Shah, S. (1995). *The Silent Minority: Children with Disabilities in Asian Families*. London: National Children's Bureau.

Shah, S. (2005). Choices and Voices: The Educational Experiences of Young Disabled People. Career Research and Development. *The NICEC Journal*, 12, 20–6.

Shah, S., Travers, C., & Arnold, J. (2004). Disabled and Successful: Education in the Life Stories of Disabled High Achievers. *Journal of Research in Special Educational Needs*, 4 (3), 122–32.

Shakespeare, T. (2000). *Help*. Birmingham: British Association of Social Workers.

Shakespeare, T. (2006). *Disability Rights and Wrongs*. London: Routledge.

Shakespeare, T. (Ed.) (1998). *The Disability Reader: Social Science Perspectives*. London: Cassell.

Shakespeare, T., & Watson, N. (2001). The Social Model of Disability: An Outdated Ideology? Exploring Theories and Expanding Methodologies. *Research in Social Science and Disability*, 2 (9–28).

Sharma, N. (2002). *Still Missing Out? Ending Poverty and Social Exclusion: Messages to Government from Families with Disabled Children*. Basildon, Essex: Barnardo's Publications.

Shaw, I. F., Arksey, H., & Mullender, A. (2006). Recognizing Social Work. *British Journal of Social Work*, 36 (2), 227–46.

Sheldon, A. (1999). Personal and Perplexing: Feminist Disability Politics Evaluated. *Disability & Society*, 14 (5), 643–58.

Shelton, N., & Johnson, S. (2006). 'I Think Motherhood for Me Was a Bit Like a Double-Edged Sword': The Narratives of Older Mothers. *Journal of Community and Applied Social Psychology*, 16 (4), 316–30.

Sherratt, N., & Hughes, G. (2002). Family: From Tradition to Diversity? In Hughes, G. & Ferguson, R. (Eds), *Ordering Lives: Family, and Welfare*. London: Routledge.

Sherry, M. (2004a). Overlaps and Contradictions between Queer Theory and Disability Studies. *Disability & Society*, 19 (7), 769–83.

Sherry, M. (2004b). (Post) Colonizing Disability. Paper presented to The American Sociological Association. Hilton San Francisco & Renaissance Parc 55 Hotel, San Francisco, CA: Aug 14.

Shildrick, M. (1997). *Leaky Bodies and Boundaries*. London: Routledge.

Siddiquee, A., & Kagan, C. (2006). The Internet, Empowerment, and Identity: An Exploration of Participation by Refugee Women in a Community Internet Project (CIP) in the United Kingdom (UK). *Journal of Community and Applied Social Psychology*, 16 (3), 189–206.

Silvers, A., & Francis, L. P. (2005). Justice through Trust: Disability and The 'Outlier Problem' in Social Contract Theory. *Ethics*, 116 (1), 40–76.

Silvers, A., Wasserman, D., & Mahowald, M. B. (1998). *Disability, Difference and Discrimination: Perspectives on Justice in Bopethics and Public Policy*. Oxford: Rowan and Littlefield Publishers.

Singh, I. (2004). Doing Their Jobs: Mothering with Ritalin in a Culture of Mother-Blame. *Social Science and Medicine*, 59, 1193–205.

Skeggs, B. (1997). *Formations of Class and Gender*. London: Sage.

Skrtic, T. (Ed.) (1995). *Disability & Democracy: Reconstructing (Special) Education for Postmodernity*. New York, N.Y.: Teachers College Press.

Sloper, P. (1999). Models of Service Support for Parents of Disabled Children. What Do We Know? What Do We Need to Know? *Child: Care, Health and Development*, 25 (2), 85–99.

Sloper, P. (2004). Facilitators and Barriers for Co-ordinated Multi-agency Services. *Child: Care, Health and Development*, 30 (6), 571–80.

Sloper, P., Greco, V., Beecham, J., et al. (2006). Key Worker Services for Disabled Children: What Characteristics of Services Lead to Better Outcomes for Children and Families? *Child: Care, Health and Development*, 32 (2), 147–57.

Sloper, P., & Lightfoot, J. (2003). Involving Disabled and Chronically Ill Children and Young People in Health Service Development. *Child: Care, Health and Development*, 29 (1), 15–20.

Sloper, P., & Turner, S. (1992). Service Needs of Families of Children with Severe Physical Disability. *Child: Care, Health and Development*, 18 (5), 259–82.

Smith, A. (1976). An Inquiry into the Nature and Causes of the Wealth of Nations. In Campbell, R. H., et al. (Eds), *Glasgow Edition of the Works and Correspondence of Adam Smith*. Oxford: Clarendon.

Smith, D. E. (1987). *The Everyday World as Problematic: A Feminist Sociology*. Milton Keynes: Open University Press.

Snell, S. A., & Rosen, K. H. (1997). Parents of Special Needs Children Mastering the Job of Parenting. *Contemporary Family Therapy*, 19 (3), 425–42.

Snow, D. A., Morrill, C., & Anderson, L. (2003). Elaborating Analytic Ethnography: Linking Fieldwork and Theory. *Ethnography*, 4 (2), 181–200.

Spandler, H. (2004). Friend or Foe? Towards a Critical Assessment of Direct Payments. *Critical Social Policy*, 24 (2), 443–54.

Speedwell, L., Stanton, F., & Nischal, K. K. (2003). Informing Parents of Visually Impaired Children: Who Should Do It and When? *Child: Care, Health and Development*, 29 (3), 219–24.

Stanley, L. (1990). Recovering 'Women' In History from Historical Deconstructionism. *Women's Studies International Forum*, 13, 153–5.

Stanley, L., & Wise, S. (Eds) (1993). *Breaking out Again: Feminist Ontology and Epistemology*. London: Routledge.

Strike, J., & McConnell, D. (2002). Parents with Intellectual Disability: Just the Same, Only Different. *Interaction*, 15 (4), 11–15.

Stronach, I. (2006). Progressivism against the Audit Culture: The Continuing Case of Summerhill School Versus Ofsted. In Lamb, A. (Ed.), *Summerhill School: A New View of Childhood*. Buckingham: Open University Press.

Stuart, O. W. (1992). Race and Disability: Just a Double Oppression? *Disability, Handicap & Society*, 7 (2), 177–88.

Sullivan, O. (2000). The Division of Domestic Labour: Twenty Years of Change? *Sociology*, 34 (3), 437–56.

Swain, J., Clark, J., French, S., et al. (2004). *Enabling Relationships in Health and Social Care: A Guide for Therapists*. London: Butterworth-Heinemann.

Swain, J., & French, S. (1999). *Therapy and Learning Difficulties*. London: Butterworth-Heinemann.

Swain, J., French, S., & Cameron, C. (2003a). *Controversial Issues in a Disabling Society*. Buckingham: Open University Press.

Swain, J., Griffiths, C., & Heyman, B. (2003b). Towards a Social Model Approach to Counselling Disabled Clients. *British Journal of Guidance and Counselling*, 31 (1), 137–53.

Taanila, A., Syrjälä, L., Kokkonen, J., et al. (2002). Coping of Parents with Physically and/or Intellectually Disabled Children. *Child: Care, Health & Development*, 28 (1), 73–86.

Tannen, D. (2006). *'You're Wearing That?': Understanding Mothers and Daughters in Conversation*. New York, N.Y.: Random House.

Taylor, S. J. (2000). 'You're Not a Retard, You're Just Wise' Disability, Social Identity, and Family Networks. *Journal of Contemporary Ethnography*, 29 (1), 58–92.

Taylor, S. J., & Bogdan, R. (1984). *Introduction to Qualitative Research Methods: The Search for Meanings*. New York, N.Y.: John Wiley and Sons.

Taylor, S. J., Bogdan, R., & Latfiyya, Z. (Eds) (1995). *The Variety of Community Experience: Qualitative Studies of Family and Community Life*. Baltimore, MD: Paul H. Brookes Publishing Co.

Terzi, L. (2005). Beyond the Dilemma of Difference: The Capability Approach to Disability and Special Educational Needs. *Journal of Philosophy of Education*, 39 (3), 443–59.

The Children Act (2004). London: Stationery Office.

The Health Act (1999). London: Stationery Office.

The Health and Social Care Act (2001). London: Stationery Office.

Thiruchelvam, D., Charach, A., & Schachar, R. (2001). Moderators and Mediators in Long-Term Adherence to Stimulant Treatment in Children with ADHD. *Journal of the American Academy of Child and Adolescent Psychiatry*, 40 (8), 922–8.

Thomas, C. (1997). The Baby and the Bathwater: Disabled Women and Motherhood in Social Context. *Sociology of Health & Illness*, 19 (5), 622–43.

Thomas, C. (1999a). *Female Forms: Experiencing and Understanding Disability*. Buckingham: Open University Press.

Thomas, C. (1999b). Narrative Identity and the Disabled Self. In Corker, M. & French, S. (Eds), *Disability Discourse*. Buckingham: Open University Press.

Thomas, C. (2001). Feminism and Disability: The Theoretical and Political Significance of the Personal and the Experiential. In Barton, L. (Ed.), *Disability Politics and the Struggle for Change*. London: David Fulton Publishers.

Thomas, C. (2006). Disability Studies and Medical Sociology. Paper Presented at The Disability Studies Association Conference. Lancaster University, Lancaster.

Thomas, C. (2007). *Sociologies of Disability and Illness. Contested Ideas in Disability Studies and Medical Sociology*. Basingstoke: Palgrave Macmillan.

Thompson, P. (1988). *The Voice of the Past: Oral History*. Oxford: Oxford University Press.

Timmermans, S., & Berg, M. (2003). *The Gold Standard: The Challenge of Evidence-Based Medicine and Standardization in Health Care*. Philadelphia, PA: Temple University Press.

Tobbell, J., & Lawthom, R. (2005). Dispensing with Labels: Enabling Children and Professionals to Share a Community Practice. *Journal of Educational and Child Psychology*, 22 (3), 89–97.

Tong, R. (2002). Love's Labor in the Health Care System: Working toward Gender Equity. *Hypatia*, 17 (3), 200–13.

Traustadóttir, R. (1991). Mothers Who Care: Gender, Disability and Family Life. *Journal of Family Issues*, 12 (2), 221–8.

Traustadóttir, R. (1999). Gender, Disability and Community Life, Toward a Feminist Analysis. In Bersani, H. (Ed.), *Responding to the Challenge: Current Trends and International Issues in Developmental Disabilities*. Cambridge, MA: Brookline Books.

Traustadóttir, R. (2004a). Disability Studies: A Nordic Perspective. Keynote Presentation at the British Disability Studies Association Conference. Lancaster University, Lancaster.

Traustadóttir, R. (2004b). A New Way of Thinking: Exploring the Intersection of Disability and Gender. In Kristjaensen, K. & Traustadóttir, R. (Eds), *Gender and Disability Research in the Nordic Countries*. Lund: Studentlitteratur.

Traustadóttir, R. (2006a). Disability Studies: A Nordic Perspective. Paper presented at the Applying Disability Studies Seminar Series. Centre of Applied Disability Studies, University of Sheffield.

Traustadóttir, R. (2006b). Families of Disabled Children: An International Perspective. Keynote Address. Enabling Practices of Care and Support for Parents with Babies with Disabilities: End of Award Conference, University of Newcastle, Newcastle.

Traustadóttir, R. (Ed.) (1995). *A Mother's Work Is Never Done, Constructing a 'Normal' Family Life*. Baltimore, MD: Paul H. Brookes Publishing Co.

Tregaskis, C. (2004a). *Constructions of Disability: Researching the Interface between Disabled and Non-Disabled People*. London: Routledge.

Tregaskis, C. (2004b). *The Perspectives of Disabled People and Disabled Parents*. Sheffield: Unpublished literature review.

Tregaskis, C. (2005). Parents, Professionals and Disabled Babies: Personal Reflections on Disabled Lives. In Goodley, D. & Lawthom, R. (Eds), *Disability and Psychology: Critical Introductions and Reflections*. Basingstoke: Palgrave Macmillan.

Tregaskis, C., & Goodley, D. (2006). Disability Research with Non/Disabled People: Towards a Relational Methodology of Research Production. *International Journal of Social Research Methodology*, 8 (5), 364–74.

Treichler, P. (1999). *How to Have Theory in an Epidemic: Cultural Chronicles of Aids*. New York, N.Y: Routledge.

Tremain, S. (2001). On the Government of Disability. *Social Theory and Practice*, 27 (4), 617–36.

Tremain, S. (2002). On the Subject of Impairment. In Corker, M. & Shakespeare, T. (Eds), *Disability/Postmodernity: Embodying Political Theory*. London: Continuum.

Tremain, S. (2006). Reproductive Freedom, Self-Regulation, and the Government of Impairment in Utero. *Hypatia*, 21 (1), 35–53.

Tremain, S. (Ed.) (2005). *Foucault and the Government of Disability*. Ann Arbor, MICH: University of Michigan Press.

Tronto, J. C. (1993). *Moral Boundaries: A Political Argument for an Ethic of Care*. London: Routledge.

Trute, B., & Heibert-Murphy, D. (2002). Family Adjustment to Childhood Developmental Disability: A Measure of Parent Appraisal of Family Impacts. *Journal of Pediatric Psychology*, 27 (3), 271–80.

Ungerson, C. (1987). *Policy Is Personal: Sex, Gender, and Informal Care*. London: Tavistock.

Ungerson, C. (2000). Thinking About the Production and Consumption of Longterm Care in Britain - Does Gender Still Matter? *Journal of Social Policy*, 29 (4), 623–43.

Ungerson, C. (Ed.) (1990). *Gender and Caring: Work and Welfare in Britain and Scandinavia*. Hemel Hempstead: Harvester Wheatsheaf.

UPIAS (1976). *Fundamental Principles of Disability*. London: Union of the Physically Impaired Against Segregation.

Vanobbergen, B., et al. (2006). 'We Are One Big, Happy Family': Beyond Negotiation and Compulsory Happiness. *Educational Theory*, 56 (4), 423–37.

Vincent, C. (2000). *Including Parents? Citizenship, Education and Parental Agency*. Buckingham: Open University Press.

Vlachou, A. (1997). *Struggles for Inclusion: An Ethnographic Study*. Buckingham: Open University Press.

Wakeford, T. (2002). Citizens Juries: A Radical Alternative for Social Research. *Social Research Update*, 37 (Summer).

Walker, A., Maher, J., Coulthard, M., et al. (2001). *Living in Britain: Results from the General Household Survey 2000–2001*. London: Stationery Office.

Watson, N. (2002). 'Well, I Know This is Going to Sound Very Strange to You, but I Don't See Myself as a Disabled Person': Identity and Disability. *Disability & Society*, 17 (5), 509–29.

Watson, N., McKie, L., Hughes, B., et al. (2004). (Inter)Dependence, Needs and Care: The Potential for Disability and Feminist Theorists to Develop an Emancipatory Model. *Sociology*, 38 (2), 331–50.

Watson, N., & Woods, B. (2005). The Origins and Early Developments of Special/Adaptive Wheelchair Seating. *Social History of Medicine*, 18 (3), 459–74.

Webb, J. (1999). Work and the New Public Service Class? *Sociology*, 33 (4), 747–66.

Wenger, E. (1998). *Communities of Practice: Learning, Meaning, and Identity*. Cambridge: Cambridge University Press.

West, C., & Zimmermain, D. H. (1987). Doing Gender. *Gender & Society*, 1, 125–51.

Whitney, C. (2006). Intersections in Identity: Identity Development among Queer Women with Disabilities. *Sexuality and Disability*, 24 (1), 39–52.

Wilkinson, S. (1999). How Useful Are Focus Groups in Feminist Research? In Barbour, R. S., & Kitzinger, J. (Eds), *Developing Focus Group Research: Politics, Theory and Practice*. London: Sage.

Williams, F. (2004). What Matters is Who Works: Why Every Child Matters to New Labour. Commentary on DfES Green Paper *Every Child Matters*. *Critical Social Policy*, 24 (3), 406–27.

Willoughby, J. C., & Glidden, L. M. (1995). Fathers helping out: Shared child care and marital satisfaction of parents of children with disabilities. *American Journal on Mental Retardation*, 99 (4), 399–406.

Wilson, A., & Beresford, P. (2002). Madness, Distress and Postmodernity: Putting the Record Straight. In Corker, M. & Shakespeare, T. W. (Eds), *Disability/Postmodernity: Embodying Disability Theory*. London: Continuum.

Wilson, E. (1993). Is Transgression Transgressive? In Bristow, J. & Wilson, A. R. (Eds), *Activating Theory: Lesbian, Gay, Bisexual Politics*. London: Wishart.

Witz, A. (1992). *Professions and Patriarchy*. London: Routledge.

Wolfensdale, S. (Ed.) (2002). *Parent Partnership Services for Special Educational Needs – Celebrations and Challenges*. London: David Fulton.

Woodgate, R. L., & Degner, L. F. (2004). Cancer Symptom Transition Periods of Children and Families. *Journal of Advanced Nursing*, 46 (4), 358–68.

Woodward, I., & Emmison, M. (2001). From Aesthetic Principles to Collective Sentiments: The Logics of Everyday Judgments of Taste. *Poetics*, 29 (6), 295–316.

Woolley, H., Armitage, M., Bishop, J., et al. (2005). *Inclusion of Disabled Children in Primary School Playgrounds*. London: Joseph Rowntree Foundation.

Wyness, M. G. (2006). *Childhood and Society: An Introduction to the Sociology of Childhood*. New York, N.Y.: Routledge.

Yuval-Davis, N. (2006). Belonging and the Politics of Belonging. *Patterns of Prejudice*, 40 (3), 197–214.

Index